PRAISE FOR

## Scandalous Women

"How can one not love a book that includes among its scandalous subjects Zelda Fitzgerald, Camille Claudel, and Calamity Jane? My only criticism of Elizabeth Kerri Mahon's engaging book on the lives of women who have helped write the pages of history is that it is not longer, given the host of others who deserve to be rescued from the footnotes of history."
—Paula Uruburu,
author of *American Eve*

"Brains, boldness, beauty, courage, and craziness all come together in this entertaining account of some of history's wildest women."
—Hallie Rubenhold,
author of *The Covent Garden Ladies* and *The Lady in Red*

"As delectable as dark chocolate on a winter night, *Scandalous Women* offers definitive proof that bad girls *do* have more fun. A thoroughly enjoyable romp through women's history."
—Kris Waldherr,
author of *Doomed Queens*

"A lively and informative look at the women from many walks of life who have shaken up history—and made it."
—Susan Higginbotham,
author of *The Queen of Last Hopes*

"With more verve than Josephine Baker's banana dance, Elizabeth Kerri Mahon brings together a pantheon of history's most scintillating women and jam-packs each and every story with fascinating details and lively humor."
—Carlyn Beccia,
author of *The Raucous Royals*

# Scandalous Women

## THE LIVES AND LOVES OF HISTORY'S MOST NOTORIOUS WOMEN

Elizabeth Kerri Mahon

A PERIGEE BOOK

A PERIGEE BOOK
Published by the Penguin Group
Penguin Group (USA) Inc.
375 Hudson Street, New York, New York 10014, USA
Penguin Group (Canada), 90 Eglinton Avenue East, Suite 700, Toronto, Ontario M4P 2Y3, Canada
(a division of Pearson Penguin Canada Inc.)
Penguin Books Ltd., 80 Strand, London WC2R 0RL, England
Penguin Group Ireland, 25 St. Stephen's Green, Dublin 2, Ireland (a division of Penguin Books Ltd.)
Penguin Group (Australia), 250 Camberwell Road, Camberwell, Victoria 3124, Australia
(a division of Pearson Australia Group Pty. Ltd.)
Penguin Books India Pvt. Ltd., 11 Community Centre, Panchsheel Park, New Delhi—110 017, India
Penguin Group (NZ), 67 Apollo Drive, Rosedale, North Shore 0632, New Zealand
(a division of Pearson New Zealand Ltd.)
Penguin Books (South Africa) (Pty.) Ltd., 24 Sturdee Avenue, Rosebank, Johannesburg 2196, South Africa

Penguin Books Ltd., Registered Offices: 80 Strand, London WC2R 0RL, England

While the author has made every effort to provide accurate telephone numbers and Internet addresses at the time of publication, neither the publisher nor the author assumes any responsibility for errors or for changes that occur after publication. Further, the publisher does not have any control over and does not assume any responsibility for author or third-party websites or their content.

First edition: March 2011

Library of Congress Cataloging-in-Publication Data

Mahon, Elizabeth Kerri.
   Scandalous women : the lives and loves of history's most notorious women /
Elizabeth Kerri Mahon.— 1st ed.
      p.   cm.
   "A Perigee Book."
   Includes bibliographical references.
   ISBN 978-0-399-53645-8 (trade pbk.)
   1. Women—Biography.  I. Title.
   CT3203.M35 2011
   920.72—dc22                    2010045764

PRINTED IN THE UNITED STATES OF AMERICA

10  9  8  7  6  5  4  3  2  1

Most Perigee books are available at special quantity discounts for bulk purchases for sales promotions, premiums, fund-raising, or educational use. Special books, or book excerpts, can also be created to fit specific needs. For details, write: Special Markets, Penguin Group (USA) Inc., 375 Hudson Street, New York, New York 10014.

*In loving memory of my parents,*
*Victor and Roslyn Mahon*

# ACKNOWLEDGMENTS

There are a huge number of people who were instrumental in the process of shepherding *Scandalous Women* from blog to book, and I owe them all a shout-out for their help and assistance. First and foremost, my awesome agent Erin Cartwright-Niumata, who always believed that we would find the right project to work on together. Thank you for having faith in me. To my editor Jeanette Shaw, for having patience as I learned the process and for her insightful comments that made the manuscript that much better. To Leanna Renee Hieber, Hope Tarr, Liz Maverick, Katrina Tipton, Stacey Agdern, Megan Frampton, and Kwana Jackson who kept telling me "This should be a book!" Thanks, guys, for keeping on me to finally sit down in front of the computer to write the proposal. To Marley Harbuck Gibson, for sharing her own experiences with writing a nonfiction proposal. To my fellow chapter members in RWA NYC for the support. To Sue Ritt-Nichol and Natalie Noel, for being the best friends in the world. And I would like to especially thank the readers of *Scandalous*

*Women*, who have followed the blog from its inception three years ago. When I started the blog, I had no idea what a journey I would end up taking and how many wonderful people I would reach through the blog. Their comments, emails, and suggestions have been a blessing. This book is for them.

# CONTENTS

# INTRODUCTION

*Well-behaved women rarely make history.*
—LAUREL THATCHER ULRICH

*Scandalous Women* isn't history, it's herstory. Ever notice those "This Day in History" sections in the newspaper or on TV? Most of those little factoids only give you half the story—the male half. If they do mention women at all, it is a scant few whose names are well known, mainly the saints and the Goody Two-Shoes of history. *Scandalous Women* aims to change that, reclaiming history one woman at a time.

In five thousand years of recorded history, from the ancient world to the present day, women have caused wars, created drama, defied the rules, and brought men to their knees. The famous and the infamous, warrior queens, spies, adventurers, and even a pirate or two have set off a ruckus during their lifetime—turning heads while making waves. These women came from all walks of life, from the royal palaces of Egypt, England, France, and Russia to the slums of St. Louis and Baltimore. Some of them, like Jane Digby and Lady Hester Stanhope, broke out of their comfort zone, leaving their homes, the lives they knew, behind them, to search for something more. Some sought fame and fortune, women like Lola Montez, Billie Holiday, and Josephine Baker.

From Boudica, who torched London to the ground in revenge against the Romans after they brutally raped her daughters, to Josephine Baker, who took Paris by storm while dancing at the Folies Bergère wearing only a belt of bananas and a smile in the Roaring Twenties, these women didn't let the mores of the time stop them from getting what they wanted. Others, like Émilie du Châtelet, battled the chauvinism of the male establishment, which held that science was no place for a woman. While others triumphed, some women, like Zelda Fitzgerald and Camille Claudel, paid a high price in their lifetime, their creativity stifled by dominant men, until they ended spiraling into madness. Not all of these women are admirable; some did questionable things, but for what they considered a noble cause, like Rose O'Neal Greenhow.

These thirty-five women represent just a taste, an amuse bouche as it were, of the many women who have rocked history. Every year more and more women's lives are being reclaimed from the mists of time, the dusty bookshelves, or the footnotes of history. But all the women in this book have one thing in common: they caused a scandal, a commotion, and they bumped up against the status quo. Some maneuvered their way around, and some used a battering ram. Each ran counter to conventional behavior, and each caused gossip, furor, and anger among her contemporaries. They were free, unafraid to take a stand, to make a mess if necessary to achieve their goals, whether it was against oppression or liquor or for religious freedom. Some were movers and shakers in terms of changing events; others left behind a legacy of brilliance and great art. Some of the women were perhaps a little self-serving in their behavior, exasperating in their wrongheadedness. Yet all of them are fascinating.

# ONE

# Warrior Queens

## Cleopatra

### 69–30 BCE

*Age cannot wither her, nor custom stale / Her infinite variety: other women cloy / The appetites they feed, but she makes hungry / Where most she satisfies.*

—SHAKESPEARE, ANTONY AND CLEOPATRA

The life of Cleopatra is one of the best soap operas ever in world history, filled with drama, romance, murder, sex, handsome men, and overwhelming ambition. More than two thousand years after her death, she still holds our fascination as one of history's most famous and mysterious women. Contemporary chroniclers claimed that she was a brazen temptress who corrupted both Julius Caesar and Mark Antony. And her legend has inspired filmmakers, poets, and playwrights over the centuries as they try to capture her elusive spirit. The last Pharaoh of the Ptolemaic dynasty was blessed with brains, charisma, and edge. A brilliant political strategist, Cleopatra used all the weapons at her disposal to keep Egypt free.

By the time Cleopatra was born in 69 BCE, the Ptolemaic dynasty had descended into depravity and an unfortunate tendency to bump each other off. As the Egyptian Empire declined, the Roman Empire was rising, spreading throughout Europe and the Middle East, until it came knock-knock-knocking on Egypt's door. Cleopatra's father, Ptolemy XII Auletes, was already in debt to Rome for help retrieving his throne from his daughter Berenice. He walked a tightrope between keeping Rome at bay and Egypt independent.

Cleopatra was never meant to be queen. Although second in line for the throne after her older sister Berenice, she was still educated to be the future Pharaoh according to an advanced Greek curriculum, which included rhetoric, philosophy, medicine, drawing, music, math, art, and the glorious history of her ancestor Ptolemy I. A passionate scholar, she learned nine languages and became the first Ptolemy to learn Egyptian. When Berenice was executed for stealing the throne from Dad, Cleopatra moved up a notch in the line of succession.

At eighteen, Cleopatra inherited the throne after her father's death, along with her ten-year-old brother/husband Ptolemy XIII, who became her coruler. She quickly moved to show who was really in charge. Inheriting a bankrupt kingdom, she managed to turn it into the richest state in the Mediterranean. Grain was distributed to the poor, the budget was balanced, and new building projects were initiated. She eventually amassed a fortune that was so great that Rome's interest rates dropped by two-thirds when her treasure was brought there after her death. She pilfered foreign libraries for scrolls to bring back to the library in Alexandria. During her reign, Cleopatra promoted herself endlessly, making constant displays of her power and her image as Pharaoh and as a goddess. She also personally led rituals that were associated with Isis, the most important Egyptian goddess at that time. By doing so, Cleopatra ensured that her people would be loyal to her.

Her brother's advisers, believing that they could control the boy king, soon forced Cleopatra off the throne. But years of familial scheming had turned her into a survivor. Fleeing into the Syrian Desert, she raised a small army of Arabs and tried to invade Egypt, but she was defeated by her brother's forces. There was only one man who could help Cleopatra regain her throne: Julius Caesar. At fifty-two, he was a seasoned military commander and embroiled in a civil war with his former coconsul Pompey. Cleopatra had seen how the power of Rome had restored her father to the throne. Luckily for her, Caesar was in Egypt in pursuit of Pompey. Unluckily for her brother, his advisers viewed Pompey as a threat to Egypt's relationship with Caesar and had him killed, pissing off Caesar, who had wanted him alive.

Seizing the advantage, and knowing that Caesar had a reputation as a womanizer, in an ingenious move Cleopatra had herself delivered to his ship rolled up in a Persian carpet. When it was unrolled, she tumbled out looking like a rumpled kitten. Charmed by this gesture, Caesar agreed to help her. He also took her as his mistress. Cleopatra impressed Caesar with her intelligence, her wit, and her abundant female charms. It was a meeting of the minds as well as the bodies. Now backed by Caesar's forces, she defeated her brother, who later drowned in the Nile while fleeing Caesar's henchmen. Caesar married her off to her youngest brother, Ptolemy XIV, who was only twelve and easily ignored.

When Caesar went back to Rome, he left Cleopatra a little present, a son she named Ptolemy Caesar but who the people of

Alexandria named Caesarion after his father. After the birth of their son, Caesar gave up his plans to annex Egypt, instead backing Cleopatra as sole ruler. Cleopatra packed up Caesarion and left Egypt in 46 BCE to be with Caesar at his invitation. While in Rome, Caesar showered his mistress with many titles and gifts, including erecting a golden statue of her, the first human image ever, in the temple of Venus, considered the mother of the republic, making her a living incarnation of the goddess. The Romans feared Cleopatra because she was unwomanly by their standards. She was independent and powerful. While Cleopatra hoped that Caesar would make Caesarion his heir, he refused to publicly claim him as his son, choosing his grandnephew Octavian instead.

Cleopatra and Egypt lost their protector in Rome when Caesar was assassinated on the ides of March in 44 BCE by a host of conspirators, including his close friend Brutus, who were afraid that Caesar would declare himself emperor. Cleopatra, fearing for her safety, fled back to Egypt. She now made her son Caesarion her coregent as Ptolemy XV after the death of her second brother/husband. Cleopatra eyed the situation as to who was going to end up on top when it came to ruling Rome. When the forces of Mark Antony defeated Caesar's murderers, Cleopatra turned her attention to him.

As she had done with Caesar, Cleopatra sized up her quarry, how best to appeal to him. Antony, although a brilliant general and popular with his troops, was also a complete party animal with a weakness for powerful women. It was showtime on the Nile. Pulling out all the stops, Cleopatra arrived at Tarsus to meet Antony on her great barge with its gold stern and billowing purple sails, inclining under a golden canopy, dressed like the goddess Aphrodite. Boys dressed like Cupids cooled her with their fans, and the most beautiful of her waiting women lined the barge. At dinner that night, she served him a banquet with the finest wines and foods, on bejeweled plates, while reclining on embroidered couches. The feast went on for four days and nights; Cleopatra spared no expense, with extravagant menus, banquets with fireworks, carpets of rose petals, and expensive presents. The spectacle was designed to show off the wealth of Egypt that would be put at Antony's disposal should he partner with her.

It worked like gangbusters; Antony was just as captivated by Cleopatra as Caesar had been. Soon they were living *la vida loca*. According to Plutarch, Cleopatra catered to Antony's every little whim, whether he wanted to go hunting or carousing and gambling. She drank with him and played practical jokes with him; basically she never let him out of her sight. She wanted to bind Antony by making herself indispensable on every level, as a way of protecting herself and her country. Antony and Cleopatra were well matched; they both enjoyed a hunger for life. But even more than lust, ambition brought them together. Cleopatra had been looking for a strong man to help her keep her kingdom. Antony likewise needed Cleopatra's support, money, supplies, and troops to invade Parthia (now a part of present-day Iran). In return, he offered protection and help getting rid of her last remaining sibling, her sister Arsinoë, who had been a thorn in her side ever since she inherited the throne.

Together they shared a glorious dream of an empire that stretched from East to West. But power struggles at home led Antony away from Cleopatra's side and back to Rome. After the death of his wife, Antony agreed to marry Octavian's sister, Octavia, to cement their alliance. Back in Egypt, Cleopatra gave birth to twins, Alexander Helios and Cleopatra Selene. It would be three years before she saw Antony again.

Remembering his plan to invade Parthia, Antony arranged to

meet Cleopatra in Antioch. To pay him back for leaving her alone for three years, she kept him cooling his heels impatiently for weeks before agreeing to meet with him. It wasn't long before the fire was rekindled but now their sexual passion soon turned into a strong emotional bond. It was a true partnership of equals; nobody would ever be as close to either of them as each other. After a few days between her golden thighs, he had agreed to give her land that included modern Lebanon, Syria, Jordan, and southern Turkey in exchange for her help. Unfortunately too pooped from partying, Antony managed to lose to the Parthians. The remaining survivors were left cold and starving, until Cleopatra arrived with supplies soon after giving birth to another son, Ptolemy Philadelphus.

Antony abandoned his marriage to Octavia and married Cleopatra; for the ceremony they dressed as the gods Aphrodite and Dionysus. He also made their son Alexander King of Armenia; their daughter Cleopatra Queen of Crete; and little Ptolemy ruler of Syria. In Rome, Octavian went to the Senate to declare war on Egypt and Cleopatra. He launched a bitter propaganda war against Cleopatra, declaring that she was the real enemy of Rome and was using Antony as her besotted plaything.* This image lasted throughout the centuries, until 1820, when hieroglyphics were deciphered that told the other side of the story.

Instead of playing to Antony's strength as a soldier, Cleopatra decided that a naval battle would be a better idea. It was a colossal mistake. While they were sailing away Octavian crushed their scattered troops in Greece, trapping them at Actium for four months. Antony's larger, unwieldy ships were no match for Octa-

---

* A king of spin, Octavian had two thousand documents destroyed after Cleopatra's death that didn't support his version of events.

vian's smaller, lighter fleet. In the midst of battle, Cleopatra took her ships, which were filled with Egypt's entire treasury, and fled the scene as was prearranged. Antony followed her, deserting his troops, who surrendered to the enemy. Defeated and feeling sorry for himself, Antony returned to the city, deciding to take his own life by stabbing himself with his sword. Unfortunately, he botched it. Cleopatra's servant discovered him and Antony was carried to the mausoleum, where Cleopatra was holed up with her two maids. He died in her arms.

When Octavian finally marched into town, Cleopatra tried to win him over, as she had Caesar and Antony. Plutarch wrote that even at the age of thirty-nine, "her old charm and the boldness of her youthful beauty had not wholly left her and in spite of her present condition, still sparkled from within." She even offered to abdicate if her children could rule in her place. But Cleopatra had finally met a man who was immune to her charms. When she heard that Octavian planned to parade her as a captive in the procession in Rome to celebrate his triumph, she refused to be humiliated. Instead, bedecked in the robes of Isis, she died poisoned by an asp that had been smuggled to her in a basket of figs, simultaneously outwitting Rome and affirming her immortality. Or at least that was the story put out by Octavian. Even Plutarch thought that story smelled fishy. There were no marks found on the body and, more important, no asp. Cleopatra, knowing her way around a chemistry kit, no doubt came up with a suitable royal cocktail of poison to make her exit from this world. However she died, it was as she had lived, a proud, independent queen.

After her suicide, Octavian ordered her son Caesarion put to death, one less challenge to his authority as emperor. What Cleopatra had fought against had happened: Egypt was now just another piece of the Roman Empire. Her daughter by Antony later married

King Juba II of Numidia, but the fate of her other two children by Antony, Alexander Helios and Ptolemy Philadelphus, remains unknown.

Cleopatra was a heroic and brilliant patriot, and the last major threat to the Roman Empire for a while, but she will always be known as the seductress of the East who lured two of Rome's greatest men away from their duties. Her legend only grew as writers from Shakespeare to Shaw shared their versions of her story with the world and by the many movies since then. She has passed from history into an icon.

# Boudica

## ?–60 CE

*All this ruin was brought upon them by a woman, a fact which caused them [the Romans] the greatest shame.*

—Dio Cassius

Boudica was a wife, a mother, a revered queen, and the leader of the most violent rebellion against the Romans in British history. The first heroine in British history, even her name adds to her legend, as it is the Celtic word for "victory." Little is known of her life before she became a thorn in the side of the Romans, although she was probably of royal descent. The historian Dio Cassius described her as tall, terrifying, and with a great mass of tawny hair hanging to her waist, wearing a large golden necklace and a many-colored tunic—a real-life Xena, Warrior Princess. We'll have to take his word for it, for he wasn't actually there. His history, like that of Tacitus, was written years after the events, and he had a keen interest in promoting the Roman point of view. Still, she must have been formidable, even if she wasn't the Amazon that Dio Cassius described.

After a century of seeing Britain solely as a useful source for tin and great oysters, the Romans came a-calling in 43 CE launching a full-scale invasion. The emperor Claudius, who needed some good PR to change his image as a drooling, limping fool, decided it was time to bring Britain under the civilizing influence of the empire. At the time Britain was divided into a hodgepodge of kingdoms large and small. When the Romans arrived, many Britons welcomed them, not thinking what it would mean in the long run. The emperor himself made a ceremonial visit, holding a huge celebration at Camulodunum (Colchester) to impress the locals with a little Roman razzle-dazzle. Most of the southern tribes, including the Iceni, chose the path of least resistance, becoming client kingdoms.

In 60 CE, after twenty years of rule, King Prasutagus of the Iceni in East Anglia* died, leaving his empire divided between the Roman Empire and his two daughters, with his widow, Boudica, as regent. Prasutagus had been one of the first to sign a treaty with Rome, but since he died without a male heir, the Romans considered the treaty to be null and void. Under Roman law, inheritance could only come through the male line. Having a woman in charge proved that the Iceni were barbarians as far as they were concerned. Women in Celtic Britain were able to rule, marry whom they liked, and own property; they had a great deal of freedom compared to their Roman counterparts, whose lives were tightly controlled.

---

* The Iceni kingdom covered an area that roughly encompasses modern-day Norfolk, Cambridgeshire, and northern Suffolk in England.

Tacitus wrote, "Kingdom and household alike were plundered like prizes of war." When Boudica protested their actions, the Romans flogged her in public and allowed slaves to rape her daughters as a warning to the other tribes. The Romans chose the wrong woman to make an example of. Boudica appealed to the Iceni as well as several of the neighboring tribes, including the Trinovantes, who had a laundry list of grievances of their own, to join her in rebelling against Rome. She was helped by the fact that the Romans, under the procurator Catus Decianus, had begun to treat the Britons like slave labor. The native population was now subjected to brutality and casual mistreatment. Army veterans helped themselves to whatever land they wanted, driving the natives out. A huge temple dedicated to the emperor Claudius had been built in Camulodunum, using the Trinovantes as unpaid labor and then taxing them to pay for it to boot.

At first Boudica's rebellion was in luck. The military governor Suetonius was off massacring the Druids on the island of Mona (Anglesey). In his absence Boudica amassed an army over 120,000 strong made up of men, women, and priests. While Boudica must have had extraordinary charisma to persuade so many Britons to follow her, she also had a powerful story that everyone could relate to. What made her a strong leader was that she was filled with outrage—she felt that she had justice on her side. The Celtic tribes had spent their lives preparing for war. When the call came, they were ready to go kick some Roman butt.

First stop was Colchester, where they took the town by surprise. Boudica prayed to the goddess Andraste for victory and released a hare into the multitude to determine by its direction whether the campaign would be a success. The omen must have been favorable since the people were unarmed and unprepared, and the town was unfortified. Boudica and her army sacked it, razing the town and setting it on fire. The nearest legion of two thousand Romans was at Lincoln. The commander hurried to meet the rebels but his forces were ambushed by the Britons on the way and cut to pieces.

Emboldened, Boudica headed toward London, the commercial heart of the Roman Empire in Britain. As soon as Catus Decianus heard Boudica was on her way, he fled the city to Gaul. Meanwhile Suetonius arrived in London from Wales with only a cavalry unit. When he had first heard the news of the revolt, he was not too concerned. The Britons must have been desperate to take orders from a woman. However, after sizing up Boudica's forces, and realizing he was lacking sufficient strength, Suetonius made the executive decision to abandon the town, telling the people to flee. After burning London to the ground, Boudica and company headed for St. Albans and sacked it, although the inhabitants had already fled.

But Boudica wasn't done; she decided to follow the Roman army north, sacking a few towns along the way. No one knows exactly where the final battle took place between Boudica and the Romans, but it was probably in the West Midlands. What is known is that Suetonius picked a place that was surrounded by a wood where he could only be attacked by the front. Outnumbered, the Romans had to rely on strategy and the fact that they were a highly trained and organized fighting machine.

Before the final battle Boudica drove up and down the front line in her chariot with her daughters in front of her, exhorting her army, "You will win this battle or perish. That is what I, a woman, plan to do. Let the men live in slavery if they will." Confident of victory, the Britons had brought their families with them, installing them in carts that were stationed at the edge of the battlefield.

In a straight-line formation, the Romans held their ground with their shields and javelins as the Britons, faces and bodies painted blue and screaming insults, charged toward them in frenzied chaos. It must have been a fearsome sight but the Romans held their ground, launching their javelins into the air. With no body armor to protect them, the first wave of Britons fell. They were no match for the superior fighting skills of the Roman legionnaires, who used the wedge formation to corner them. When they tried to turn and flee they were hemmed in by their own wagons on the edge of the field. When the dust settled, untold numbers of Britons were dead, but only four hundred Romans. It was the last significant rebellion against the Roman Empire. It is believed that Boudica poisoned herself and her daughters rather than end up in Roman hands.

It took sheer guts and bravery for Boudica to mount a rebellion against the greatest world power in existence at that time. And she almost won. Boudica's revolt actually had Nero, Rome's emperor during the uprising, considering withdrawing all Roman forces from Britain. Her fatal flaw was that she seemed to have no clear plan other than kicking Roman ass. If she had been able to capitalize on her earlier victories, she might have gained more support and led Rome to finally give up on Britain.

Centuries after her defeat, Boudica became known as a heroine, a patriotic queen who died defending the liberty of her country against a ruthless and alien power. But it was the Victorians, with their penchant for romanticizing ancient British myths like hers and King Arthur's, who really took Boudica to heart. Her statue now stands proudly on the Thames near the Houses of Parliament, as a reminder of the might of the British Empire and a symbol of national patriotism. It is a fitting memorial to the woman who has now passed into legend.

# Eleanor of Aquitaine
## 1122–1204

*A woman without compare.*

—RICHARD OF DEVIZES

Eleanor of Aquitaine was one of the most famous women in medieval Europe and one of the most infamous in history. Wife to two kings and mother of two kings, she founded a dynasty that would rule England for the next 330 years. In her lifetime, she was the subject of scandalous rumors: that she rode bare-breasted on crusade; that she slept with her uncle; that she murdered her husband's mistress. She was a warrior who helped her sons revolt against their father, and she served as regent while Richard the Lionheart went on crusade.

Born in 1122, Eleanor's family history was filled with romance and drama. Her grandfather was a flamboyant figure, acknowledged as the first troubadour. He was also no stranger to love or to scandal. Having discarded two wives, and been excommunicated twice, he decided to abduct a married woman named Dangereuse, who became his mistress. Indifference to public opinion and doing pretty much what one pleased ran in Eleanor's blood.

With the death of her brother when she was eight, Eleanor became the heiress to the duchy of Aquitaine. It was a major chunk of real estate, encompassing one-fourth of modern France, and whoever married her would be incredibly powerful. Proud of having such a beautiful, lively, and intelligent daughter, her father made sure that she was highly educated. She traveled with him throughout the duchy, observing the skillful way he handled his subjects. When she was fifteen, her father died from food poisoning while he was on a pilgrimage to Spain. In order to protect Eleanor from being vulnerable to bride snatchers after he was gone, on his deathbed he dictated a will making her a ward of Louis VI of France. Eager to get his chubby fingers on the duchy of Aquitaine, Louis, nicknamed "the Fat," quickly married Eleanor off to his son, the future Louis VII. There was only one tiny catch. Aquitaine would remain independent of France for the moment, but if the union was blessed by a son, he would be both King of France and Duke of Aquitaine.

The bride wore scarlet, which would turn out to be appropriate given her later reputation. Eleanor's first glimpse of her husband was not promising. Louis was quiet and pious, as unlike her warrior father and grandfather as it was possible to be, and he definitely knew nothing about girls. "I thought to have married a King," she complained, "but I find I have wed a monk." Louis on the other hand was thrilled with his half of the bargain. His new bride was highly sophisticated, blessed with beauty and brains. She had seen more of the world than her cloistered husband. Before Eleanor could adjust to her married life, she became queen when her new father-in-law died a few days after the wedding.

Paris shocked Eleanor; it was a backwater compared to Poitiers, and the royal palace left a lot to be desired. Rolling up her sleeves, she started by giving the palace an Extreme Makeover: Medieval Edition, tearing down the musty tapestries and filling her apartments with light, perfume, and color, bringing a little bit of Poitiers to Paris. Flouting convention, she enlivened the court with party games after dinner and minstrels who sang ribald songs. Determined to civilize the court, she introduced new innovations like napkins and tablecloths and insisted the servants wash their hands before serving food.

Eleanor was seen as a foreigner, importing her decadent southern ways and corrupting the court. When her mother-in-law called her flighty and a bad influence, Eleanor dispatched her to her dower lands. Her conduct was criticized by church elders, who constantly harangued her to spend more time praying and less time singing. Louis continued to be in awe of his wife. He consulted her often on matters of state, much to the chagrin of his ministers. He even invaded Champagne to try to impress her, burning down a church filled with people in the process.

When Louis decided to go on the Second Crusade in 1147 to atone for the church incident, Eleanor announced that she was joining him along with a company of three hundred women and their attendants (one can only imagine how much luggage they brought) to nurse the wounded. Louis' advisers were completely against it until Eleanor sweetened the deal by offering the services of a thousand men from Aquitaine.

The crusade turned out not to be the adventure that Eleanor had signed up for. Traveling was difficult, the weather sucked, and Eleanor once had to trade her jewelry for food! Louis didn't have the first clue how to lead an army. While crossing Mount Cadmos en route to Antioch, disaster struck when Eleanor and her vassals ignored instructions and went ahead to find a better place to camp. When the king and his men arrived at the campsite, they were ambushed by the Turks, causing heavy losses. The king was only spared because he wasn't recognized. Eleanor was blamed because it was rumored the rear was slowed down by her luggage. Since she already had a dubious reputation, it was easy to use her as a scapegoat.

Things went from bad to worse in Antioch, where they were welcomed by Eleanor's handsome uncle who was only seven years older than his niece. At the royal palace, Raymond wined and dined his beautiful niece, speaking to her in their native tongue. Gossip of an affair spread, fueled by Eleanor's clear preference for her uncle's company and sparking her husband's jealousy. Louis and Eleanor had been growing apart, and the crusade just emphasized how incompatible they were. When Raymond advised Louis not to attack Jerusalem, to help hold Antioch against the Muslim Turks instead, Eleanor took his side. When Louis refused, Eleanor declared that not only was she staying in Antioch but she wanted a divorce. Louis finally grew some balls and forced Eleanor to go to Jerusalem with him.

The attack on Jerusalem went badly and Eleanor couldn't help saying, "I told you so." Things were so bad that they took separate ships back to Europe. Stopping in Rome for a little marriage counseling, the estranged couple ended up sharing a bed thanks to Pope Eugene III's maneuvering. Their daughter Alix was born nine months later, but it was too late to save the marriage.

Louis was convinced by his advisers to let Eleanor go, although losing Aquitaine must have hurt. Still, he had the future of the throne to think about. After fifteen years of marriage, they had only two daughters and no sons. Eleanor, of course, countered that it wasn't her fault; if he wanted an heir, he needed to sleep with her once in a while. On March 11, 1152, the marriage was dissolved, on the grounds of consanguinity. The king was given sole custody of their two daughters.

At twenty-nine, Eleanor was still a catch, so much so that while on her way home to Poitiers she was ambushed by two knights who wanted to marry her. But she already had husband number two all picked out even before she and Louis divorced. The lucky guy was Henry Fitz-Empress, Count of Anjou, Duke of Normandy, and heir to the throne of England. Sure, he was eleven years younger, but he was the antithesis of the monkish Louis, exuding animal magnetism.

Eleanor and Henry were well matched. They shared similar backgrounds; both were highly intelligent and strong willed. His physical courage and keen political mind meshed well with her ambition for power. And they were powerfully attracted to one another. Eleanor must have been in heaven to be in the arms of a real man after sleeping with a saint. Defying his father, who was against the match; the ambitions of his younger brother, who also wanted to marry her; and the wrath of her ex-husband, Henry married her six weeks after her annulment came through.

Eleanor had gambled successfully. Two years after their marriage, Henry of Anjou was King of England and Eleanor was now queen of a kingdom that stretched from the Pyrenees to the Cheviots. At first they were happy, producing a steady stream of princes and princesses, eight in all. But they soon grew apart. Eleanor wanted to exercise her intelligence doing more than just hanging around the nursery or supervising her ladies-in-waiting. Henry wasn't about to share his power with a coruler. Although he allowed Eleanor to act as regent during his absences from court, that meant little more than signing her name to give authority to his ministers, who had the real power. Henry was also busy with other women, in particular, Rosamund Clifford, fair and many years younger than the queen.

It's not that Eleanor expected fidelity; no, what put her knickers in a twist was Henry flaunting his mistress in public, setting her up like a queen in Eleanor's own rooms at Woodstock. Eleanor wasn't going to put up with that. There are legends that Eleanor attempted to do away with her rival by poisoning her or stabbing her, take your pick. None of them are true. Rosamund spent her remaining years in a convent after Henry grew bored with her.

Refusing to play second fiddle to his mistress, Eleanor convinced Henry to let her return to Poitiers in an attempt to control the unruly barons in Aquitaine. There she was in her element. For five years, Eleanor was free from Henry's dominance. Though Henry was the ruler of Aquitaine, Eleanor made sure that her lords knew that their loyalty was to her and her favorite son, Richard, who would rule after her, and not to the king. She undid many of his oppressive laws, recalled exiled vassals, and held feasts, festivals, and tournaments to please the people. Creating a court to her liking, she welcomed young knights and troubadours, who flocked to sing her praises. Along with her daughter Marie of Champagne, Eleanor held mock Courts of Love, where the real world—where men treated women like property—didn't exist. In the Courts of Love, women had the upper hand, handing down verdicts on the behavior of men toward their loved ones.

In 1173, Eleanor brokered the alliance of her three oldest sons, Henry, Richard, and Geoffrey, and her ex-husband against Henry. It was a startling act of aggression that Henry didn't see coming. He was enraged that his sons would dare to rebel against him and that Eleanor would back them. The plan failed and all three sons fled to France. Eleanor was not so lucky; she was caught trying to flee dressed like a man. She was sent back to England and imprisoned for the next fifteen years in various royal residences around the country. On brief occasions, she was let out of her prison, mainly for Christmas celebrations at the court, and to see Richard installed as Duke of Aquitaine after Eleanor renounced her title. Occasionally she was allowed to have family members as visitors, but Henry never let her forget that she was his prisoner.

Henry died in 1189 and Eleanor really came into her own.

While the newly crowned Richard went off on the Third Crusade, Eleanor ruled England with distinction in his place, going from city to city and castle to castle holding "queenly courts," releasing prisoners and exacting oaths of loyalty to her son, while simultaneously keeping the greedy fingers of her other remaining son, John, off the throne in his brother's absence. When Richard was captured by the Duke of Austria, not only did Eleanor manage to raise the money to ransom Richard, but she went all the way to Austria to bring him back; not bad for a broad in her seventies. On their return, she managed to get the two brothers to reconcile.

After Richard's death and John's ascension to the throne, Eleanor decided to retire in 1202 to Fontevrault Abbey, where she spent her remaining two years of life seeking advantageous matches for her relatives. But she was not done yet. Besieged in her castle at Mirabeau by the forces of her grandson Arthur, who was warring with John for the English throne, Eleanor told her attackers that she would be damned before she surrendered. She died at the age of eighty-two, a remarkable age in a remarkable life, outliving most of her children. She is buried beside her husband at the abbey.

Eleanor was a woman of extraordinary power and influence even while constantly having to operate from behind the men who controlled the throne. Contemporary chroniclers, uneasy with the idea of a woman wielding power, tended to focus on Eleanor's romantic relationships. Some accused her of being a demon in league with the devil. Modern historians, who have been able to cut past the detritus to examine her influence, have given her the credit and recognition she deserves. Eleanor of Aquitaine was an extraordinary woman for any age, refusing to be bound by the rules of proper behavior for women. She played a major role in political events, unusual for her time, helping to create an empire for her descendants through diplomacy and clever marriages. Brave and independent, she remains one of history's most impressive women.

⚹

# Joan of Arc
## 1412–1431

*Even little children repeat that oftentimes people are hanged for having told the truth.*

—JOAN OF ARC AT HER TRIBUNAL

She was just a small-town girl living in a small-town world, called Domrémy, France, population two hundred. But in a few short years everyone in the medieval world would know her name. Her actions helped turn the tide in the Hundred Years' War with England. Not bad for an illiterate peasant girl from the French countryside whose public career lasted less than two years!

Joan was born around January 6, 1412. Unlike the image of her as a poor, barefoot peasant girl, Joan came from a family of well-to-do farmers who owned a nice two-story home with a slate roof that's still standing. Her father, Jacques, was well respected by the villagers; he was responsible for the defense of the town and collected the taxes. Until the age of twelve, Joan lived an ordinary life, going to church, helping her mother with the housework, and tending the sheep, with marriage or the convent in her future. But God and history had other plans for her.

Joan first started hearing her "voices," which she claimed were those of the saints Michael, Catherine, and Margaret, when she hit puberty. Nowadays if a teenager claimed to be hearing voices, she would probably be diagnosed as schizophrenic and pumped full of psychotropic drugs. But this was the medieval world, where no one put you in a padded room if you heard voices, particularly if they came from God. However, Joan's voices told her to do something extraordinary. She was to lead an army against the English, and crown the Dauphin, who was heir to the throne, King of France. At first Joan refused to listen. How could a teenage girl with no connections hope even to meet the Dauphin, let alone lead an army? The task was so daunting that she kept her voices to herself, not even telling her priest.

The French and English had been fighting over who got to wear the French crown for nearly one hundred years. Thanks to the longbow, the English kept winning, soon occupying huge chunks of France. In 1415, Henry V scored a major victory at Agincourt, along with a French princess and the promise of the crown. After the deaths of Charles VI of France and Henry V in 1422, half of the kingdom now believed that Henry's son, the child king Henry VI of England, was their king, while the other half supported the Dauphin. Joan's hometown was smack in the middle of the war zone. While Domrémy was true to the forces of the King of France and his allies, it was surrounded by those loyal to the Duke of Burgundy, who had allied with the English. But Joan couldn't refuse God's orders, and she had her voices to guide her. She just needed to find a way to the Dauphin.

Leaving home without telling her parents, Joan convinced her uncle to accompany her to Vaucouleurs to see the powerful lord in her area, Robert de Baudricourt, to tell him that she had heard the voice of God and to ask him for his help in meeting the Dauphin. She reminded him of the prophecy that France would be lost by a woman* and regained by a virgin from Lorraine. Annoyed, Baudricourt sent her home and told her uncle to give her a good beating. Not willing to take no for an answer, Joan came back two more times. The third time several of his knights were persuaded by her sincerity and determination and asked for permission to accompany her. Baudricourt finally gave in and agreed to give her his support.

Joan made her way to Chinon with an escort of six men. Before they left, she made the radical decision to cut her hair and put on men's clothing. She was now a soldier of God and needed to dress like one. They crossed France in eleven days in the middle of February, passing through English territory miraculously without a hitch. Joan had dictated a letter asking to be put on the Dauphin's calendar. What she found at Chinon didn't inspire confidence. Charles was insecure, introverted, and indecisive. He wasn't exactly jonesing to be king. It hadn't done his father any favors. Charles VI had ended up mad as a hatter, thinking he was made of glass. His mother wasn't exactly Mother of the Year material either, claiming he was illegitimate. Joan pulled him aside to talk privately and revealed to him information that only God or his confessor would have known. Nobody knows exactly what she said but it was enough to convince him.

Charles was now a believer but just to make sure, he sent Joan to Poitiers to be questioned by various senior clergymen to make sure she hadn't been sent by the devil or the English. Only the conclusions from the inquiry at Poitiers survive but Joan must have aced it because the churchmen gave her their seal of ap-

---

* Possibly referring to Charles VII's mother, Isabeau of Bavaria, who signed a treaty basically giving France to England after Agincourt.

proval. Charles now made her his captain of war. The idea was angrily denounced by the court and his generals.

Before she could lead an army Joan needed a crash course in war games, under the tutelage of the Duc d'Alençon. Luckily she absorbed knowledge like a sponge. Within months, she was as skilled as if she had been fighting for twenty years. She carried a huge banner made with images of Jesus and angels that read "De par le Roi du Ciel," which translates as "On the side of the King of Heaven." Her sword came from St. Catherine's Church at Fier-bois, where it was buried behind the altar—Joan claimed that her voices directed her to it. Medieval press releases were sent out in the form of theological treatises, linking Joan to the biblical fig-ures of Judith, Deborah, and Esther, announcing her to the world—sort of like the Good Housekeeping Seal of Approval.

As an officer, Joan was a skillful leader. She rebuked her force of four thousand men when they swore; she reassured them when they expressed fear. Even though she was a young woman, she slept rough like her men, never asking for special treatment. She forced them to give up their "camp followers" if they wanted to be in her army, haranguing any women she found hanging around. Her army prayed every day and sang hymns while they marched. Hardened and seasoned soldiers didn't take kindly at first to taking orders from a seventeen-year-old girl. When they disobeyed, which they often did, she furiously invoked God. Kind of hard to object when God is giving the orders. Despite their close proximity, none of her soldiers seem to have found her desir-able. They claimed they feared and respected her too much.

Joan's first test was the city of Orléans, which had been be-sieged by the English for seven long months. Everyone knew that it was make-or-break time. The city was the gateway to the south of France. If the French lost, it was time to fold up their tents because they would be drinking tea and eating scones before they knew it. For Charles, sending Joan to Orléans was a no-brainer. If Joan failed, it was her fault. If she won, he came out smelling like a rose.

When she arrived in Orléans, she was greeted by an enormous crowd who wanted to touch her or her horse. Joan was impatient to get the show on the road. The French had gotten so used to losing that although they outnumbered the English, Joan practically had to push them onto the battlefield. She dictated a letter to the English and had it shot by arrow to the fort where the English were entrenched. "I've been sent by God to drive you out of France. We will strike you wherever we find you." The English laughed themselves silly at the idea of surrendering to a girl. But Joan had the last laugh. She led several furious assaults and sent the English running with their tails between their legs.

While scaling a ladder, she was wounded by an arrow in the shoulder but continued fighting. Even though her troops were exhausted and her captains suggested retreat, Joan demanded they press on. By the next day, the French held both sides of the river, and the English retreated. Joan had her first real victory. The city of Orléans rejoiced, ringing the bells in the city. As she prepared to leave, she was offered gifts, which she refused, never taking credit for the victory. More victories followed in June at Jargeau, Meung, Patay, and Beaugency. Men now flocked to fight for her.

But while her supporters thought her deeds were miracles, to the establishment Joan was a threat on many levels. Her claim that she'd talked directly to God without benefit of a priest threatened the church. She managed to instill among the French a sense of nationalism and patriotic pride in the king, which threatened powerful men like the Duke of Burgundy. And she stepped outside the bounds of what was acceptable behavior for women, which meant that she must be a witch.

Joan now decided that it was time to crown the Dauphin at Reims, where French kings traditionally had their coronation. She believed that once Charles was crowned, the power of his enemies would be diminished. Though a teenage girl, with no education, she understood the power of symbols and propaganda. Reims was deep in the heart of Burgundian territory, which didn't faze Joan a bit, although it made Charles tremble. With the future king by her side, she fought her way to the city. On July 17, 1429, with Joan at his side, Charles was crowned King of France. Joan's father, Jacques, traveled all the way to see her triumph, and the king rewarded them by exempting their village from taxes.

The coronation was the turning point of Joan's short career. She believed that France could not be unified without Paris, which was under the control of the Duke of Burgundy. Joan wanted Charles to fight on to Paris but now that he was king, Charles didn't feel that he needed Joan anymore, and he and his advisers certainly didn't see any need for more fighting. They preferred negotiating with the Duke of Burgundy. Joan also had powerful enemies at court, such as Georges de La Trémoille, who disliked her influence over the king and her popularity with the people.

Only when his diplomatic efforts with the Burgundians failed did Charles turn to Joan. By the time he actually agreed to fight, Joan had been cooling her heels impatiently for weeks. Because of the delay, the Burgundians had had time to fortify the city against attack. She was wounded, her page was killed, and her banner tumbled to the ground. After two days the king called off the siege. Joan was crushed at her first failure. The king, hoping that she'd take the hint and go away, ennobled her and her family. Joan couldn't have cared less but her brothers and their descendants took advantage of the opportunities nobility brought. The only advantage to her was that now she didn't need the king's permission to fight.

The Burgundians had taken the city of Compiègne. With only three hundred men, Joan's army traveled through the night to take the Burgundians by surprise. At first it worked, and they were able to make several assaults. But the Burgundians were able to send for reinforcements. Joan was trapped when the governor of the town ordered that the gates of the city be closed. Riding at the rear, Joan didn't make it through them to safety before they were shut. She was left outside the city walls, with no hope of escape. It was May 23, 1430, and Joan only had a year left to live.

Medieval etiquette held that important prisoners of war were held for ransom. Joan's was set at ten thousand ecus. Charles made no move to pay the ransom, despite the people begging him to. In Tours, the entire population appeared in the streets, barefoot, singing in penance. In Orléans, the site of her first victory, they made public prayers for her safety. Still Charles did nothing. The king was embarrassed that he'd needed her help. His chief minister was said to be delighted by the outcome. Talk about ingratitude!

When Charles wouldn't pay, the Burgundians handed her over to the English, who were salivating at their good fortune. Life with her English jailers was difficult. For four months she was subject to brutal pressure, given meager rations, and regularly deprived of sleep. They interrogated her relentlessly. She had no privacy; three guards stayed inside her cell and two outside her door at all times. An iron cage was placed in her cell to intimidate her. Her ankles were shackled and she was chained to her bed. Joan insisted that she needed her masculine attire to keep from being assaulted and her jailers relented. Finally she was sent to Rouen for trial, which began a few days after her nineteenth birthday.

Joan was brought before the ecclesiastical court, accused of twelve counts of heresy, witchcraft, and idolatry. The English wanted her discredited; they didn't want to create a martyr. If she was found guilty, her punishment would be execution. Joan had no legal counsel, and none of her friends or family were called as witnesses to defend her. For days, she was questioned relentlessly and repeatedly, in an effort to wear her down. She held up well at first, answering their questions concisely in a clear voice. To every single charge brought against her, she staunchly replied that she answered only to the judgment of God.

Since they couldn't prove her guilty of heresy and witchcraft, they focused on a third charge, the claim that dressing like a man violated the Bible. The clergy was obsessed with this one; it was offensive to them, because she said that God was the one who told her to wear them. Only when Pierre Cauchon, the Bishop of Beauvais, pointed at the scaffold where she would be burned did she finally break down. She signed a statement confessing that her voices were false, although the brief statement she was shown was not the one the church later claimed that she agreed to. That one was much longer.

Back in her cell, Joan realized that she had traded in the stake for life in an English prison, not the ecclesiastical church, where she would have been protected. Defiantly, she put her menswear back on, rejecting her recantation. Some historians believe that it was a trap, that Joan's dress, which she had consented to wear, was stolen and she had no choice but to put on men's clothes again. Joan knew what she was doing; she was committing a crime punishable by death. She was now a relapsed heretic.

After the church pronounced her guilty, she was taken to be executed in the marketplace of Rouen. Before her death, Joan was allowed to take Holy Communion privately, although she was publicly excommunicated. On May 30, 1431, she was led barefoot to the marketplace. Seeing the stake, she couldn't control her emotions anymore and she burst into tears. Her last request was that a cross be held before her. An Englishman, John Tressart, said, "We are lost, we have burned a saint." Her ashes were scattered in the Seine to prevent them from being saved as holy relics.

Her death did not have the desired effect the English had hoped for. As Joan had prophesied, the English grip on France was now broken, thanks to her efforts, although England continued to hold some territory until Henry VIII. Despite his less than encouraging start, Charles VII became a strong king who left France in better shape than it was given to him in. Joan's myth started before her ashes were cold. Many claimed that her heart was not touched by the flames. Over twenty years after her death, Joan was vindicated by a new trial in 1455, ordered by Charles VII. This time, witnesses were called for the defense, including Joan's mother. When the trial ended in 1456, Joan was declared a national hero, the symbol of France. In 1920, nearly five hundred years after her death, Joan was canonized as a saint by the Roman Catholic Church, the same church that had found her guilty and ordered her execution.

So was Joan a hysteric or a saint? Or perhaps she was just a rebellious teenager who devised a clever way to escape a dull provincial life. There are as many versions of Joan as there are books in the library. In her short life she left her village, led an army, crowned a king, and was renowned throughout Europe. Her story has proved irresistible to the world's greatest artists for the past five hundred years.

# Grace O'Malley
## (Gráinne Ní Mháille)
### 1530–1603

*She was nurse to all rebellions in the province for this forty years.*

—Sir Richard Bingham

In the summer of 1593, an elderly woman traveled to England to plead her cause before Queen Elizabeth I. Her name was Grace O'Malley and she wasn't just any woman. For over forty years, she had ruled the sea in Connacht, plundering ships and causing trouble for the English in Ireland. Now at the age of sixty-three, she faced an uncertain future. Her only hope was to deal with the queen in person. It was an unprecedented meeting. Although other Irish chieftains had gone to England to parley with the queen, most ended up in the Tower of London. The meeting between these two queens would pass into folklore and legend, with the Pirate Queen of Connacht getting the best of Elizabeth I.

Grace O'Malley (Gráinne, her Gaelic name, means "sun") was born sometime in 1530 at the family castle on Clare Island off the west coast of Ireland. The O'Malley clan motto was *Terra marique potens* ("Powerful by land and sea"). Her father, Owen "Black Oak" O'Malley, had long made his living mainly on the sea, some of his activities legal (selling fishing rights, trading, and levying tolls for right of passage) and some of them not (piracy and ferrying mercenaries—the Gallowglass—from Scotland). His control over the sea was so extensive that in 1556, Philip of Spain had to pay Owen O'Malley one thousand pounds a year for twenty-one years of fishing rights.

Although she had an older half brother, it was clear that Grace was her father's pride and joy. Owen groomed her to take over the clan's fleet and fortune, making sure that she had a first-class education from the local monks. Her mother would have preferred that Grace be a proper lady but, like all the O'Malleys, Grace was born with salt water in her veins. Dressed like a boy, with her hair short, Grace would accompany her father on his trading trips. Legend has it that on a return trip from Spain their ship was attacked by the English. When her father ordered her to safety, Grace refused, instead climbing up the rigging. While watching the fighting, she leaped on the back of a man attacking her father, saving his life. She was barely a teenager when she took the wheel as captain of her first vessel.

Although Irish women had more freedom than their English counterparts, there were a few things forbidden to them. Grace's role as a ship's captain was unusual. Sailors were a superstitious lot, and women were considered to be bad luck on a ship. In fact, the only women generally allowed were the figureheads that graced the bow. The fact that Grace, for over forty years, was able to lead her men successfully despite being a woman says much about her personality and leadership skills.

Despite her abilities as a sea captain, like most girls of the period Grace couldn't escape marriage. At the age of sixteen, she married Donal O'Flaherty. Nicknamed "Donal of the Battles" because of his tendency to fight first and ask questions later, her husband was the heir to the O'Flaherty, the leader who ruled all of Iar-Connacht, a huge chunk of Ireland that the English were dying to get their hands on. Marriage and three children didn't stop Grace from continuing to captain ships, make raids on vessels, and basically lead an active, seafaring life. There is no mention of what Donal thought of her continuing to work after marriage. Apparently he had his hands full, what with being accused of murdering his stepnephew and trying to keep the peace among the unruly clans in Connacht.

Grace eventually commanded two hundred fighting men and three raiding ships. It was a hard life for a man, let alone a woman, but Grace loved being out on the sea. When she wasn't raiding English ships or ferrying mercenaries from Scotland, Grace did have legitimate business interests. The O'Malleys had long traded with other European countries such as France and Spain, bringing spices, wines, and other goods back home to sell. It was, however, as a pirate that Grace ruled the seas. It was rumored that she had buried more than nine tons of treasure, taken from her raids of castles and clans along the Irish coast. She was even tougher than the men she commanded; she loved gambling and could curse a blue streak when provoked. Grace earned the respect of her men because she wasn't afraid to fight alongside them with her cutlass and pistols.

Grace's husband, Donal, was killed at the hands of his old enemies, the Joyces, in revenge for an attack on their island fortress on Lough Corrib. Not content with killing Donal, the Joyces launched an attack on "Cock's Castle," one of the O'Flaherty strongholds. They reckoned without Grace, who with her husband's clansmen defended the castle with such skill that the name was permanently changed to "Hen's Castle."

She soon had to fend off a strong force of English soldiers who besieged her and her followers at the castle. Conditions soon grew desperate but Grace was not going down without a fight. Thinking quickly, she and her men melted down the lead roof of the castle and poured the molten liquid onto the soldiers, who beat a hasty retreat to the mainland. She sent one of her men under cover of darkness to light a beacon on the Hill of Doon as a signal. Soon the rest of her followers arrived to assist her in routing the English.

By Gaelic law, Grace was entitled to a widow's portion, one-third of her husband's estate. But this rarely happened, and Grace had three children to support. With her men, she established herself on Clare Island at the mouth of the mainland's Clew Bay. She had a splendid view of the ships coming in the harbor, the better to plunder. Sometimes, depending on her mood, she offered pilot services or charged protection money for safe passage.

On St. Brigid's Day, Grace's crew rescued a half-drowned man named Hugh de Lacy. Grace decided that he was a better prize than a casket of gold, took him home, and nursed him back to health and into her bed. The lovers' idyll was short-lived when Hugh, out deer hunting, was killed by the MacMahons of Bally-roy. Grace tracked them down while they were on pilgrimage, killing the ones she held personally responsible for Hugh's death. Not content with just that, she sailed to their castle in Blackhood Bay and tossed out or killed everyone who couldn't run fast enough, taking the castle for herself and adding to her list of nicknames "the Dark Lady of Doona."

In 1566, when she was thirty-six and still a fine figure of a woman, Grace married another chieftain, named Iron Richard Burke, whose family owned Rockfleet Castle, a key fortress in Clew Bay. Tradition has it that Grace only married him for his castle, the only piece of land in the area not owned by the O'Malleys. Once she had established herself and her followers, she locked him out and, taking advantage of the Gaelic custom that allowed divorce after a one-year trial period, divorced him by shouting down the words, "Richard Burke, I dismiss you."

Despite the divorce, Grace and Burke continued to live together as man and wife. She soon gave birth to their son, who was nick-named "Tibbot of the Ships" because legend has it that he was born while Grace was at sea. The ship was soon attacked by Turkish pirates. As the battle raged on deck, her captain came down below, where Grace lay with her baby, and begged her to come on deck to rally her men. With the words, "May you be seven times worse off this day twelve months, who cannot do without me for one day," Grace wrapped herself up in a blanket, grabbed a cutlass, and joined her men to defeat the Turks.

For the next twenty years, the battles between England and Ireland continued. The English were growing increasingly frustrated at the unwillingness of the Irish to become English. A policy began of surrender and regrant. The deal was that after submitting to the authority of the king, a chieftain would be "regranted" his lands. He would also receive an English title suited to his rank. While many of the clan chieftains, seeing which way the wind was blowing, submitted to English domination, Grace was not willing. Some battles she won, and there were many that she did not. Her good luck eventually ran out and she was captured by an old enemy, the Earl of Desmond, and spent two years in prison in Limerick and Dublin before she was released, promising to behave herself. Amazingly no one at the time seemed surprised that one of Ireland's greatest pirates was a woman. To the English, it just seemed confirmation that the Irish were barbarians.

Her greatest foe arrived in Ireland in 1579. Richard Bingham was sent to aid in the suppression of the Second Desmond Rebellion. For his efforts, he was appointed Lord President of Connacht in 1584. He hated Grace with a passion, calling her the "nurse to all rebellions in Connacht." He murdered her eldest son, Owen Flaherty, and convinced her second son, Murrough, to switch sides. In retaliation for Murrough's betrayal, Grace sailed to his town while he was away and burned it, stole all the cattle she could grab, and had several of his men killed for resisting.

By 1593, Grace was tired of fighting a losing battle. The Ireland that she had known in her childhood was disappearing. She was widowed a second time, Iron Dick having gone to that great pirate ship in the sky. The last straw was when her son Tibbot Burke and her half brother, Donal-na-Piopa, were taken captive by Bingham. Bingham also impounded Grace's ships, endangering her livelihood. Not one to accept defeat, Grace wrote a wily and flattering letter to Queen Elizabeth, requesting a meeting and explaining that she was only protecting her people against her neighbors, "which in like manner constrained your highness's bond subject to take arms and by force to maintain herself by land and sea." She also asked for a pardon for her sons, and requested that in spite of her age she be allowed "to roam the seas freely and to invade with sword and fire all your highness's enemies."

In September 1593 at Greenwich Palace, surrounded by guards and members of Elizabeth's court, these two legends finally came face-to-face. No one knows exactly what the two talked about; the only thing historians agree on is that their conversation was probably in Latin, the only language they had in common. On the surface the two women couldn't have been more different. Elizabeth I bedazzled with jewels and gorgeous fabrics to distract from her fading looks. Grace, weather-beaten by her years at sea, didn't even try to compete in the glamour stakes. She wore her finest dress, which was probably no longer in fashion, in the clan colors of yellow and green, and with her only jewel a silver clip in her gray hair, she was no match for Gloriana.

Both women were charismatic leaders, politically shrewd, and neither was used to taking orders from anyone. More important, both were survivors. Despite the legends that have sprung up around the meeting—that Grace refused to curtsy, that she tossed the queen's handkerchief into the fire after blowing her nose—it's hard to believe that Grace would insult or antagonize the queen with so much at stake. Grace was too canny for that.

She must have done a good snow job because Elizabeth agreed to some of her demands, one of which was the removal of Richard Bingham from power in Ireland as well as pardons for her son and her half brother. Grace in turn agreed to stop supporting the Irish lords' rebellions in Ulster and to make sea raids only for the English. Feeling victorious, Grace sailed back to Ireland, but, contrary to their agreement, the queen gave Bingham just a slap on the wrist. Several of Grace's other demands (the return of the cattle and land that Bingham had stolen from her, for instance) remained unmet, and within a rather short period of time, Elizabeth sent Bingham back to Ireland. Upon Bingham's return, Grace realized that the meeting with Elizabeth had been useless and went back to supporting Irish rebellions.

The Irish kept on battling the English until their defeat at the battle of Kinsale in 1601. Heartsick over the loss, Grace retreated to Clare Castle. She lived long enough to learn of Elizabeth's death in 1603 before dying several months later. It is said that after her death, no Irish chieftain was able to preserve the Gaelic way of life as Grace and her family had done. While Grace's place in Irish history was given short shrift in the chronicles of Ireland, her fame and exploits were kept alive by the bards who created poems and songs about her, including "Oró Sé do Bheatha 'Bhaile."

In 2007, Grace sailed on to the Great White Way, docking at the Ford Center as the heroine of a new musical entitled—what else—*The Pirate Queen*, bringing her story to a new generation.

# Wayward Wives

## Émilie du Châtelet
### 1706–1749

*When I add the sum total of my graces, I confess I am inferior to no one.*
—ÉMILIE DU CHÂTELET TO VOLTAIRE

Émilie du Châtelet was regarded as one of the most beautiful and brilliant women of the Enlightenment, even by her enemies; but for more than two centuries she was better known for being Voltaire's mistress. "Judge me for my own merits," she once protested. "Do not look upon me as a mere appendage to this general or that renowned scholar." Few women of the period could write, much less conduct experiments in physics, chemistry, and mathematics, compose poetry, and translate Greek and Roman authors into French with ease as she did. Her work contributed to energizing the school of theoretical physics in France. She would have been extraordinary in any era, let alone the one she was born in. In her lifetime, she fought for the education and publication that she craved, but struggled under the burdens of society's expectations for women of her class.

Gabrielle-Émilie Le Tonnelier de Breteuil grew up in the lap of luxury surrounded by servants in a three-story town house near the Tuileries gardens. She was doted on by her father, who encouraged her in her studies, refusing to let her mother send her to a convent. He made sure that she had the same education as her brothers, including fencing and riding lessons along with Latin, Italian, Greek, and German. She was so precocious that her father enjoyed showing her off to his intellectual friends. Her mother despaired at having such an unnatural daughter who refused to appreciate proper etiquette. But Émilie had a hunger for learning that just couldn't be quenched with talk of fashion and gossip. When her father's income shrank, and there was no money for new books, Émilie used her mathematical skills at the gaming tables to get her fix.

Tall and clumsy as a child, Émilie seemed destined for spinsterhood. Her father worried that "no great lord will marry a woman who is seen reading every day." But suddenly at the age of fifteen, she grew from an ugly duckling into a swan. Although she was almost a giant at five foot nine in era when even most men were an average height of five foot six, she was also blond with a supermodel figure and a face that could launch a thousand ships. Raised away from court, Émilie took joyous delight in everything, and soon bets were being made by the court rakes to see who could seduce her first. Émilie nipped that idea in the bud the day she verbally fenced with a colonel with consummate skill. This display of her rapier wit served to keep the rest at bay. They soon turned their attentions elsewhere.

Émilie went husband hunting with a vengeance. She had a laundry list of requirements: he had to be older, of higher rank, and he had to be content that she was beautiful and bright since her dowry was pathetic. She found him in the marquis Florent-Claude du Chastellet,* who was twelve years older, a career soldier from one of the oldest families in Lorraine, who preferred wars to court. Out of all of her suitors, he was the only one that Émilie felt she could tolerate. The marquis promised not to interfere with her studies, and Émilie promised to turn a blind eye to his infidelities. They were married on June 25, 1725, at Notre Dame. The story goes that the bride halted the ceremony to correct the clergyman's pronunciation of a Latin phrase.

After bearing three children, Émilie was bored out of her mind. She moved to Paris to pursue her studies further while her husband stayed in the country. She hired the best tutors in math and physics from the Sorbonne, studying like a fiend. Since women weren't allowed at Gradot's, the "in" coffee shop for the scientific crowd, Émilie donned breeches and a frock coat to talk shop with her peers. The proprietors pretended they didn't notice. Émilie still made time for high society, but she did it her way, dripping in diamonds and wearing gowns of gold and silver cloth, normally reserved for royalty, that were cut low enough to show off rouged nipples. She chatted happily about Descartes to her throngs of admirers. She held a salon in her newly renovated town house, decorated tastefully but expensively. When she ran out of money for the renovations, she gambled until she'd won enough to continue.

Once she'd given her husband an heir, Émilie indulged herself

---

* It was Voltaire who introduced the spelling Châtelet, which became the standard.

in a love affair with the duc de Richelieu.* The duke was rich, powerful, and extremely handsome; men wanted to be him, and women threw themselves at his feet. Émilie was a different kettle of fish. He fell for her because he liked to talk to her. She was witty and chattered a mile a minute about the things she loved, mainly science and the theories of John Locke. The affair didn't last long, as the duke couldn't be faithful to anyone, and the very qualities that made Émilie different began to pall after a while. Still, they managed to end their affair with dignity and remain friends.

Émilie yearned for a man who could satisfy her both intellectually and sexually. She found him in Voltaire. They were introduced by mutual friends in 1733 after Voltaire's return from a long exile in England. Already he was famous for his plays and poems and his ability to get into trouble. It was the coming together of two geniuses who defied social conventions. They were immediately attracted to each other and became lovers soon after they met. "Why did you reach me so late? What happened to my life before? I hunted for love but found only mirages," he wrote to her. They broke the conventionally accepted rules of adultery, showing their affection in public, romping indiscreetly all over the city.

They made an odd couple. Not only was Émilie a head taller than her lover but she was twenty-six and Voltaire was thirty-nine. Voltaire had finally found a woman who was intellectually his equal, although his superior in rank, and who respected and adored him. Émilie finally had a man who respected her brain as well as her body. He was also one of the few men rich enough to

---

* Louis François Armand de Vignerot du Plessis, third duc de Richelieu, was a French soldier and statesman. A notorious womanizer, he is considered the model for Valmont in Choderlos de Laclos' novel *Les liaisons dangereuses*.

afford her expensive tastes. Voltaire taught her how to speak English so that they could converse without anyone understanding what they were talking about. She read his work and gave him gentle criticisms.

Not long after they met, they moved into the Château Cirey, a tumbledown mansion owned by Émilie's husband in the country between Champagne and Lorraine. The move was precipitated by Voltaire getting into trouble again for his radical political views. For the next fifteen years, they lived there together, embroiled in a private world of intense intellectual activity intertwined with romance. Émilie described their life at Cirey as "Paradise on Earth." Voltaire lent the marquis forty thousand francs to pay for renovations to make the château livable, including a tub for Émilie's daily baths. Playing architect, Émilie installed a kitchen inside the château, a novel idea at the time. They quickly amassed a library of twenty-one thousand volumes, more than in most universities in Europe. The marquis was happy with the renovations because the restored house gave him a place to hunt. His visits also gave their affair an aura of respectability. The marquis was not a jealous man. Since Émilie had no objections to his affairs, he refused to meddle in hers.

The château became something like a modern-day think tank. Émilie and Voltaire entertained some of the best minds from Paris, Basel, and Italy, including her former lover Pierre Maupertuis, Francesco Algarotti, and Clairaut, hailed as France's new Isaac Newton, who at first came to scoff, but then hung around, impressed by what they saw. Visitors to the château were only entertained in the evenings since Émilie typically put in twelve to fourteen hours a day at her work. She had taken over the great hall as a physics lab, testing Newton's theories with wooden balls hanging from the rafters. Eventually the hall became so cluttered that it was an impenetrable maze. Émilie had prodigious energy, often sleeping only three or four hours a night. When she was on a deadline, she plunged her hands into bowls of cold water to stay awake.

Rooms were dimly lit and the curtains were shut, the better for mental stimulation. Guests were expected to entertain themselves. Dinner was at no set time, just when Émilie and Voltaire decided they were hungry. Émilie would arrive at the dining room table powdered and perfumed and dressed as if at a court ball, dripping in diamonds, her fingers stained with ink. Guests served themselves from the dumbwaiters. Conversation was fast and furious as the lovers discussed what they were working on or argued mathematical equations. After dinner it was back to work. Late at night, they would put on plays in the little theater or Émilie would play the pianoforte and sing entire operas. There would be poetry readings at 4:00 a.m. or picnics in the middle of winter.

Émilie and Voltaire decided to collaborate on a major project: a treatise on the works of Newton, covering the entire spectrum of his philosophical, scientific, and mathematical studies. When word first leaked, all of Paris ridiculed the idea. But when it was finally published after two years of work, Émilie had the last laugh. It was hailed as a masterpiece by every scientist of note. Although Voltaire's name was on the cover, he acknowledged her as coauthor. She was recognized as a woman of powerful intellect and finally treated with the respect that was due her. *The Elements of Newton's Philosophy* was so influential that it persuaded the French to abandon the theories of their national hero, René Descartes, and jump on the Newton bandwagon.

Now Émilie made the most unorthodox decision of her life: to submit an essay to the Royal Academy of Sciences yearly competition. This year the theme was fire. Émilie had been helping Voltaire with his essay but she felt that his conclusions were wrong. Her thesis was that light and heat were the same element while Voltaire believed the opposite. She had an unfair advantage since she knew what Voltaire had written. In two weeks she wrote her essay, 139 pages long. She didn't tell Voltaire that she was entering, although she did tell her husband; she needed his permission to enter. She submitted her entry anonymously, wanting it to be judged on its own merits. Neither Voltaire nor Émilie won, but he later persuaded the academy to publish her paper under her own name. It was the first time the academy had ever published a dissertation by a woman.

In her spare time, when she wasn't conducting science experiments or learning advanced calculus, Émilie wrote poetry, translated Latin and Greek classics, and mastered law to defend her husband's interests at court. For fun, she wrote one of the first self-help books, entitled *Discourse on Happiness*, which went through six editions. In it, Émilie taught women how to be as happy as she was. She advised them to cultivate "strong passions," enjoy sex, enrich their minds through education, and make themselves mistresses of the "metaphysics of love." Émilie translated the book into English herself and it was also translated into Dutch and Swedish.

But the idyll couldn't last. Voltaire fell out of love first. It was hard living with a genius, particularly one who was almost always right. He had taken up history and given up science, realizing that Émilie was far ahead of him intellectually in that field. "I used to teach myself with you," he wrote, "but now you have flown up where I can no longer follow." Émilie grew tired of having to tend to his ego, when she wanted to do her own research; and she became upset over the time Voltaire spent at the court of Frederick the Great of Prussia, whom she didn't like or trust. They both found solace in other lovers. Voltaire secretly began having an affair with his widowed niece Madame St. Denis. Émilie fell in love with the poet and soldier Jean François de Saint-Lambert, who was ten years younger. Their relationship eventually dwindled into a loving friendship. Although no longer lovers, they couldn't do without one another. No one understood them as well as each other.

At the age of forty-two, she found herself inconveniently pregnant. The relationship with Saint-Lambert petered out at the news. Voltaire, however, stayed by her side and her husband graciously offered to accept paternity. In a letter to a friend she confided her fears that, because of her age, she would not survive her confinement. During her pregnancy she moved into a suite at Versailles, where she redoubled her efforts to finish her book on Newton's *Principles of Mathematics*, staying up until the wee hours of the morning. She finished the book a few days before she went into labor in September. Émilie bore the child, but died six days later from an embolism. The child, a daughter, soon died as well.

Voltaire was distraught: "I've lost the half of myself—a soul for which mine was made." Months after her death, his servant Longchamps would find him wandering through the apartments that he had once shared with Émilie in Paris, plaintively calling her name in the dark. He helped to prepare Émilie's book, called *The Principles of Mathematics and Natural Sciences of Newton*, for publication. It came out ten years after her death, just in time for the return of Halley's comet, which stimulated a burst of interest in Newton. To this day it is still considered to be the standard translation of Newton in French, a lasting testament to the woman Voltaire described as "a great man whose only fault was being a woman."

# Lady Caroline Lamb
## 1785–1828

*I fear nobody except the devil, who certainly has all along been very particular in his attentions to me.*

—LADY CAROLINE LAMB

Lady Caroline Lamb famously remarked about the poet Byron that he was "mad, bad, and dangerous to know." By the time their affair ended nine months later, Byron was the one crying for mercy. "Let me be quiet. Leave me alone," he wailed in a letter to her, sounding unlike the hardened womanizer that he was. Even the rather louche Regency society was scandalized by her reckless behavior and flouting of convention.

The only daughter of the Earl and Countess of Bessborough, she was born in November 1785. Caroline came from a family noted for its eccentric, strong-willed, and scandalous women but she would surpass them all. Her aunt, the beautiful and glamorous Georgiana, Duchess of Devonshire, lived in an unorthodox arrangement with her husband

and his mistress, who happened to be her best friend. Caroline's mother occupied her time with her lover Lord Granville and fending off the playwright Sheridan.

Caroline had a chaotic upbringing, alternately running wild with her cousins at Devonshire House or restrained during her stay with her grandmother, the austere Lady Spencer. From early childhood, Caroline showed a vivid and volatile nature, high-spirited and fearless. She was also nervous and hyperactive, asking questions incessantly, sometimes the same question over and over again even after it had been answered, and getting on everyone's last nerve. To calm her down, she was given liquid opium. While most kids outgrow the inclination to say whatever comes into their heads, Caroline never did.

In 1805 Caroline married William Lamb, heir to Viscount Melbourne, after a three-year courtship. At the reception, Caroline broke into tears at leaving her family and had to be carried out by William to the waiting carriage. It was a sign of things to come. The couple was forced to move in with his family, occupying the upper floor of the mansion in Whitehall, because William's father refused to increase his allowance after their marriage. It was an uneasy fit. While her family was sophisticated and tolerant, the Lambs were a rowdy, boisterous family devoted to practical jokes. They made fun of her and jeered at William's devotion to his wife. His sister Emily in particular took against her and did her best to come between them.

If living with her in-laws wasn't bad enough, it was soon clear that the couple was incompatible. Darkly handsome, William was easygoing, with a mocking smile and an air of cultivated bored indifference. Caroline, on the other hand, was high-strung and childish. Although William loved her, he was also reserved, unable to give Caroline the petting and coddling she desired. He soon set about disabusing her of what he thought of as her old-fashioned notions, in particular her belief in God. She once remarked that William "amused himself with instructing me in things I need never have heard of or known." The physical side of marriage shocked Caroline as well, who probably had learned very little about sex before she was married.

After suffering two horrible miscarriages, Caroline finally gave birth to a son, Augustus, in 1807. Unfortunately, it soon became apparent that he was not only mentally handicapped but suffered from epilepsy as well. Caroline refused to send him away, ignoring the pleas of her family and her in-laws. Despite his affliction, she was devoted to him, but there would be no more children.

As her husband spent more time away from home on parliamentary business, Caroline grew bored and resentful. To provoke him and to be noticed, she wore risqué dresses cut almost to the nipple and flirted outrageously. Her behavior caused comment. "The Ponsonbys are always making sensations," one caustic observer wrote, referring to Caroline's family. She had a brief, publicly flaunted affair with Sir Godfrey Webster. Lady Melbourne was appalled, not because of the affair, but because Caroline committed the cardinal sin of being indiscreet. Not only did she accept jewelry and a puppy from Webster, but she also confessed the affair to her husband, who forgave her. She later admitted, "I behaved a little wild, riding over the downs with all the officers at my heels."

In March 1812, Caroline read an advance reading copy of Byron's *Childe Harold's Pilgrimage* and wrote him an anonymous fan letter. Her friend Samuel Rogers told her that Byron had a club foot and bit his nails but she replied, "If he is as ugly as Aesop, I must see him." Byron at this time had yet to become the rock star of the Regency that he was soon to be. He'd had some verses published in 1806 and 1807, but *Childe Harold* made his reputation after the first two cantos were published. Caroline wrote him an anonymous poem in iambic pentameter à la *Childe Harold*.

Byron later described Caroline to a friend as "the cleverest, most agreeable, absurd, amiable, perplexing, dangerous, fascinating little being that lives now or ought to have lived two thousand years ago." Caroline was beautiful and charming but, in the words of one of her friends, "had a restless craving after excitement." Byron received hundreds of what were essentially fan letters from women. But when he received Lady Caroline's poem, he was impressed, particularly when he discovered that the anonymous writer was the aristocratic and eccentric Lady Caroline Lamb. When she first saw him at a party at Lady Westmorland's, surrounded by beautiful women, she turned on her heel and declined to be presented, which intrigued the poet. That night in her journal she wrote, "That beautiful pale face will be my fate."

Soon after, while out riding, she placed an impromptu call on Lord and Lady Holland. When she was told that Byron was expected as well, she protested that she couldn't meet him dusty and disheveled. She ran upstairs to freshen up and when she came downstairs, Byron was entranced by the elfin creature before him, with her bobbed golden curls and boyish figure. Bending toward her, he whispered, "The offer was made to you before. Why did you resist it?"

She couldn't resist it now. What followed was an affair that lasted only nine months, but the repercussions continued for years. Caroline was totally besotted with Byron and, initially, he was equally smitten by her, although she wasn't his usual type; he normally preferred voluptuous, uncomplicated women. It was not just a sexual attraction but also an intellectual attraction. They shared a love for dogs, horses, and music. They wrote constantly to each other, sometimes every day. By the end of their affair, around three hundred letters had exchanged hands.

The public nature of the romance presented no problem to Caroline. Most of her family, including her mother-in-law, had little regard for fidelity, but they kept their liaisons quiet. This was not Caroline's style. She enjoyed making scenes, and with Byron, there was ample opportunity. Caroline didn't care about other people's opinions, a trait that Byron admired. She also had no use for the hypocrisy of the times, where as long as one was discreet, one could get away with anything. At first Byron was charmed by her enthusiasm, but eventually he got bored. He preferred the chase. As he summed it up, "Man's love is of man's life a thing apart, / 'Tis woman's whole existence." On the other hand, he also wanted all her love and devotion solely for him. It killed him when Caroline admitted that she loved her husband, and that she wouldn't tell him that she loved him more than William. The more he demanded of her, and the more she gave, the less he wanted her once the initial thrill was gone.

Byron soon pulled back, wounding Caroline, who wanted him to admit that the relationship mattered to him. Her infatuation became obsessive. She begged to be invited to suppers where she knew he was going to be. If she wasn't invited, she would wait in the garden. She made friends with his valet, in order to gain admittance to his rooms in St. James, where she rifled through his letters and journals. Hostesses began ridiculing her behind her back, as they smugly gossiped over tea.

His friends advised him that his affair with Caroline was ruining his reputation. He removed himself to his country estate, where Caroline bombarded him with letters he didn't answer. But Caroline persisted. She became that woman we all fear becoming, the crazy ex-girlfriend, unable to walk away with her dignity intact when it was clear that he was no longer interested. She sent him some of her pubic hair tinged with blood and dressed herself in a page costume to smuggle herself into his rooms. The campaign was so intense that Byron would refuse to attend social engagements for fear of meeting her. Byron's passive-aggressive behavior didn't help matters. He couldn't—or wouldn't—just end things. And William refused to play the outraged husband and demand she end the affair.

Byron detested "scenes" unless he was the one making them and he finally found the intensity all too much. He eventually broke off the affair, but Caroline wouldn't give up. She claimed that she and Byron intended to elope. Her father-in-law called her bluff, telling her, "Go and be damned! But I don't think he'll take you." Caroline ran off, her family panicked, and her mother had a stroke. It was left to Byron to bring her back, but she would only go after William promised to forgive her. Her parents eventually whisked her off to Ireland, where Caroline tried to forget Byron and repair the damage to her marriage.

While she was gone, Byron took up with Lady Oxford, an older woman with six children, who was also a friend of Caroline's. Lady Oxford encouraged her lover's disdain for Caroline, effectively ending their friendship. When Caroline wrote to Byron from Ireland, he would compose his replies to her with Lady Oxford's help. As she was arriving back in London, she received a letter from Byron, sealed with Lady Oxford's initials, that read: "I am no longer your lover; and since you oblige me to confess it, by this truly unfeminine persecution,—learn that I am attached to another; whose name it would be of course dishonorable to mention."

The shock made Caroline physically ill; she lost weight, and her behavior became increasingly erratic. During Christmas, she held a dramatic bonfire at Brocket Hall. While village girls danced in white, Caroline threw copies of Byron's letters into the fire, while a figure of the poet was burned in effigy. She forged a letter from Byron to his publisher, John Murray, in order to take possession of a portrait of him that he had long refused her. She would visit at inappropriate hours, once leaving a note in one of his books on his desk: "Remember me!"

At a party at Lady Heathcote's, as they exchanged barbed remarks about dancing the waltz, suddenly Caroline took a knife and slashed her arms. Horrified guests tried to stop the bleeding; someone offered a glass of water. Caroline broke the glass and tried to gash her wrists with the slivers. Finally Byron felt the only way to truly end Caroline's obsession was to tell her that not only had he slept with his half sister Augusta but that he'd also had affairs with men, hoping to turn her desire to disgust.

The nineteenth-century term for what ailed Caroline was "erotomania," dementia caused by obsession with a man. More likely Caroline was bipolar. Nowadays, she'd be given Prozac or lithium to balance out her moods, but back then the only treatment was laudanum, a concoction derived from opium and alcohol. It was used for everything from menstrual cramps to nervous ailments, from colds to cardiac diseases. The problem was that it was also addictive. Caroline began to use laudanum and alcohol indiscriminately to ease her nerves and the sting of Byron's betrayal.

Byron married Lady Melbourne's niece Annabella Milbanke in 1815, but after their first child was born, a daughter named Ada Augusta, the couple separated in 1816. Caroline at first was on Team Byron, writing to him, urging him to reconcile with his wife or to give her a large settlement so that a scandal could be avoided. If Caroline was hoping for a big thank-you from Byron, she was mistaken. All bets were off when she learned from John Murray that Byron had been so violent and cruel that Annabella feared for her life. Caroline swore to have no more communication with Byron. She also informed Annabella that he had confessed to an incestuous relationship with Augusta at their last meeting, although she begged Annabella not to tell Byron that she was the one who told her. When Annabella spread the word, Byron was forced to leave England.

Caroline got her own revenge of a sort in 1816 with the publication of her novel *Glenarvon*, a thinly disguised account of her relationship with Byron. She even quoted one of his letters in the novel. A gothic melodrama, her husband, William, also appears in it as the heroine's cynical husband who destroys his young wife's faith, while Byron is the hero/villain accredited with every crime from murder to incest to infanticide. The roman à clef also satirized the Holland House set so perfectly that twenty years after the book appeared, friends still called Lady Holland the Princess of Madagascar, after the character modeled on her, behind her back. Although the book was published anonymously, the ton were aware of the author and began to shun her. To Caroline's delight and everyone else's dismay the book sold out. When Byron heard the news, he told his publisher John Murray, "Kiss and tell, bad as it is, is surely somewhat less than f*** and publish."

The reviews of *Glenarvon* were encouraging enough for Caroline to continue to write, but the only opinion that she cared about was Byron's. She took other lovers but they could never replace Byron in her heart. The affair made her life afterward seem dull by comparison. In 1820, she appeared at a masquerade ball dressed like Don Juan, after the first cantos of Byron's now classic poem had been published. Four years later, she had a nervous breakdown after accidentally encountering Byron's funeral cortege as it passed through Welwyn, near Brocket Hall. As her health declined, she began abusing alcohol and laudanum and gave up regular meals and all semblance of order.

William's parents had encouraged him for years to formally separate from Caroline for the good of his career. They had even gone so far as to try and have her committed. However, every time he took steps to do so, they would reconcile. Despite her bad behavior, he continued to love her, although her tantrums and affairs took a toll on him. Finally in 1825, after William dithered about the separation one too many times, his sister Emily viciously and aggressively attacked Caroline, threatening a public trial. Caroline agreed to the separation.

By 1827, she was an invalid, under the full-time care of a physician. William had been given the post of Secretary for Ireland and was away when she took a turn for the worse. Despite the past, he was still devoted enough to her that he came back from Ireland in inclement weather to be by her side when she died on January 26, 1828. She was only forty-two years old. After her death, William never remarried. He told Lady Brandon, soon to become his mistress, that he felt "a sort of impossibility of believing that I shall never see her countenance or hear her voice again."

# Jane Digby

## 1807–1881

*Being loved is to me as the air that I breathe.*

—JANE DIGBY, WRITING TO KING LUDWIG OF BAVARIA

Jane Digby was born into an aristocratic family with every conceivable advantage—beauty, money, and privilege—yet she shocked her upper-class world by collecting husbands and lovers like a nineteenth-century Angelina Jolie before ending up in the arms of a desert prince. She had uncanny powers of fascination, luring men with her wit and charm. In her lifetime, no fewer than eight novels were written about her, most of them unflattering portraits. Cutting free from tight-laced English society in exchange for the life of a passionate nomad, she spent her life searching for that one perfect love.

Born in 1807, Jane was much loved and spoiled by her parents and relatives, who hated to discipline their golden-haired little darling. From childhood, Jane showed the reckless courage, independence, and taste for adventure that marked her ancestors, once wandering off with a band of gypsies because she liked their lifestyle. Jane's delicate beauty of blond ringlets, violet eyes, and creamy complexion was noticed at a very early age, as well as her power to attract the attention of men. It was her beauty that convinced her mother that it was prudent to get her married off as soon as possible.

At her coming-out ball, Jane met Edward Law, Baron Ellenborough. He was seventeen years her senior and a widower. On paper, it seemed a brilliant match. Ellenborough was a rising politician, handsome, and rich, and his maturity would curb her childish impulses. Flattered by the attentions of an older, experienced man, Jane accepted his proposal. She had visions of the grand life she would lead, the London house, the balls and parties, taking her place as a leading political hostess. On his part, Ellenborough was looking for two things: a decorative partner and an heir. After a short courtship, they were married by special license.

The old adage "Marry in haste, repent at leisure" could have been written about Jane's first marriage. No sooner had they shaken the rice out of their shoes than Jane realized why her husband had been called "Horrid" Law at school. Ellenborough was ambitious and totally devoted to his career. He thought nothing of spending long hours at the House of Commons late into the night, writing speeches, and hanging out with his political cronies. Instead of attention and affection, he gave her jewelry, cold diamonds that wouldn't keep her warm at night. Not only did Jane have to contend with the memory of his late wife, she soon discovered he had a mistress tucked away in Brighton.

Jane was not a woman who could live without love and passion in her life. If her husband was not willing to give it to her, she would look elsewhere. Dressed in décolleté gowns, Jane fell in with the glittering and sophisticated international society set led by Princess Esterházy. She soon found her cousin George more than willing to console her. When Jane found herself pregnant, she passed the baby off as her husband's. When her cousin finally dumped her rather than risk his career, Jane moved on to her grandfather's librarian. He later wrote that she had "blue eyes that would move a saint, and lips that would tempt one to forswear heaven to touch them."

It was at one of Almack's famous Wednesday night balls in late May 1828 that Jane, newly turned twenty-one, met the darkly handsome and courtly Prince Felix Schwarzenberg, an Austrian diplomat who had just been posted to London. The prince was instantly smitten and laid siege to her heart with flowers, poems, and presents until she succumbed to his ardor. It was more than a physical attraction for Jane. The prince had an air of mystery; he literally oozed adventure with his talk of the faraway places he had seen. Jane fell madly, ecstatically in love with him and didn't care who knew it, practically shouting it from the rooftops. Jane would visit him at his flat on Harley Street, wearing a veil to hide her identity, but before long they became reckless. She was seen by a neighbor in Schwarzenberg's embrace, the prince lacing up her stays. Soon the gossip about them was so flagrant that Schwarzenberg was sent packing back to the continent before his career was totally ruined.

When Jane realized she was pregnant, she decided to risk everything by joining her lover on the continent. Her parents pleaded with her to at least attempt to repair her relationship with her husband. Her father, in particular, tried to impress upon her what she was giving up by leaving him to go abroad. If she stayed in England, and they formally separated, she could still take her place in society after a suitable amount of time. But Jane was not to be denied. As far as she was concerned, her life and her fate lay with the prince. He was the only man she wanted to be married to.

When Ellenborough found out about the affair, he decided that the only hope he had of maintaining his career and saving his honor was to divorce her. The divorce case was so sensational that for the first time, the *Times* of London featured the story on its front page instead of among the classified advertisements that were a mainstay of the paper until the 1960s. Despite the fact that he was the "innocent party," Ellenborough was chastised for allowing his wife to associate with "undesirable persons." In exchange for Jane not introducing evidence of his own indiscretion in court, Lord Ellenborough settled a generous sum on her for the rest of her life.

While the divorce proceeded in England, Jane gave birth to Schwarzenberg's daughter. The prince soon proved to have feet of clay. Schwarzenberg's family was adamant that he break up with her. The family was Catholic and marriage to a now notorious divorcée would be ruinous. Realizing that he was out of his depth and fearing for his career, Schwarzenberg left her for good.

On the rebound, Jane fled to Munich and into the arms of King Ludwig I of Bavaria, who was captivated like many men before him by her beauty and intelligence. Her portrait joined the pantheon of other beautiful women in his "Gallery of Beauties." She also caught the attention of Baron Karl von Venningen-Üllner, who worshipped her and pursued her relentlessly while she pined for Felix. After months of rebuffing him in the hopes that Felix would return to her, she finally succumbed to his attentions and promptly became pregnant. Although she didn't love Karl, Jane succumbed to pressure from her parents, the baron, and the king to get married, but not before giving her daughter by Schwarzenberg to his sister, where she grew up with no memory or knowledge of her beautiful mother.

For a time she was content, but her husband wanted to turn

her into a German hausfrau in the country, while Jane was lively and intelligent and loved parties. Even a second baby couldn't tie Jane down. At a ball, during Oktoberfest, Jane met a young Greek count named Spiridon Theotoky, who awakened her sleeping passion. He was young and carefree, the antithesis of her sober and conservative husband. When the lovers tried to elope, her husband followed them and challenged the count to a duel. Although Theotoky was wounded, he managed to survive. Despite his hurt and humiliation Karl generously agreed to release Jane from their marriage. He received custody of their children, and he and Jane stayed friends for the rest of her life.

Jane moved to Greece and married her count, converting to the Greek Orthodox faith. They had a child, Leonidas, who became Jane's favorite, the only one of her five children that she felt any affection for. It seemed as if Jane had finally met her soul mate, until the family moved to Athens and Spiridon began drinking and spending his nights out. After fifteen years together, she discovered that not only was he unfaithful, but he was also stealing from her accounts, so she left him. No sooner had she settled into a new home, when she suffered the devastating loss of her six-year-old, Leonidas, who died falling from a balcony when he tried to slide down the railing to greet her.

Jane, beside herself with grief, believed it was a punishment for her actions. Leaving Greece, she wandered disconsolately around the Mediterranean. For a time she became the mistress of an Albanian general and was thrilled to share his rough outdoor life as queen of his brigand army, living in caves, riding fiery Arab horses, and hunting game in the mountains for food—until she found that he, too, was unfaithful, with her maid, no less, and left him on the spot.

Now middle-aged but still stunningly beautiful, and vowing to renounce men, she headed for Syria, to see Damascus. Speaking Turkish, dressed in a green satin riding habit, she hired a Bedouin nobleman, Sheikh Medjuel el Mezrab, who was twenty years her junior, to escort her. Smitten by her courage and zest for life, Medjuel proposed but Jane wasn't interested. On her second trip to Damascus, she began to see him in a different light. When he proposed again, she asked for only two things: that he divorce his wife and that he remain faithful to her. Despite the advice of the British consul and her family, she threw caution to the wind. At the age of forty-six, she had finally found the great love of her life. Medjuel gave her the love and devotion that she had been longing for, and an adventurous life among the Bedouin.

Jane made one last visit to England in 1856. She found English society rigid and straitlaced under the reign of Victoria and Albert. They found her shocking; not only had she married an Arab but she also had three ex-husbands who were still living! Jane realized just how far she had moved away, not just physically but mentally. Victorian England was no place for her. After six months, she kissed her family good-bye and returned to Medjuel and the desert.

During the remainder of her life she adopted for six months of each year the exotic but uniquely harsh existence of a desert nomad living in the famous black goat-hair tents of Arabia; the remaining months she spent in the splendid palace she built for herself and Medjuel in Damascus. Accepting Arab customs, although she never converted to Islam, she dressed in traditional robes, her blond hair dyed black. As wife to the sheikh and mother to his tribe she found genuine fulfillment. She learned to milk camels, she hunted, she rode into battle at Medjuel's side during the frequent intertribal skirmishes, and she raised Thoroughbred horses. Diplomats and scholars came to visit her, regarding her as an authority in the area. Middle Eastern expert and adventurer Sir Richard Burton called her the cleverest woman he'd ever met.

With her husband by her side, she passed away at the age of seventy-four. Obeying her final wishes, he had her buried in the Protestant cemetery in Damascus. Then her grief-stricken widower rode out into the desert and sacrificed one of his finest camels in her memory.

Jane Digby's worst sins were an overwhelming hunger for love and adventure, and an astonishing naiveté about men. Despite her romantic disappointments, she never allowed herself to become bitter or jaded. She always believed that the perfect lover was out there, one who would fulfill her body and soul. Some historians and biographers have regarded Jane as promiscuous or a nymphomaniac. But Jane was a serial monogamist. In every relationship, she gave her full heart; each time she was sure that she had found "the one." She could never be content with maintaining the discreet appearance of respectability. Jane also had a healthy sexual appetite in an era when women weren't supposed to enjoy sex. If she had been a man, she would have been admired and patted on the back.

Jane lived a remarkable life but she paid a high price for the choices she made, ostracized by most of her relatives and polite society and alienated from her children. She saw her name become a byword for scandal. Despite all this, Jane was able to look back on her life with no regrets. She had lived fully and loved.

# *Violet Trefusis*
### 1894–1972

*Across my life only one word will be written: "waste"—waste of love, waste of talent, waste of enterprise.*

—Violet Trefusis

It was to be the wedding of the year. St. George's Hanover had been booked, the invitations sent, the *Times* of London had reported on the impressive list of wedding gifts, including a diamond brooch from the king and queen, but London society wondered whether the bride would show up. There was an audible sigh of relief in the church when, wearing a gown of old Valenciennes lace over chiffon, Violet Keppel walked down the aisle on her father's arm and became Mrs. Denys Trefusis. But before the thank-you notes were written, Violet was back in the arms of her lover. It was a scandal that people could only whisper about behind closed doors. For the lover that Violet Trefusis refused to abandon was another woman: the writer Vita Sackville-West.

There were two great loves in Violet Keppel's life. The first was her mother, Alice Keppel, known as "La Favorita," mistress of Edward VII for the last twelve years of his life. Violet and her sister, Sonia, from an early age were in awe of their vivacious and charming mother. Violet once wrote, "I wonder if I shall ever squeeze as much romance into my life as she had in hers." Violet's father, the Hon. George Keppel, was a rather shadowy figure in their lives, his chief job to stay discreetly out of the way.

Violet was ten when she met her second great love, Vita Sackville-West, at a party. Although Vita was two years older, they bonded over their mutual love of books and horses. Both also had glamorous, dominating mothers and complacent fathers. The two young girls attended school together and wrote each other when they were apart. Violet, from the beginning, idolized Vita and bombarded her with letters. When Violet was fourteen and Vita sixteen they traveled together to Italy, where Violet had been sent to perfect her Italian. Violet declared her love to Vita and gave her a Venetian doge's lava ring she had wheedled from an art dealer when she was six. "I love in you what I know is also in me, that is, imagination, a gift for languages, taste, intuition, and a mass of other things. I love you, Vita, because I have seen your soul," she wrote.

After the death of Edward VII in 1910, the Edwardian era was over and with it Mrs. Keppel's reign as La Favorita. The new king and his queen ushered in a more conservative age with a less glittering court, at which Mrs. Keppel was not welcome. Practical as always, she took herself abroad as a sort of "discretionary" leave before reentering British society. Violet spent those years in Germany, Italy, and France, developing her fluency for languages.

Violet returned to England in 1913, dressed in the latest Paris fashions, to make her debut. With a glamorous, desired mother, it was difficult for Violet to feel as lovable, good-looking, or success-ful. Feeling she couldn't compete with her mother, she determined to be as different as possible. Wanting to be the center of attention, Violet usually managed it with her gift for mimicry, her low, husky voice, and her large gray eyes. She became a terrific flirt, becoming engaged to several men, including the nephew of the Duke of Westminster.

But underneath the gay exterior, Violet was desperately un-happy. She found her mother's world boring and straitlaced, full of old people talking about old ideas and obligations that she hated but was scared to defy. She had also never forgotten Vita. But their lives had gone in different directions. Vita had gotten married to diplomat Harold Nicolson and settled down to the life of a country matron, giving birth to two boys. She also adored her husband, whom she'd nicknamed "Hadji."

In April 1918, Violet invited herself to stay with Vita at Long Barn, the Nicolsons' home in the country, with the excuse that she was frightened by the threat of bombs in London. Vita was not too thrilled; they had seen little of each other during the war, and she thought they might end up bored with each other. Still, it would be impolite to refuse. One night Harold didn't return from London, staying the night at his club. The two women spent the day together, tramping through the woods; Vita shared her dreams with Violet of being a great writer. She also shared a secret about her marriage: that Harold had contracted a sexually transmitted disease from a man he had had a brief affair with at a country house party. While Vita was initially shocked, she and Harold came to an understanding that they would both be allowed to pursue outside affairs as long as their own bond was paramount. That agreement was soon to be tested. That night, wearing a red velvet dress exactly the color of a rose, Violet once again declared her love, but this time Vita reciprocated. In her diary, which her son Nigel later published as part of his biography of his parents, *Portrait of a Marriage*, Vita paints Violet as a seductress that she couldn't resist.

The two women became lovers, going off on holiday together to Cornwall. Emotionally, spiritually, and physically they were now united. It was a raging fire that threatened to torch everything in its path. Violet later wrote, "Sometimes we loved each other so much we became inarticulate, content only to probe each other's eyes for the secret that was secret no longer." They pretended to be gypsies and called each other Mitya and Lushka. They spent an increasing amount of time together, much to the dismay of Vita's husband, Harold. In the autumn of 1918, Vita and Violet began work on *Challenge*, Vita's romantic novel about the conflict between love and duty, in which she depicted herself and Violet as the lovers Julian and Eve. Vita took to wearing corduroy trousers; with her short hair, she looked like a man. Harold was incensed at the idea of Vita going off on holidays without him. She wrote him a letter, uncomplimentary toward Violet, telling him that she needed new experiences and horizons but it didn't dim her love for him.

Gossip about the two women wormed its way into all the smart drawing rooms in London. Mrs. Keppel worried that her eldest daughter was in danger of ruining herself. She had no problem with what people did behind closed doors, but appearances must be maintained. She didn't understand the new generation, who, having survived a war, had no interest in living as their parents had. Violet was unrepentant despite the gossip that was buzzing through London society. She was obsessed with Vita, spending her days in agony until the next time she could see Vita or would receive a letter from her. She and her mother fought when Mrs. Keppel caught her writing to Vita. "I hate lies," she wrote to Vita. "I'm so fed up with lies." Violet's dream was for Vita to leave Harold and go off to France with her to live openly as a couple.

In the meantime, Mrs. Keppel determined that it was time Violet got married. Society dictated that no matter what one's proclivities were, one still got married, particularly in the case of upper-class women who depended on marriage for support. Violet had no skills to support herself with independently; her only income was the allowance Mrs. Keppel gave her. No marriage, no allowance.

She even had the perfect candidate in mind, Major Denys Trefusis. The son of an old aristocratic family, he was twenty-eight and attractive, with reddish gold hair and blue eyes. An officer in the Royal Horse Guards, he had served heroically during the war. Awarded the Military Cross for his services during the war, Denys was tall, handsome, kind, and intelligent, with a sardonic wit similar to Violet's own. Violet met him in London when he was on leave and she had written him lively, chatty letters while he was at the front, seducing him by post.

Mrs. Keppel began actively promoting the match, hoping that marriage would settle her. Violet saw Denys as a way to get her mother off her back and to goad Vita to leave Harold, but she didn't intend to marry him. Vita, however, hoped that Violet would gain more freedom by marrying. Harold Nicolson, trying to be a good and reasonable husband, suggested that Vita buy a little weekend cottage in Cornwall where she could do whatever she wanted, and he wouldn't ask questions. This was exactly the type of life that Violet abhorred and wanted nothing to do with, a life of secrets and hypocrisy.

Denys proposed to Violet but she put him off. Instead, she and Vita went off to Paris for ten happy days. They attended the opera, ate in the cafés. They made a striking pair, Violet delicate and feminine, Vita tall with the elegance of a handsome boy. Instead of returning home, they went off to the south of France. In Monte Carlo, they scandalized everyone by dancing together at a tea dance at their hotel. Violet tried to extract promises from Vita that they would stay together indefinitely, threatening to kill herself if she didn't agree; these scenes would repeat whenever Vita tried to escape. But Vita didn't try too hard. Harold Nicolson later wrote to Vita, "When you fall into Violet's hands, you become like a jellyfish addicted to cocaine." The pair didn't return for four months.

If Violet wouldn't save herself, then Mrs. Keppel would do it for her. She sprang into action, demanding that Violet stop dithering and marry Denys. The engagement was announced after Denys agreed to Violet's condition that the marriage would remain unconsummated. He was genuinely in love with Violet and was prepared to let her have her way. Nigel Nicolson suggests in *Portrait of a Marriage* that Denys may also have been partially impotent, which would explain why he agreed to her demands, or perhaps he just thought that eventually the affair with Vita would peter out. Violet was in a quandary. Her life was about to become the very thing that she loathed. She wrote to Vita, panic-stricken, "Are you going to stand by and let me marry this man? It's unheard of, inconceivable. You are my whole existence."

On the day of her wedding, she wrote to Vita, "You have broken my heart, goodbye." Vita went off to Paris with Harold to keep herself from stopping the wedding. The marriage was doomed from the beginning. The newlyweds went to Paris for their honeymoon and ran smack into Vita and Harold. Vita met Violet at the Ritz, where they resumed their relationship. "I treated her savagely. I had her. I didn't care, I only wanted to hurt Denys,"

Vita wrote later. She promised Violet that in the autumn they would go away together. The next day, the two women confronted Denys with the truth about their relationship. Leaving Violet to deal with the wreckage of her marriage, Vita went off to Geneva with Harold.

The marriage between Violet and Denys continued to disintegrate as she heaped emotional abuse on the poor man, declaring that she would never care for him. He began tormenting Violet by burning her letters from Vita and checking her alibis whenever she went out. Denys was starting to show signs both of post-traumatic stress syndrome and tuberculosis. Violet didn't want to stay with him but it would have looked bad if she had abandoned a sick husband. A compromise was reached that nothing would be done about the marriage until after her sister Sonia's wedding. Her fiancé's family was already against the marriage because of Mrs. Keppel's affair with the late king. A scandal now would ruin everything.

Vita again told Violet that she would elope with her, that she would leave her old life behind. Finally the day came for the two women to leave. While Violet went ahead, Vita encountered Denys, who was looking for Violet, while she was waiting for the boat to France at Dover. The two struck up an unlikely friendship, which strengthened on the boat. In Calais, Violet refused to return with Denys. Harold Nicolson caught up with them in Amiens to complete the unhappy foursome. Accusations were flung, including that Violet was unfaithful to Vita with Denys, which Violet denied. The whole thing was too much for the two women. Finding that they were trapped on either side, Vita folded up her tent and returned with her husband to London. Although the affair continued intermittently for a year, the handwriting was on the wall. While Vita was everything to Violet, Vita had a life independent of her, with Harold, their sons, her gardening for which she would also become famous, and her writing. Violet felt she had been beaten by the bounds of convention.

Denys threatened not only to sue for divorce but to bring Vita's name into it, and Mrs. Keppel said no way. Violet was not going to disgrace the family any more than she already had. More to the point, if there were a divorce, she would have nothing to do with Violet emotionally or financially. Violet, who adored her mother, could not live without her approval. She had learned a hard truth, that society would never condone the love that she shared with Vita; it led to social ostracism and self-loathing.

Violet thought she was a rebel, that by openly flaunting convention, she would show the world that there was more to love than people dreamed of. She gave no thought at all to the pain she caused her parents, her sister, or particularly Denys. She never once realized how much she had wronged him or hurt him or even apologized for what she did to him. In her romantic fantasy, love should have conquered all. But there was the reality of life. As much as she deplored the hypocrisy of her mother's life and her aristocratic set, she also longed to emulate her mother and please her.

She and Denys settled in France, to avoid further scandal, where they led separate lives until his death in 1929. Chastened, Violet modified her behavior, but not her sexuality, learning the value of discretion to become more socially acceptable. She became involved with the American-born Princess de Polignac, who preferred to keep her private life private. The relationship relieved the boredom and loneliness Violet had felt since the end of her relationship with Vita. But she was never again to give herself so completely. Relationships would always be tempered with reservations.

She wrote novels, including her own account of her affair with Vita disguised as a heterosexual relationship; threw dinner parties; told witty stories; and hobnobbed with members of Parisian literary society. Colette nicknamed her "Geranium." Violet became a notable eccentric who embellished stories; but she was still in thrall to her mother, who, she wrote, still treated her like a little girl. When she and Vita reconnected in England during World War II, neither one wanted to stir the embers of the still burning fire. After the war, Violet resumed her life in France but her mother's death in 1947 was a great blow. She wrote, "What has happened to me since is but a post scriptum. It really doesn't count."

Increasingly fragile as she got older, Violet passed away in 1972, ten years after Vita, at L'Ombrellino, a villa overlooking Florence that she had inherited from her parents. Her ashes are buried with her mother's in Florence.

## *Zelda Fitzgerald*
### 1900–1948

*Both of us are very splashy vivid pictures, those kind with the details left out, but I know our colors will blend, and I think we'll look swell hanging beside each other in the gallery of life.*

—ZELDA FITZGERALD TO SCOTT,
TWO MONTHS BEFORE THEIR WEDDING

On a hot summer night in July 1918 at the Montgomery Country Club, Zelda Sayre sauntered out onto the dance floor and captured the heart of First Lieutenant Francis Scott Key Fitzgerald. She was a few days short of turning eighteen, but already a celebrity by Montgomery standards. Zelda had a reputation as something of a wild child. Flirtatious and flamboyant, she enjoyed scandalizing her proper Victorian father, Judge Anthony Sayre, who was one of the leading citizens of the capital.

There were Southern belles and then there was Zelda Sayre. Tall and slender, with honey blond hair and a Kewpie doll pout, Zelda had teenage boys and college students tripping over themselves to get to her. She had so many beaus that she was attending parties every single night of the week. When her father forbade her from going out so much, Zelda just climbed out the window and shimmied to the ground. Zelda was vivacious and fearless, and she genuinely didn't care what people thought of her. Whether wearing a form-fitting swimsuit that appeared almost nude or roller-skating down the steepest hill in town, Zelda was noticed. She wore makeup and bobbed her hair, drank "dopes" (Cokes with aspirin) at the drugstore, and parked with boys on Boodle's Lane. But she knew just how far to go in her behavior without ending up with a reputation for being "fast."

Not yet twenty-two when they met in the summer of 1918, Fitzgerald was on the five-year plan at Princeton University and hadn't graduated. In his Brooks Brothers uniform, his handsomeness almost made him look feminine. "He smelled like new goods. Being close to him, my face in the space between his ear and his stiff army collar was like being initiated into the subterranean reserves of a fine fabric store," Zelda later wrote.

Soon he was joining the throngs of men who hung about at the Sayre house on Pleasant Avenue, vying for Zelda's attention. In a matter of a few weeks, the two were in love. They courted, sitting on her front porch sipping lemonade and dancing all night at the country club. As a gesture of his affection, he carved their initials into a tree. They slept together almost immediately, leaving Scott wondering who else might have been to paradise with her before him. For two years he and Zelda carried on a long-distance relationship. Scott was tormented by Zelda's letters, which included details of all the parties and dances she was going to while he was gone.

Zelda still continued to see other men; she was young, why shouldn't she have fun? After all, Scott was all the way up in New York City. He certainly couldn't expect her to sit home playing tiddlywinks, could he? The biggest obstacle to their getting married was Fitzgerald's lack of money. Zelda had been raised to be a rich man's wife. Quitting his advertising job, he holed up back in St. Paul, Minnesota, subsisting on Coke and cigarettes, to rewrite his first novel, published in 1920 as *This Side of Paradise*. The heroine in the book owed much to Zelda. He even used portions of her diary and her letters to create the character of Rosalind Connage.

Now that he was about to be a published author, Scott took the train down to Montgomery to propose to Zelda. Fitzgerald's friends warned him not to marry "a wild, pleasure loving girl like Zelda." While he conceded that he might be in over his head, he explained, "I love her and that's the beginning and the end of it." As for Zelda, now almost twenty years old, she was ready for a new adventure. Scott wove tales of what their life would be like in New York. After four years of being the most popular belle in Montgomery, perhaps Zelda sensed that her time was coming to an end. There were younger and prettier girls just waiting in the wings to take her place.

The first years of their marriage were spectacular. Scott and Zelda were the celebrity couple of the Jazz Age. Stories abounded of their antics: Zelda and Scott riding on top of a taxicab, Zelda jumping full-clothed into the fountain in Union Square, the pair spending a half hour going through the revolving door at the Commodore Hotel. Everything they did was news. They were good-looking and risqué. Soon they were hobnobbing with the glitterati of Manhattan's café society as well as its literary lights. They met everyone from Dorothy Parker to Sinclair Lewis. Silent screen star Lillian Gish said of them, "The Fitzgeralds didn't make the twenties, they were the twenties." They seemed to symbolize a generation that had been baptized by fire in the Great War. Their lives were filled with an aura of excitement, bathtub gin, and romance.

Fueled by bootleg liquor, they spent several weeks drinking, attending the theater or rooftop parties, and going through Scott's book royalties faster than they came in. They lived in hotels for the most part, since Zelda was crap at housekeeping, throwing lavish parties in their suite. Soon they were doing outlandish things just for the effect; they were the Spencer Pratt and Heidi Montag of the Jazz Age but with charisma and talent. Scott quickly shed his Midwestern morals, performing a striptease along with the talent onstage one night, which got him and Zelda evicted from the theater. Zelda had no qualms about taking off her clothes and having a bath in other people's homes.

Because of her status as Mrs. F. Scott Fitzgerald, people were clamoring for her views on the "New Woman," as well as the phenomenon known as "the flapper," a young woman free from the conventions of the day, smoking, drinking, and doing what she pleased. Zelda was the flappers' patron saint. She turned out to be a natural as a writer with a distinctive voice. Scott had no qualms about having Zelda's stories published either under their joint names or under his name alone. There was a practical reason for this. Stories under his name paid top dollar, as much as four thousand dollars at the height of his popularity, while stories with Zelda's name alone rarely fetched as much.

Zelda at first had no objection to Scott not only publishing her work under his name but also advancing the idea that she was his Muse. In fact, they both encouraged the idea. The cover of *The Beautiful and Damned* featured a couple that looked amazingly like Scott and Zelda. She wrote a tongue-in-cheek review of the book for the *New York Tribune* entitled "Friend Husband's Latest," in which she said that Fitzgerald "seems to believe that plagiarism begins at home." From the beginning Zelda considered herself Scott's literary partner. She read his drafts and discussed story ideas, and soon she was line editing and creating dialogue.

But as the years passed, Zelda became less sanguine about the situation. The cracks began to show beneath the façade of the Jazz Age flapper and her consort. While they were courting, Zelda had held all the power, with her elusiveness and her ability to torment him with her other flirtations. The only way that Scott could hold Zelda was to marry her. Once they were married, however, the balance of power shifted in Scott's favor. Zelda became dependent on him, and not just financially—her notoriety derived in part from being his wife. Even her small forays into writing were supported solely due to her marriage to Scott. For his part, Scott was surprised when people he admired, like the critic George Jean Nathan, were interested in Zelda, as an individual apart from her connection to him.

And then there was the drinking. At Princeton, Scott had had a reputation for being a hard drinker. Initially, he would stop drinking while he wrote, but as the years passed and it took longer and longer to write his novels, he began to drink in order to write.

Zelda could knock back a few cocktails as well as Scott, but there was a darker side to Scott's drinking. He could be verbally abusive and belligerent while drunk.

They lived an increasingly nomadic existence, as they criss-crossed the country from Connecticut to St. Paul and Montgomery, finally settling in Great Neck for two years while they tried to economize and Fitzgerald wrote. When Scott wrote, he required a life free from distractions, which left Zelda at loose ends. While he holed up in his study working feverishly on the short stories that kept them afloat between novels, she spent her days swimming, playing tennis, or waiting for the bootlegger to show up with their booze. Even the birth of their daughter, Scottie, didn't completely fill up her days.

Attempting to save money, the Fitzgeralds sailed for Europe, where the dollar was strong and drinking was legal, along with fifty-five pieces of luggage, and settled in the south of France. They would spend the better part of the next five years abroad. While Scott hunkered down to finish what would be his masterpiece, *The Great Gatsby*, Zelda was bored. She and Scott became friendly with a group of French pilots stationed nearby. For Zelda, it brought back memories of her glory days in Montgomery when pilots from the nearby airfield would fly over her house. Zelda became particularly friendly with one in particular. When she told Scott that she had fallen in love and wanted a divorce, he locked her in the villa. Depressed, Zelda took an overdose of sleeping pills. Still only twenty-four, she felt as if life was passing her by. Her unhappiness manifested itself in illness; she began to suffer from anxiety attacks and colitis.

They continued to quarrel and make up incessantly, seeming to egg each other on to see who could be the more outrageous. Once

Zelda threw herself under the wheel of their car and goaded him into driving over her, which he almost did. They fought over his drinking, which was getting in the way of his work. When Scott flirted with an aging Isadora Duncan in a café in the south of France, Zelda threw herself down a flight of stone stairs.

Needing a creative outlet of her own, Zelda was drawn back to her first love, ballet. Despite the fact that ten years had passed since her last dance class, Zelda became fanatical about practicing. She installed a mirror and a barre so she could work sometimes for eight hours a day. As Scott was stalled in writing his new novel, he resented Zelda's determination to revive her dance career. He was unwilling to admit that she might have real talent, that she needed to be seen as more than his wife. Despite her age, Zelda was offered a position with a company in Naples, dancing a solo in *Aida*. No one knows exactly why she turned it down. Perhaps just the offer was enough for her.

In 1930, Zelda had her first breakdown. The sparkle had gone out of her; she seemed tired and distracted. Her blond hair turned dark brown, and she lost weight. She complained of hearing voices in her head, and her speech became confused. Diagnosed with schizophrenia, for the rest of her life she would be in and out of institutions, most of the time voluntarily. Scott blamed her breakdown on her obsession with dancing. She agreed to cease dancing if he would stop drinking but he refused to see he had a problem.

While recuperating at the Phipps Clinic at Johns Hopkins in 1932, Zelda began secretly working on her first novel, *Save the Waltz*. It was the semiautobiographical story of a young woman from the South who marries a famous artist. Without telling Scott, she sent the manuscript to his editor, Maxwell Perkins, at Scribner. When Scott finally read the manuscript he felt betrayed; as Zelda's biographer Nancy Milford writes, he believed that Zelda had directly invaded what he considered his domain. How dare Zelda use her own life for her work? Her life belonged to Scott, not to her. It was as if she were his personal property, not just his wife. He was writing his own book, one that would become *Tender Is the Night*, which used some of the same material.

During a joint session with her doctor, the transcript running 116 pages, Scott blamed her for the fact that he hadn't published a novel in seven years, refusing to see the role that alcohol played in his inability to work. He disparaged her, calling her a third-rate writer and a third-rate ballet dancer. Zelda wearily responded that he was making quite a violent attack on someone he considered third-rate. She assured him that she was not trying to be "a great artist or a great anything." She just needed a creative outlet, to have a sense of self. Nevertheless she changed the novel according to his wishes and it was published in October of 1932. The reviews were poor and it sold less than half of its three-thousand-copy print run. Zelda earned $120.73 from her novel.

Although they never lived together as husband and wife again, Scott never abandoned his wife during her years of mental illness. In 1936, Zelda entered the Highland Hospital in Asheville, North Carolina, where she would spend the next twelve years on and off. Scott died in Hollywood in 1940, having last seen Zelda a year and a half earlier. She was too unwell to attend his funeral. Fitzgerald left her an annuity to help pay for her medical bills. When she was well, she lived with her mother in Montgomery until her demons came back, and she would go back to the hospital. She submitted to electroshock therapy, which helped but also damaged her memory.

Zelda spent her remaining years working on a second novel,

which she never completed, and she painted extensively. In 1948, a fire broke out on the top floor of the hospital, causing her death. It took some time before her charred body could be identified. Scott and Zelda are buried with the other Fitzgeralds at Saint Mary's Catholic Cemetery. Inscribed on their joint tombstone is the final sentence of *The Great Gatsby*: "So we beat on, boats against the current, borne back ceaselessly into the past."

# THREE

# *Scintillating Seductresses*

## *Anne Boleyn*
### 1501?–1536

*I never wished to choose the King in my heart.*

—ANNE BOLEYN

Anne Boleyn is probably one of the most maligned queens in English history. During her lifetime, she was considered an enchantress who seduced Henry VIII through witchcraft; she was accused of having a sixth finger and a third breast; she was called "the concubine" or worse. Historians since then have been divided about Anne's true nature and motives. Was she the instrument of an ambitious family that craved power above all else, or was she a devout evangelical Christian who believed that God had put her on earth to lead England toward the true religion? By capturing the heart of Henry VIII she set in motion the action that changed the course of English history.

Born sometime around 1501, she was the middle child of Thomas Boleyn and his wife, Lady Elizabeth; through her mother she was a niece of the man who would become the powerful third Duke of Norfolk. At the age of twelve, Anne was sent to the continent as lady-in-waiting at the courts of Margaret of Austria and Claude of France. There she picked up the sophisticated élan that set so many male hearts aflutter at Henry's court. She learned to speak French like a native, to dance with flair, and to flirt in the continental fashion, promising everything but giving away nothing. It was at the court of Francis I that Anne may have come into contact with his sister, Marguerite de Navarre, who was the patron of Christian humanists, such as François Rabelais, who espoused reform within the Catholic Church.

Anne was recalled to England in 1521 to marry her cousin. When that engagement fell through, she was sent to court, this time to serve Henry VIII's first wife, Catherine of Aragon. She quickly became popular, at least among the men. She wasn't beautiful by sixteenth-century standards, which favored plump, blue-eyed blondes, but she knew how to make the most of what God gave her. She dressed impeccably in rich colors to enhance her dark hair and olive complexion. Rejecting the unflattering gabled hood then in vogue, which looked like a house sitting on one's head, Anne brought the chic French hood into fashion.

Anne was vivacious and flirtatious and not afraid to speak her mind. She must have seemed like an exotic bird to the Englishmen used to women who demurely lowered their eyes and spoke in soft voices. Her years on the continent had polished her talents to a high sheen. One courtier wrote, "Albeit in beauty she was to many inferior, but for behavior, manner, attire, and tongue, she excelled them all, for she had been brought up in France." She was chased by several admirers, including the married poet Thomas Wyatt;

however, she had her eye on Henry Percy, eldest son of the Earl of Northumberland, one of the most powerful nobles in the north of England. The fact that he was already betrothed to the daughter of the Earl of Shrewsbury didn't stop him from falling under Anne's spell. They secretly became engaged, until Cardinal Wolsey, Henry's chief minister, got wind of it and took Percy to task, reminding him of his obligations and Anne's unworthiness to be married into the Percy family. Wolsey's prevention of her marriage to Henry Percy would eventually end up costing him dearly.

It wasn't long before Anne caught the eye of an even bigger fish at court. Grown tired of his wife, Catherine of Aragon, Henry VIII turned his icy blue eyes Anne's way. This Henry wasn't the corpulent, sore-ridden, cantankerous monarch that he became in his later years. Then thirty-five, he could have been the centerfold in "Hot Renaissance Princes." He stood six foot one, towering over most of the other men at court, with the famous Tudor red hair. He was a musician, poet, linguist, scientist, and star athlete. How could Anne resist? And yet she did.

Henry hunted her like one of the deer in Richmond Park, beating her down with the chase. He wrote her ardent letters, seventeen of which later ended up in the Vatican archives, filled with racy bits where he begs, "give your heart and body to me," and talks of her "sweet duckies [breasts] I trust soon to kiss." Anne tried to subtly reject his advances; she didn't write back often and she stayed away from court. Her unavailability just spurred his obsession. Pulling out all the stops to woo her to be his mistress, he even sent her a buck that he had killed with his own two hands. Even when Henry wrote and told her that she would be his only mistress it didn't sway her.

What Henry didn't understand was that Anne was a *rules* girl. No ring for Anne, no ring-a-ding-ding for Henry. She was determined not to end up like her sister, Mary, discarded by the king after their liaison with no decent jewelry to show for her time on her back. But because of Henry's interest in Anne, no other man would step forward as a possible suitor, for fear of offending the king. Anne was now twenty-five and in danger of ending up on the shelf. The stalemate went on for a year before the king finally capitulated and offered to make Anne his wife.

It would take six long years for Henry to end his marriage and make Anne his queen. They were turbulent years that involved never-ending papal entreaties, courtroom drama, bribery, and finally the cherry on top of Anne's sundae, the disgrace and death of her enemy, Cardinal Wolsey. Anne wasn't a passive participant; it was she who encouraged Henry in the idea of breaking with Rome. She had been reading a banned book, by the heretic William Tyndale, that suggested that kings ruled by divine right and must be obeyed in everything. It was just what he was looking for. Henry was not a man to be thwarted, he wanted a son, he wanted to be rid of Catherine, and he wanted Anne, even if it meant that he had to break with the Church of Rome to do it.

In the meantime, Anne continued to keep Henry on a leash, allowing him to get just close enough before pushing him away. She sang, she danced, and she hunted with him, but at night she closed the door to her room, leaving him to take a cold shower. It's impossible to say when or if Anne fell in love with Henry. She certainly loved what he had done for her and her family, the power she now wielded. Whether that led to true love is anyone's guess.

As Anne's star rose, so did the Boleyn family's, racking up peerages, lands, honors, and enemies. Her father became the Earl of Wiltshire, her brother Viscount Rochford, and Anne herself was made Marquess of Pembroke in her own right. As Catherine became marginalized, Anne took her place at Henry's side, queen in all but name.

As soon as the archbishopric of Canterbury became open, Henry appointed reformer Thomas Cranmer to the job. His first order of business was to make Henry head of the Church of England (with a little help from Parliament) and to push through the divorce. In one fell swoop, Henry had gained more power than any English monarch before him, but he had also pissed off a segment of the population still loyal to Rome and opened wounds between Catholic and Protestant that took years to heal.

Finally, with the divorce all but signed, sealed, and delivered, and an engagement ring safely on her finger, Anne gave in to Henry's desires. To Henry's great joy, she was soon knocked up. After the new Archbishop of Canterbury pronounced Henry's marriage to Catherine null and void, Anne and Henry were free to be husband and wife. They wed in England in a secret ceremony. Now that she was carrying what Henry hoped was his son and heir, Anne was crowned with all due pomp and ceremony on June 1, 1533. Befitting her newly royal status, she was dressed in purple edged in ermine fur, her hair loose under a caul of pearls. When the heavy crown of St. Edward, the same as worn by the sovereign at his coronation, was placed on her head at Westminster Abbey, Anne must have heaved a sigh of relief. She had achieved the hat trick; it was a big middle finger to those who considered the Boleyn family ambitious upstarts. Hopefully Anne savored that Kodak moment because from that high point it was a slow, slippery slide to her date with the swordsman.

Instead of the boy that many astrologers had predicted, Anne gave birth to a daughter, and Henry already had one of those. The marriage was less than a year old and Anne had proved to be a disappointment. Soon it was *The War of the Roses, Part Deux*, complete with loud fights, broken crockery, and passionate recon- ciliations. The very qualities that had attracted Henry to Anne, her independent spirit and intellectual bantering, began to bug him. He expected his wife to obey him in all things. Instead of the ar- dent lover who had given her dead animals as love tokens, Anne now had a husband who had grown increasingly paranoid and suspicious as he aged. And there were problems in the bedroom; Anne imprudently confided in her sister-in-law Jane that there was very little fire in the royal cannon.

Anne had expected to be Henry's partner, to reign beside him. She believed that God had chosen her to be queen to reform a corrupt church. Her first order of business was to appoint evan- gelical chaplains to her household and to secure bishoprics for reform-minded clergymen. Anne helped religious exiles, and because of her influence, many reformers were able to return to England. She also made the poor and the lower classes one of her missions. On progress, she distributed clothes to the poor, helped pregnant women, and even paid for farmers in difficulty to receive new livestock. Anne was discreet about her charity work, although it is estimated that she donated almost fifteen hundred pounds a year.

Anne soon began to crack under the strain, turning her sharp tongue on her husband, flaying him like a piece of leather. One successful pregnancy and two miscarriages in three years must have had her hormones completely out of whack. Henry's eyes began to roam the court looking for a diversion from his harridan of a wife. When she complained, Henry told her to remember where she came from and that if he had to do it all over again, he wouldn't! Anne must have started to panic. She knew that she was only safe as long as the king loved her. She grew thin and brittle, looking older than her years. To compensate for her unhappiness, and hoping to provoke Henry's jealousy, she began to flirt outrageously at court.

Anne became increasingly isolated. Her arrogant and high-handed behavior on her way to the top had made her many enemies eager to see her fall. Catherine of Aragon still had friends at court, who called Anne "the goggle-eyed whore" behind her back. Her poor treatment of the young princess, Mary, appalled even her friends at court. She was blamed for the deaths of Sir Thomas More and Bishop Fisher, who refused to sign the Acts of Succession. Even her uncle the Duke of Norfolk, once one of her biggest supporters, began to turn his back on her. Norfolk liked his women docile and obedient and was not pleased that Anne was not willing to be his puppet. He was willing to support his niece as long as it was politically expedient; otherwise he was perfectly willing to throw her under the bus to save his own skin. Anne lost Thomas Cromwell's support when she differed with him about where the resources of the church should be spent. She wanted education and relief for the poor. Cromwell began to resent her growing power. He now made it his mission to take Anne down before he met the same fate as Wolsey.

Her rise had set a dangerous precedent, as other ambitious ladies-in-waiting batted their eyes at the king. One in particular was Jane Seymour, who had been one of Catherine of Aragon's attendants. She was the antithesis of Anne, barely literate and meek. At twenty-eight, she was even older than Anne was when Henry was first courting her. Taking a leaf out of Anne's book, she was keeping her legs crossed until marriage. Encouraged by her brother Edward and Thomas Cromwell, Jane encouraged Henry's disillusionment with his wife.

The only happiness in Anne's life was her daughter, Elizabeth.

Any disappointment she might have felt over Elizabeth not being a boy was swept away on a tide of maternal love. She had wanted to breast-feed the baby herself, but Henry nipped that idea in the bud. Refusing to be separated from her daughter, Anne brought the infant to court, laying her on a velvet cushion next to her throne. When Elizabeth was finally moved to her own establishment, Anne spared no expense to make sure her little darling was the most stylishly dressed baby in the kingdom. An attentive mother, not only did she visit her daughter regularly but made sure she was brought to court, the better to show her off. She was also ambitious for Elizabeth, wishing her to be well educated, in preparation for her role as Henry's heir.

Anne's inability to bear a son added fuel to the vitriol and rumors spread by her enemies. Henry began to fret that he would never have a legitimate heir to his kingdom. He began to question his marriage, claiming that Anne had bewitched him. In January 1536, Henry had a jousting accident; thrown from his horse, he lay unconscious for two hours. Anne had another miscarriage, this time a boy. It was the final nail in her coffin.

On May 2, 1536, Anne was arrested and charged with adultery, incest, and intent to murder the king. Surprised and frightened, she fell to her knees, claiming that she had committed no crime. She was taken to the Tower of London, to occupy the same rooms she'd occupied before her coronation. Five men were accused and charged with committing adultery and incest with the queen: a young musician, Mark Smeaton; her brother, George; Sir Henry Norris; Sir Francis Weston; and William Brereton. Four of them denied the charges, but Smeaton confessed to adultery under torture. They were all tried quickly, found guilty of treason, and summarily executed.

Anne's own trial was a sham from the beginning. Even her

greatest enemies didn't believe the charges against her, the most heinous being that she had tried to conceive a child with her own brother. None of her ladies were charged as conspirators to her adultery. The evidence against Anne and her brother came solely from his wife, Jane. Jealous of his relationship with his sister, Jane stuck the knife in Anne's back so deep it's a wonder it didn't come out the other side. Anne defended herself eloquently but the sentence was a forgone conclusion. Anne's own uncle, the Duke of Norfolk, pronounced the guilty verdict, as her former love Henry Percy looked on.

Showing some mercy, the king paid twenty-four pounds for an expert swordsman to come over from Calais to perform the deed on Tower Green, but not before he divorced her. Yes, just to rub salt in the wound, Henry had his marriage to Anne annulled two days before her execution. And irony of ironies, it was on the grounds that she had been previously contracted to marry Henry Percy! Even though this technically nullified the charge of adultery, the king was still determined that her head would roll. Still, to the very last minute Anne hoped for a reprieve. She was doomed to be disappointed.

On May 19, 1536, Anne dressed carefully for her final public appearance, wearing an ermine cloak and a gabled hood. Underneath the cloak, she wore black damask and a kirtle of red, the color of martyrdom, proclaiming her innocence. As she walked through the vast crowd, she distributed alms to the poor, her last act as queen. Carrying her book of psalms with her, she mounted the scaffold. As was the custom, Anne made a final speech from the scaffold; she refused to condemn Henry for his actions, to protect her daughter, Elizabeth. With her final words, Anne knelt down and prayed before being beheaded with one stroke of the sword. Eleven days after Anne's death, Henry VIII married Jane Seymour, who took the motto "Bound to Obey and Serve." He never again spoke of the woman he had once promised "ever truly to honor, love and serve."

Anne's reign of a thousand days had more of an impact on English history than Henry's other five wives combined. The crown broke with the Church of Rome, putting the power into the hands of the king. There would be other ambitious families who jockeyed for position close to the crown using the weapons that Anne wielded so effectively in the beginning. In the end, it wasn't sex that caused Anne to lose her "little neck," but politics. The transition from mistress to Queen of England turned out to be a rocky one, strewn with pitfalls that Anne couldn't have imagined. She gambled and lost but her legacy lived on in her daughter, Elizabeth I, one of the greatest monarchs England has ever known.

# *Barbara Palmer*
## 1640–1709

*A woman of great beauty but most enormously vicious and ravenous, foolish but imperious.*

—Bishop Burnet

In the court of Charles II, there came a point when people began to wonder just who really ruled England, the amiable but amoral king or his beautiful mistress Barbara Palmer. Her power over him was absolute, her avarice insatiable, and her temper formidable. During her reign, Barbara was loathed, feared, and envied by men and women at court, including people who relied on her patronage. Lord Clarendon, the chancellor of England, couldn't bear to utter her name. He referred to her as "That Lady," and diarist John Evelyn, disgusted at her lack of morals, called her the "curse of the nation."

Barbara was a member of the Villiers family, an ancient family who had been successful courtiers since the Norman Conquest. Her father had died fighting for Charles I at the battle of Bristol when she was still an infant. Barbara grew up in reduced circumstances, hankering after the wealth and luxury she felt was her due. Raised in the country among relatives, by the time she hit puberty, Barbara realized that she had the goods to attract the type of lifestyle she wanted. At fifteen she was brought by her mother to London, where she fell in with a wild group of royalist society, earning a tarnished reputation.

At eighteen, she was married off to Roger Palmer, the son of another Cavalier family. Her mother may have hoped that marriage would tame her wild, wanton daughter, but Barbara had other ideas. The cou-ple was mismatched from the start; the bride was vivacious with a quick wit, and an even quicker temper, while the groom was quiet, studious, and a devoted Catholic. He had married her against his parents' wishes, his father predicting at their wedding that she would make him one of the most miserable men on earth. At first Palmer kept her in the country, away from temptation, but before long Barbara was bored. She seduced the libertine Philip Stanhope, Earl of Chesterfield, a man who once claimed he would sleep with any woman who wasn't ugly or old. Barbara was neither.

Palmer might have thought his worries were over when Chesterfield was forced to flee abroad but it was nothing compared to what happened when Barbara took up with the king. In 1659 she and her husband, as true-blue royalists, rushed to the continent to offer the exiled king their support on his restoration to the throne of England. At nineteen, Barbara was striking with her long chestnut hair, eyes so deep a blue that they appeared almost black, voluptuous figure, and easy manner. She and the king immediately became lovers and when Charles returned to England in triumph, he allegedly spent his first night in London with Barbara. Soon she became known as "the lewdest as well as the fairest of King Charles' concubines."

At first the lovers were relatively discreet about their affair. They took care always to be in the company of his two brothers, the Duke of York and the Duke of Gloucester. But tongues still wagged about the king's visits to her home, which was conveniently located near the palace of Whitehall. Their relationship finally became public after the birth of her first child, Anne, in early 1661. Eventually she bore five children acknowledged by the king.*

For his pains, her husband was created the first Earl of Castlemaine, an Irish peerage. The terms of the title made it embarrassingly clear that it was for services rendered by Barbara. Although he accepted the honor, Roger never took his seat in the Irish Par-

---

* Her children were given the surname Fitzroy. The current Duke of Grafton still carries that surname to this day.

liament. Barbara reveled in her new title because it provided her with the rank befitting a king's mistress. The couple finally separated after Barbara gave birth to her first son, named Charles after the king. Out of spite, Roger had him baptized a Catholic. When Barbara found out, she flew into a rage, packing her bags to go live at her brother's house in Richmond. They never lived as husband and wife again. The baby was rebaptized Anglican in front of the king, who publicly proclaimed the child as his own.

Just when things were going swimmingly, Barbara was brought down to earth with a bang. The king had decided to get married and hinted that her position would be different when his bride arrived. "The whole affair," Samuel Pepys noted maliciously in his diary, "will put Madame Castlemaine's nose out of joint." When Catherine of Braganza arrived from Portugal in 1662, Barbara angled to be appointed a lady of the bedchamber, which would give her an income and rooms at the palace. However, the queen had been warned about Barbara. When she saw her name on the list of appointees, she immediately struck it off. Barbara was pissed, and she let the king know it in no uncertain terms.

The king was not a man to be thwarted by his wife. Instead he brought Barbara to be presented to the queen at court. When Catherine discovered who she was, she fell into a faint, blood pouring from her nose. The king was incensed by what he considered to be her stubbornness. Determined to bring her around, he dismissed her Portuguese ladies, allowing the queen to retain only a few priests and one elderly, blind attendant. The poor queen was left friendless and alone. The few friends that she had made at court turned from her rather than face the king's wrath. Catherine eventually gave in and accepted Barbara as one of her ladies.

These were the glory years for Barbara. She sat several times for the king's official court painter, Sir Peter Lely. The images were engraved and sold like hotcakes, making Barbara one of the best-known women in England. She received an annual income of almost five thousand pounds a year from the post office, and also other sums from customs and excise. She also did a brisk business taking money from those seeking to advance at court. Even the French and Italian ambassadors sought out her influence with the king. The Earl of Clarendon, her greatest enemy, remarked bitterly, "That woman would sell every place if she could."

Barbara was extravagant; after a childhood of deprivation, she was making up for it big-time. Her carriage and barge had to out-shine her rivals. It wasn't uncommon for her to wear thirty thousand pounds' worth of jewelry to the theater and then lose the same amount at the gaming tables later that night. The king paid her gambling debts and also deeded over the Tudor palace of Nonsuch to Barbara, which she proceeded to have dismantled, the contents sold.

She was the best thing to happen to the fledgling tabloid press. The public was eager to read about the doings of the royal court. Barbara was credited with every vice known to man and some that were invented, from being a lesbian to biting off the private parts of a corpse with her mouth. Barbara's enemies were as legion as her lovers. One night she was accosted while walking through St. James' Park by three masked men who shouted obscenities at her and chased her back to the palace.

The first crack in her power came from the arrival of a new lady-in-waiting, fifteen-year-old Frances Stuart. The king fell head over heels for the innocent teenager and chased her relentlessly. She was the anti-Barbara, sweet, childlike, with no interest in politics. Barbara's own cousin George, the second Duke of Buckingham, turned against her, becoming part of a faction at court actively promoting Frances to replace her. The plot backfired when Barbara and Frances became best buds. When the queen fell seriously ill and almost died, giving hope that the king would marry Frances, Barbara prayed like she never had before in her life for her recovery.

Barbara never forgot anyone who had slighted her and when she had the opportunity, she took her revenge. She even managed to bring down the Earl of Clarendon. Despite the fact that he had been the king's trusted adviser during his years of exile, and his daughter Anne had married the king's brother, the Duke of York, the king had finally had enough of Clarendon's puritanical attitude. Push came to shove when Clarendon was so unwise as to speak out against Barbara and her meddling in politics. Clarendon underestimated the king's attachment to her, thinking her nothing but a whore, but she was a dangerous one. The king was furious and told him to turn in his seal of office. Barbara had won.

Clarendon's banishment convinced Barbara that she was untouchable and that she could do anything with the king. Barbara was strong, bold, and uninhibited, and the king was turned on by dominating women. She saw no reason to be faithful to her royal lover. Henry Jermyn, the playwright William Wycherly, the acrobat Jacob Hall, and the young John Churchill,* who later became Duke of Marlborough, are just a few who passed through her bed. She was generous with her lovers; John Churchill was able to purchase an annuity because of her financial help.

The couple had ferocious arguments and she was not above threatening Charles. Whenever things weren't going her way, Barbara would withdraw from court until the king mollified her, usually with an expensive gift—like the time he gave her all the New

---

* When the king caught them in flagrante delicto, he said to Churchill, "I forgive you, for you do it for your bread."

Year's gifts from his wealthier subjects. When she was expecting her sixth child in 1672, Barbara swore that if he denied paternity, she would dash the infant's brains out in front of him. Her power over Charles was such that once she even forced him to grovel at her feet for forgiveness in front of the entire court. Still, the king continued to visit Barbara four nights a week at her apartments in Whitehall.

But by 1674 Barbara found herself supplanted by Nell Gwynn and Louise de Keroualle. Ultimately, Barbara's demands were so great, her temper so fierce, and her infidelities so brazen that Charles tired of her. He wanted peace, and so did the kingdom. She lost her position as lady of the bedchamber but not before she was created Duchess of Cleveland, Baroness Nonsuch, and Countess Southampton in her own right and she had secured the futures of her children by Charles. He paid for lavish weddings for their daughters, Anne and Charlotte, but the people protested this latest extravagance of "the King's Whore."

With the death of Charles II in 1685 and her beauty and arrogance faded with age, the days when Barbara had dominated the court were over. Her gambling debts were huge, and she had to sell the contents of her house in Cheam. After her husband's death in 1705, Barbara married an opportunist by the name of Major General Robert "Beau" Fielding, who had been married twice and squandered at least two fortunes. The match was the talk of the town and the subject of cruel satires. When Fielding discovered that Barbara was not as wealthy as he'd been led to believe, he beat her so badly that she feared for her life. The marriage was voided when it turned out that Fielding already had a wife still living and he was marched off to jail for bigamy.

Barbara died in 1709 after suffering from dropsy at the age of sixty-eight. She'd spent her last few years in her house in Chiswick

Mall, near the Thames. But her spirit, always restless and dissatisfied in life, is said to haunt the mall to this day.

Barbara Palmer's distinction was that she was a master politician who studied the inner workings of the court like a great chess player. No royal mistress has ever had as great an influence on a monarch as she did. So much ink has been spilled about her beauty, her lovers, her greed, but Barbara Palmer's strength lay in her ability to deal with each threat to her power as it came, accepting the king's need for a little variety without losing her hold over him. For more than a decade, she was a woman who could not be ignored, dominating Charles II and the court with her beauty and her wit and becoming a symbol of the Restoration.

## Emma Hamilton

### 1765–1815

*I must sin on and love him more than ever. It is a great worth going to hell for.*

—EMMA HAMILTON ON NELSON, 1804

Maid, celestial goddess, courtesan, artist's model, and ambassador's wife, Emma Hamilton had lived more lives by the time she met Horatio Nelson than most women. Born to a dirt-poor family, she started life as plain Amy Lyon on April 26, 1765, in Ness, a small village twelve miles from Liverpool. Nearly illiterate but beautiful, by the time she was thirteen, young Amy had already worked as a low-end servant in various households before heading off for the bright lights of London. She lasted about a year working for a family named Budd before she was let go, probably because she was enjoying the entertainments of the big city too much.

Soon she had exchanged the drudgery of housework for the more exciting and lucrative life of a high-class prostitute. There are stories that she worked as a "Goddess" at Doctor Graham's Temple of Health, singing and dancing while infertile couples paid for the privilege of sleeping in the "Celestial" bed. She did find work at Mrs. Kelly's Piccadilly brothel, where, now calling herself Emma Hart, she found her first protector, Sir Harry Fetherston-haugh, a spoiled young squire. Legend has it that she danced naked on his dining table for the entertainment of his friends at his country estate. The relationship lasted until Emma found herself pregnant with his child, whom she named Emma. Sir Harry refused to acknowledge the child as his, kicking Emma to the curb. But she had already met her next protector, Charles Greville, the son of the Earl of Warwick.

Greville paid for her daughter to be fostered with a family in Wales, and he set Emma up in a small house. Emma's mother moved in to play housekeeper and chaperone. In exchange, Emma promised to curb her temper, live frugally on twenty pounds a year, and improve herself. She sat for the artist George Romney, who adored her chastely and painted her over and over again, as Circe, Venus, Cassandra, Joan of Arc, and herself, making her one of the most painted women in Europe. According to Emma's most recent biographer, Kate Williams, there are more portraits of Emma than Queen Victoria. Emma loved to pose; she was a born entertainer, using her skills in dance and posture to reinvent herself as other characters. Before long Emma was in demand by other well-known artists of the day, including Sir Josiah Reynolds and Thomas Lawrence.

Soon her portraits were available everywhere, not just as

prints, but also on cups, fans, screens, and sometimes clothing, making her sort of an eighteenth-century sex symbol. With her chestnut hair and classical profile, Emma had the type of beauty that transcends time and fashion. Looking at her portraits one sees a young woman who radiates on the surface an innocent sensuality but with a slightly knowing look in her eye. When Greville began to tire of her after four years, he passed her on like a secondhand sweater to his uncle Sir William Hamilton, who had long been the ambassador to the Kingdom of Naples. In exchange, he received property at Pembroke, assuring himself of a preferred place in his uncle's will.

When Emma found out that Greville had shoved her off onto his uncle, she wrote him a warning. "You don't know the power I have here. Only I will be his mistress. If you affront me, I will make him marry me." Emma realized the opportunity she had been given. She was a tender twenty and her new protector was pushing fifty-five. Always anxious to please, she made herself indispensable to Sir William, fussing over him when he was sick, learning to speak French and Italian, and taking singing and dancing lessons. After several years as his mistress, they were secretly married, on September 6, 1791. Now respectable, she was presented at the Neapolitan court, becoming a confidante of Queen Maria Carolina and using their friendship to promote British interests in the kingdom. Dressed in a fetching Greek tunic, she entertained English visitors and foreign guests with her "Attitudes" from classical sculpture. Emma soon found herself the toast of Naples.

For the next seven years, Emma and Sir William were content with each other, until Admiral Horatio Nelson arrived to protect Naples from the advancing French. Like Emma, Nelson was a self-made man. Born in Norfolk to a country rector, he joined the navy

at the age of twelve as a midshipman. While in Nevis, he'd married
Fanny Nisbet, a widow with a young son, thinking he was marrying a great heiress. He was soon disappointed, and the marriage
floundered when it became apparent that there would be no children. They also had nothing in common. Nelson was ambitious
and headstrong, while Fanny was cautious and retiring.

Emma and Nelson had met before, in 1793, when he was plain
Captain Nelson. Now he was the hero of the battle of the Nile and
Emma was determined that Nelson would fall in love with her.
Not only would it be her crowning achievement but it would cat-
apult her onto the world stage. Before he'd even arrived, she'd
primed him by writing a passionate fan letter to him. "How shall
I begin? It is impossible to write. . . . I am delirious with joy and
assure I have a fervour caused by agitation and pleasure." When
Nelson arrived at the docks to a hero's welcome, Emma, wearing
a blue shawl with anchors, rushed to the dock and threw herself
into his one arm, weeping over his wounds. Their lives would
never be the same again.

When Nelson fell ill, Emma fussed over him and nursed him
back to health. The Hamiltons threw a dinner party for his fortieth
birthday, inviting eight hundred guests, but Emma and Nelson only
had eyes for each other. Emma listened to him and flattered him,
threw huge parties in his honor, and went out of her way to make
friends with his stepson, Josiah. At forty, Nelson was not exactly a
looker. Under five foot six and scrawny, with one good eye and one
arm, he couldn't believe this beautiful woman found him exciting.
He soon found himself falling passionately in love with her.

For her part, Emma basked in the glory of being loved by a
living legend. She soon made herself indispensable to Nelson, acting as his secretary and political adviser. She translated for him and
guided him around the court, introducing him to Queen Maria

Carolina. They became confidants, sharing intimate secrets. Emma confided her sadness at not having children with Sir William. He was soon writing home to his wife about how wonderful Lady Hamilton was, which must have gone over like a lead balloon.

Everyone was soon gossiping about the two. As Napoleon swept through Naples they retreated with the royal family to Sicily. The headiness of the Mediterranean spring combined with the exhilaration of the escape and carried them away. It wasn't long before the rumors were made truth, and they were not terribly discreet about it. The news reached as far away as London, which was buzzing about the scandalous affair; caricatures soon appeared in the print shops depicting the relationship. England's Hero and England's Mistress coming together seemed designed to sell newspapers and magazines. Not since Antony and Cleopatra had the world seen anything like it. Their romance was a publicist's dream come true. Nelson was so in love that he was soon neglecting his duties, reluctant to leave his mistress. Sir William turned a blind eye to the relationship. He was fond of Nelson and may even have been happy to have someone else entertain his energetic young wife. The three settled into a happy existence, with Nelson spending all his time with them onshore.

When the happy trio returned to England, the public waited with bated breath to see what happened next. Lady Nelson was sure her husband would see the error of his ways and get rid of his mistress but it was too late. As soon as Emma set foot on English soil it was clear that she had the upper hand. She was about to give Nelson the one thing that his wife couldn't: a child, preferably a son. During her pregnancy, Emma started a fashion craze for high-waisted dresses, which was essentially a maternity dress. Lady Nelson was toast. Nelson insisted on a separation, making her a generous settlement.

In January 1801, she was granted her wish, when she gave birth to Nelson's daughter, whom she named Horatia. After the birth, Nelson wrote, "I love, I never did love any one else. I never had a dear pledge of love til you gave me one, and you, thank my God, never gave one to anybody else." Emma found them a country home just outside London for the three of them to live in, adding Horatia under the guise of an adopted child. Nelson bought it sight unseen and Emma decorated it like a mini Nelson museum filled with memorabilia. She entertained lavishly to promote Nelson's career, inviting his nieces and nephew to give the whole thing an air of respectability, while Sir William fretted about the incessant partying and the bills. He tried desperately to get the government to pay him back for all the antiquities he'd lost in the flight from Naples and to secure a pension for his thirty years as ambassador there.

The idyll ended with Nelson's death in 1805 at the battle of Trafalgar. Emma had already lost Sir William in 1803, but Nelson's death sent her into despair. She collapsed, crying, "My head and heart are gone." She was too ill to view the body while it lay in state at Greenwich Hospital, and she was pointedly excluded from his funeral at St. Paul's Cathedral. Emma had to queue up to see her lover like everyone else. He belonged to the nation, no longer just to her. She spent the day of the funeral in tears, surrounded by her mother and Nelson's female relatives.

She was also deeply in debt. Emma had always lived beyond her means, and now with limited funds from Sir William's estate,* she was hard-pressed. Despite Nelson's dying wish that the nation

---

* Sir William left Emma an annuity of eight hundred pounds, her known debts paid, and a lump sum of three hundred pounds but she was dependent on his heir, Charles Greville, who doled it out sparingly.

should take care of his mistress, no money was ever forthcoming. For the next several years Emma tried to keep up appearances, giving lavish parties for her friends. She was also supporting several of Nelson's relatives as well as her own poor relations. Three years after his death she owed thousands of pounds to a host of creditors. Worst of all, her mother died in 1810, leaving Emma without the one person she could truly rely on. Soon she was forced to sell Merton, the home she had shared with Nelson, and many other mementos of their life together, including his letters.

A wiser woman would have quickly tried to find another husband or at least a protector. But when one has been the beloved of one of the greatest heroes England had ever known, how could any mortal man compete? Emma finally fled with Horatia to Calais in 1814 to escape her creditors. By now her health was ruined from too much rich wine and food. Taking to her bed, she was nursed by a distraught Horatia, who begged to know the truth about her parentage, but Emma refused. Although Horatia had been told that Nelson was her father, Emma never admitted that she was her natural mother. Racked with pain, Emma died on January 15, 1815. She was buried in Calais, far from her lover Nelson. Horatia was taken in by one of Nelson's sisters. She later married a clergyman and had eight children. Like a true Victorian matron, Horatia was happy to claim the naval hero Lord Nelson as her father, but she refused to believe that the notorious Emma was her mother.

Emma's story continues to fascinate because it is a story about ambition and heartbreak, love and pain. She rose from the depths of poverty to the heights of fame and fortune, only to end up back where she started. Her childhood had left her ambitious, and hungry for the limelight, but it was a hunger that could never be appeased. Emma always wanted more. Like Icarus in the Greek myth, perhaps she flew too high.

## Lola Montez
### 1820–1861

*I have known all the world has to give—ALL!*

—Lola Montez

Lola Montez was the International Bad Girl of the Victorian era, wrecking havoc on three continents. Victorians lived vicariously through stories of her adventurous life, whether they were true or not, the more outrageous the better—that she bathed in lavender, dried herself with rose petals, that a man once paid one thou-

sand dollars for an evening's performance. She was an actress, a writer, a lecturer, and the most famous Spanish dancer in the world who wasn't actually Spanish. Even the minor incidents of her life could fill hundreds of romance novels.

Lola started life as the less exotically named Elizabeth Rosanna Gilbert in 1820, although some biographers claim that she was born earlier, in 1818, and Lola herself shaved years off her age. Her father was a soldier in the British army, and her mother was the fourteen-year-old illegitimate daughter of the High Sheriff of Cork and an Irish MP. The young family set off for Calcutta, where Eliza's father died from cholera soon after they arrived.

Her mother soon remarried, to another career army officer. Only eighteen, she became caught up in the social life in Calcutta and had little inclination for motherhood. Eliza's stepfather, while he adored her, felt that she was growing up wild in India and decided to send her back to live with his relatives in Scotland. The contrast between the heat and lush climate of India and the harsh winters of Scotland must have been a shock to the little girl, who had been abandoned first by her father's death and now by her mother and stepfather. She became rebellious and chafed against life in a small town. "The queer, wayward Indian girl," as Eliza was known, once scandalized the town by running down the street naked.

There was a short stint in a boarding school in Bath, until her mother came to England to whisk her back to India to marry her to a "rich and gouty old gentleman of 60 years," as she put it in her memoirs. Looking for a way out, Eliza eloped instead with Lieutenant Thomas James, an army officer on leave from India. Eliza quickly realized that she had jumped out of the frying pan into the fire. Eliza had known very little about her husband before they eloped. She claimed that he started to drink heavily and to slap her around. She returned to India with him, but the marriage was doomed. In 1842, he either abandoned her for another woman or she left him when she couldn't take his violence and infidelity anymore. Shunned by her mother for bringing disgrace to the family, Eliza sailed to England to live with her stepuncle. She never made it.

During the long journey home, Eliza carried on a scandalous shipboard romance with a dashing army officer named Charles Lennox. When they arrived in London, they continued their affair and Lennox introduced her to several influential men. When word of their affair reached her husband, he filed for divorce, citing her adultery with Lennox. Unfortunately Lennox proved no better than her husband. He dumped her with no means of support. Only twenty, Eliza had already caused multiple scandals through a failed marriage, elopement, and adultery. What was a girl with few skills to do? Why, go on the stage, of course!

With no talent for acting, she decided to become a dancer. Too old now to launch a ballet career, Eliza headed for Spain for six months to learn flamenco and Spanish. When she arrived back in London she was no longer Eliza Gilbert James but Maria Dolores de Porris y Montez, "the proud and beautiful daughter of a noble Spanish family." Lola Montez was born.

Lola was engaged to perform at Her Majesty's Theatre, where her debut was a great success, but it was revealed in the papers that she was a fraud. Her contract was subsequently canceled by management. Lola later claimed that London audiences were incapable of appreciating the subtle quality of her dancing.

The truth was, Lola sucked as a dancer. She had no sense of rhythm or timing, and all her dances had a tendency to look alike; but at the same time she knew how to work that spotlight. She wore a costume of a black lace dress with a high collar, the better to frame her face and her magnificent bosom, with a decoration of red roses. She had the advantage of being beautiful, with lustrous dark hair, ivory skin, and stunning blue eyes. Her most famous dance, the Tarantula, consisted of Lola conducting a frenzied search of her person for the elusive spider. Inevitably she would reveal a great deal of leg, shocking the audience. The secret of her success was that she was utterly shameless. Audiences either loved or hated her.

Lola decided to take her act on the road, where she danced and caused scenes wherever she went. She was like a beautiful untamed animal who believed that the rules didn't apply to her. Try to keep her out of the royal enclosure when Russia's tsar is in town? A policeman was struck in the face with Lola's riding crop in Berlin when he tried that. Try to take liberties? Well, a man might find himself stabbed, as one unwanted suitor found out in Warsaw. Hissing during one of her performances meant one felt the lash of Lola's tongue, as she berated the audience.

Noticing that Franz Liszt was performing in Berlin, Lola decided that he would be her next conquest. When Lola aimed, she aimed high. What Byron was to poetry, Liszt was to classical music, a Victorian rock star. He'd already cut a swath through the women of Europe, who threw themselves at him, and he had a longtime mistress, by whom he'd had three children, when he met Lola. The love affair lasted a week but Lola dined out on the story for years.

It was in Bavaria that Lola would pass into history as legend. After auditioning for the State Theatre, Lola was told by the theater's manager her dancing might cause moral offense. Lola stormed the palace unannounced to plead with the king himself for help. When the king asked her if her bosoms were real, Lola grabbed a pair of scissors and cut open her bodice, revealing her magnificent breasts. Whether or not this is what really happened, Lola got her wish. Ludwig, a Hispanophile, was defenseless against her "Latin" charms. Her career on the Munich stage lasted a scant two performances. The sexagenarian monarch became smitten by Lola, and the dancer enjoyed a new role—as his mistress.

Within weeks she had a powerful hold over Ludwig. She agreed to sit for a portrait, which would be included in Ludwig's renowned Gallery of Beauties. During her sittings, Ludwig would join her, spending the time getting to know her. He wrote reams of bad love poetry extolling her beauty. Soon the king remodeled a stately home for her, spending millions of dollars along the way. Lola quickly announced her retirement from the stage after a career that encompassed less than two dozen performances in four years.

The affair was an international sensation, selling papers in England and France, where they reported that mobs were rioting in Bavaria and disclosed Lola's sordid past. Lola openly boasted about her relationship with the king, although later in life she claimed that the relationship was strictly platonic. Perfecting the art of the tease, she indulged his foot fetish, letting him kiss and suck her toes. Ludwig's advisers, friends, and family warned him that Lola was nothing but an adventuress, but the more they tried to persuade him, the more stubborn he became. He refused to believe what he considered to be lies about his Lola. Lola, convinced of her own nobility, wanted a title of her own. Ludwig obliged by making her Countess of Landsfeld, despite the fact that only Bavarian citizens could be ennobled, and the Council of Ministers refused to grant Lola citizenship.

Lola hungered for social acceptance from the nobility in Munich but it was not forthcoming. If she had been more diplomatic, like Louis XV's mistress, Madame de Pompadour, coating her requests with sweet nothings and a pleasing disposition, things might have been different, and her reign as Ludwig's mistress might not have ended in disaster.

Lola was her own worst enemy. She was known to entertain

men at all hours of the day and night, although she claimed to Ludwig that she was completely faithful to him. At the theater, she would remain seated when the king came to greet her, a complete breach of protocol. It was as if the more the citizens of Munich rejected her, the uglier Lola's actions became, as if she were giving them the proverbial middle finger.

Lola made her fatal mistake when she convinced Ludwig to close down the university after the student protests against her and her supporters. An irate crowd of two thousand students gathered and made their way to city hall, where a petition was presented to the king asking him to reopen the university. Ludwig refused. When a mob of students gathered outside her home to heckle her, Lola strode out on her balcony and toasted them with champagne. In the end her affair with the king toppled the government. Lola was forced to flee the city, taking refuge in Switzerland. Ludwig was pressured into rescinding her citizenship, revoking her title, and publishing an order for her arrest. The king decided to abdicate in favor of his son. The whole sorry affair lasted less than two years. Despite having cost him his throne, Ludwig continued to write to Lola for several years and to send her an annual allowance of twenty thousand florins. But Ludwig never saw his beloved Lolita again.

After one has conquered the heart of a king, what else is there to top that? Only America offered Lola the challenge of a fresh start and a whole new continent waiting to experience the Lola magic. Immediately after her arrival in New York, she set to work giving interviews, espousing liberal ideas. Deciding to give the people what they want, Lola commissioned a five-act play, called *Lola in Bavaria*, detailing her version of her relationship with Ludwig. It was an early version of the docudrama, and probably the first time in a historical play that the protagonist played herself. The play was enormously successful and Lola took it on the road, crisscrossing the country.

But where Lola went, trouble was sure to follow. A visit to a boys' school in Boston had people in an uproar, accusing her of corrupting the morals of youth. She smoked in public and got into a scuffle with a prompter in New Orleans. Lola decided to retire and settle down in the West. While living in California, Lola showed another side to her character than that of the horse-whipping femme fatale. Madame Lola became a model citizen of Grass Valley, much admired by the other townsfolk, devoting her time to helping troubled women. She kept a menagerie of pets in her white cottage on Main Street, including a tamed grizzly bear named Major, which she took for walks. But the money soon ran out, and Lola was back on tour.

Lola wasn't exactly without a man in her life. She married two more times, first to a young blade, then to an Irish charmer; neither marriage was successful or legal. One of her lovers drowned mysteriously after they returned from a tour in Australia, leaving Lola distraught. She entertained numerous male friends at her Wednesday night soirees in Grass Valley. Later she was jilted by an Austrian baron who conveniently forgot he had a wife and children tucked away in upstate New York. Unlucky in love, she wrote, "Love is a pipe we fill at eighteen and smoke until forty. Then we rake the ashes till our exit."

Realizing that her career was on the wane, Lola reinvented herself once again, this time on the lecture circuit. Wearing a simple black dress and no jewelry, she made her debut in Hamilton, Ontario, in 1857 with a piece entitled "Beautiful Women," which discussed famous women in history. It turned out that Lola was a formidable and eloquent lecturer, far better than she was a dancer.

A Buffalo newspaper reported, "Rarely if ever was a Buffalo audience better pleased, we may say more fascinated, with a lecture than it was with Lola Montez." The *Boston Bee* declared her the "unquestioned Queen of the lecture room." Lecturing was a win-win situation for Lola. No expensive sets or costumes, and she could perform in town halls, which were cheaper to rent. Better yet, she didn't have to share the box office with anyone but her manager. That meant more money in Lola's pocket.

She added to her repertoire titles like "Gallantry" and "Heroines of History and Strong-Minded Women." Lola felt that she was the epitome of the strong-minded woman; it was her most personal lecture. In it, she espoused the theory that the beauty and wit of women "controlled the councils of diplomacy and the state." Referencing her own recent history in Munich, she added, "And this is as true of modern as of ancient courts." She believed that deeds, not words, were the measure of a strong-minded woman, having no use for women like Susan B. Anthony, whom she considered scolds. Lola was no feminist; although she defended the right of extraordinary women to take a role in public life, she also extolled the virtues of women who had "no ambition outside the hearth and home." For three years, she plied her new career up and down the eastern seaboard to great success, along with a short European tour.

She also wrote several books, including her autobiography and a book called *The Arts and Secrets of Beauty, or Secrets of a Lady's Toilet with Hints to Gentlemen on the Art of Fascinating*, based on her most popular lectures on beauty and grooming. It was filled with interesting tips, such as binding slivers of raw beef around the face to help stave off wrinkles.

Lola's mind also began turning toward religion, her own spiritual state, even thoughts of death. It seemed that she had become remorseful over her life. She spent most of her time quietly reading and studying the Bible and making frequent visits to the Magdalen Asylum for wayward women. As New York, where she now lived, sweltered in a heat wave in June 1860, she suffered a stroke. The condition left her unable to move or speak for several months. News of Lola's illness reached her mother, who traveled to America on the pretext of seeing her daughter for what might be the last time, but it appeared her actual purpose was to find out whether or not Lola still had any of the jewels that Ludwig had given her. She returned to Scotland disappointed and empty-handed. After her mother's visit, Lola made sure to make out her will.

By December, she had recovered enough to hobble outside for a breath of fresh air on Christmas Day. It was to prove the death of her. Lola developed pneumonia and, on January 17, 1861—a month before her forty-first birthday—she died. Her life quickly passed into legend. She's buried in Green-Wood Cemetery in Brooklyn. Her headstone is inscribed with a name she never used—her maiden name of Eliza Gilbert.

# Mata Hari
### 1876–1917

*The evil this woman has done is unbelievable. This is perhaps the greatest spy of the century.*

—LIEUTENANT ANDRE MORNET, PROSECUTOR, 1917

Her name is now synonymous with femme fatale, a slinky seductress luring men to their doom, but who was Mata Hari exactly? Was she the treacherous spy who sent thousands of men to their death or was she used as a convenient scapegoat by not only the British, but the Germans and the French as well? Two decades after her death, a French journalist investigated the claims of espionage but came away unenlightened. Of the three hundred men and women who were executed for espionage during World War I, only Mata Hari became a household name. Mata Hari came to embody everyone's fears about enemy aliens, the way- ward woman, and sexual decadence.

Mata Hari began life as Margaretha Zelle in a small town in northern Holland, the daughter of a prosperous store owner. The life that Margaretha knew came to a screeching halt when she was thirteen, when her father's business failed and he declared bankruptcy. The humiliation and horror was an experience that would scar her for the rest of her life. Within a year, her parents had separated, and by the time she was fifteen her mother had passed away. Her father took off for Amsterdam, where he quickly remarried. He eventually sent for her brothers but not for her. Margaretha never got over her father's abandonment of her and would spend her life seeking the same attention he once gave her from the men in her life.

A short stint training as a kindergarten teacher went nowhere when it was discovered that the headmaster had flirted outra- geously with her. At nineteen, and with no prospects, Marga- retha, on impulse, answered a personal ad in the paper. Rudolph MacLeod was thirty-nine, almost twice her age, and had served in the Dutch East Indies for almost twenty years. Bald and good- looking, he wore a uniform well. Margaretha always was a sucker for a man in uniform. After a two-month courtship, they were married. It was a disaster from the beginning; her husband pre- ferred drinking and whoring to his young wife. They quarreled bitterly about everything from child care to how much money she spent on clothes. Margaretha refused to conform to the image of an obedient army wife. Not even the birth of two children and a transfer to Sumatra changed things. When their son died under mysterious circumstances, the marriage was over. After a brief reconciliation, MacLeod abandoned her, taking their daughter with him.

La Belle Époque in Paris would now be her home. When she was asked by a journalist why she had chosen Paris, she replied, "I don't know. I thought all women who ran away from their husbands went to Paris." Since her husband refused to pay alimony, Margaretha tried to get a job modeling for artists but with little success. Finally she found a job with an equestrian circus run by Ernst Molier. It was he who suggested that she turn to dance. And not just any dance—she would turn herself into Mata Hari. Translated from Malay, it meant "the eye of the day." Her costume consisted of a jeweled metallic bra; long colored veils that represented beauty, love, chastity, voluptuousness, and passion; and a jeweled headdress of Javanese design. Her dancing, what there was of it, consisted of her striking erotic and exotic poses while slowly removing the veils from her body. Even Mata Hari admitted, "I never could dance well. People came to see me because I was the first who dared to show myself naked to the public."

Making her debut at the home of a society hostess, she was an instant smash. Within a year she had given thirty performances, both public and private. She created a suitable background for her creation, which changed from one interview to the next, but generally she said that she had learned the dances from her mother, who was a Javanese temple dancer. The critics raved, falling over themselves to come up with new adjectives to describe her undulating arms and swarthy complexion. *The Gallic* praised her as "so feline, extremely feminine, majestically tragic, the thousand curves and movements of her body trembling in a thousand rhythms." They bought into her exotic story. She also found the first of many lovers who paid the bills and kept her in the style she had become accustomed to as a child. But she had extravagant tastes and was constantly in debt.

For ten years, Mata Hari managed to hold sway over Europe, dancing in Monte Carlo, Berlin, Vienna, and Spain, becoming one of the highest-paid dancers in Europe at the time. She danced in opera houses and in music halls. But time was running out; she was pushing forty, and in the wake of her success came imitators. She took to holding concerts in her mansion in Neuilly, where she danced accompanied by a Sufi holy man and master musician, Inayat Khan. Otherwise, she was supported by her various lovers, many of whom were officers.

Everything changed for Mata Hari when World War I started. She was in Berlin, where she had been engaged to perform, and she tried to get out of her contract. Her dresser kept her jewels and furs for lack of payment and her bank accounts were frozen by the Germans. With very little money, Mata Hari took a train to Switzerland but ran into difficulties because she didn't have a Dutch passport. She finally made it back to Holland, where she became the mistress of Baron Edouard Willem van der Capellan. But Holland was too staid for her after the bright lights of Paris, so Mata Hari resolved to go back to France.

It was in Holland that Mata Hari was approached by a man named Karl Kroemer, the honorary German consul in Amsterdam, to spy for Germany. He offered twenty thousand francs, the equivalent of sixty-one thousand dollars today, with the promise of more if she was successful. She was to sign all communications "H21." Mata Hari accepted the money, but she had no intentions of spying for Germany. She felt that the money was owed to her for having to leave her furs and jewels behind and having her accounts frozen.

Looking back at it now, for either Germany or France to recruit Mata Hari as a spy makes no sense. She was well known in Europe, her every move reported in the gossip columns of the day. Even without her fame, Mata Hari was a striking woman; she stood out in a crowd, not just because of her height but also because of her beauty. A spy's skill lies in blending in. She was also incredibly apolitical, sharing her favors with soldiers from all sides of the conflict. And she barely knew what was going on in the war. As far as the French and Germans were concerned an amoral woman who had already exposed herself onstage and been seen to take money from men would do anything.

While en route from Holland to France soon after, Mata Hari had to pass through Britain to avoid the Germans. She gave a British security officer conflicting reasons for her trip, which instantly raised alarms. Initially she said that she was going to perform, but when questioned further, she told a different story, that she was going to join her lover Baron van der Capellan. A notation was placed in her file that she was now considered "undesirable" and should be refused permission to return to the U.K. From that moment on, Mata Hari was under constant surveillance by British intelligence.

It was Mata Hari's love for a Russian officer named Vladimir de Massloff that led her to the man who would be her downfall. At twenty-one de Massloff was eighteen years her junior. From the moment they met in July 1916, they developed a deep relationship; she called him Vadime, and he called her Marina. Mata wanted to settle down with Vadime; she was tired of the years of travel and sleeping with other men for money. When she went to see Georges Ladoux to get a pass to travel to Vittel to see Vadime, she unknowingly walked into a trap.

Georges Ladoux was the head of the Deuxième Bureau, the military office of espionage and counterespionage. He already knew that the British considered Mata Hari to be dangerous and possibly a German spy. It was on his orders that she was being tailed. He was in a tricky situation. France was not doing well in the war, and arresting a high-profile spy would do wonders for morale and restore French pride. In his memoirs, Ladoux implied that it was his intent from the start to entrap Mata Hari. She was a juicy target; she was glamorous with a steady supply of lovers. He admitted to her at their initial meeting that she was under suspicion. He then asked her to spy for France. Mata Hari didn't agree right away. On her return from Vittel, she agreed but asked to be paid one million francs, believing that this money would set her and Vadime up after the war.

The entire encounter with Ladoux was strange. If indeed Mata Hari was a German spy, giving her a pass to a war zone was foolhardy to say the least. And then telling her at their next meeting that he believed her to be a German spy, how could he trap her? And why would she now agree to spy for France?

Mata Hari traveled to Holland to await Ladoux's instructions, not knowing that she was playing into his hands. On her way to the war, Mata Hari again had to pass through Britain. She was detained once again, under suspicion that she was a spy named Clara Benedix. Mata Hari told the arresting officer that she had been recruited by Ladoux to spy for the French; unbeknownst to her, Ladoux informed the British that contrary to what she had told them, she was suspected of being a German spy, just not the one they were looking for.

Mata Hari was released but she was not allowed to enter Holland. Instead she was sent to Spain, where she waited for word from Ladoux. Stuck with no money, Mata Hari decided to improvise. She made the acquaintance of a German military attaché named Arnold Kalle. Mata Hari took the opportunity presented in front of her to do a little spying for France. "I was my most charming self, I played with my feet and did everything a woman does when she wants a man to fall for her and I knew that Kalle had fallen," she later told the investigating magistrate Pierre Bouchardon. She managed to discover that the Germans knew that the French had finally broken their second code. In exchange, Mata Hari fed him some gossip that she'd gleaned from the newspapers. Writing all the information down that she was given by her new lover, she took the information to the French consulate in Madrid to be sent to Ladoux. Back in Paris, Mata Hari was ready to reap the reward for all her hard work. Instead, Ladoux refused to see her. When she finally did see him, he was amazed at the information she had been able to uncover, but he made no move to verify it. To Mata Hari's shock, instead of being rewarded for her work, she was arrested in February 1917 as a German spy. She was brought in front of Captain Pierre Bouchardon, who was an investigative magistrate of the Third Council of War.

At first, Mata Hari didn't realize the seriousness of what she was being charged with, and she waived the right to counsel. Naturally flirtatious, she thought that she could just charm her way out of the interview. But Bouchardon was not inclined to be merciful. Sending her to one of the worst prisons in France, Saint-Lazare, Bouchardon continued to interrogate Mata Hari repeatedly, trying to break her, but she stuck to her story that she was a spy for France. But the dismal conditions inside the prison began to break her spirit. After years of luxury, first-class accommodations, and a fastidious detail to her personal hygiene, Mata Hari couldn't cope with the freezing cell and dirty conditions that she was forced to accept. She wrote repeatedly to Bouchardon to be released or at least moved to better accommodations.

The investigators were stuck. They had examined her accounts, her jewelry, and even her makeup (to see if she had anything that could be turned into invisible ink). Fifty-three officers whom Mata Hari had "entertained" were called in for questioning but every single one told the investigators that she had never asked them about anything regarding the war or the military. They read the reports of the surveillance on her, but they still had no evidence that Mata Hari was a spy for the Germans.

Finally Ladoux revealed the contents of messages that had been transmitted from the German military attaché in Madrid to Berlin, concerning the spy known as H21, later identified as Mata Hari. Remarkably, the messages were in a code that German intelligence knew had already been broken by the French, leaving some historians to suspect that the messages were contrived by Ladoux to implicate Mata Hari.

The fact that she had been in custody for two months before these cables were given to Bouchardon was highly suspect. It seems likely that either the Germans threw Mata Hari into the mix to deflect suspicion away from the double agents that they had working for them or Ladoux faked the cables as an act of unbridled ambition. Ladoux claimed that it was Mata Hari who offered to spy for France, not the other way around. Whatever the case, Mata Hari was doomed from that point on. Her subsequent admission that Kroemer had given her money to spy for Germany and that she had kept the money as payment for her stolen furs and clothing added to her supposed guilt. Even her own country, Holland, didn't seem to care what happened to her. When the government learned of Mata Hari's arrest, it remained largely silent.

Her trial in July 1917 was a travesty. Her lawyer was out of his depth defending Mata Hari in court, and it never seems to have occurred to either one of them to try to find another attorney who had experience with espionage trials. Only one of her lovers, Henry de Marguerie, came forward to defend her. Of the eight charges brought against her, Mata Hari was found guilty of every single one, despite the lack of evidence that she had caused the deaths of fifty thousand soldiers.

On October 15, the day of her execution, at barely five o'clock in the morning, Mata Hari dressed carefully in a pearl gray dress, a long black velvet cloak, and a tricorned hat with gloves. She wrote three letters, one to her daughter, Jeanne, the others to intimate friends, but they were never sent. Accompanied by two nuns from Saint-Lazare and her lawyer, she was taken by automobile to the barracks where the firing squad awaited her. When she saw the firing squad she whispered cheekily to one of the nuns, "All these people! What a success." She refused to be tied to the stake or to wear a blindfold, impressing everyone with her courage. She was forty-one years old. After the final bullet was put into her brain, a sergeant major declared, "By God, this lady knows how to die."

Rumors flew that she hadn't died, that she'd been whisked away by a mysterious stranger, that she'd tried to dazzle her executioners by opening her coat to reveal her naked body. None of it was true, but it no longer mattered. She had now passed into legend. No criticism of the execution was allowed in the papers. The official line was that France had been saved by Mata Hari's death. Four days after her execution Ladoux was arrested for being a double agent. He was eventually acquitted of the charges of espionage but his career was effectively over. He later wrote a book about Mata Hari, a highly colored tale of how he brought down the most infamous spy in World War I.

It wasn't until 2000 that some of the files pertaining to her arrest and trial were released that proved that Mata Hari was innocent of espionage. The rest of the files will not be released until 2017. Despite the new evidence, the myth of Mata Hari continues to hold sway. After her death, stories abounded that she had blown a kiss to her executioners, that she had appeared naked before the firing squads. Books and films perpetuated the myth of the sexy, sultry spy luring men to their doom. So who really was Mata Hari? Perhaps she explained it best herself. At her trial, Mata Hari made the distinction that there was Margaretha Zelle MacLeod and then there was Mata Hari. But the woman who was once called "an orchid in a field of dandelions" was much more than a promiscuous courtesan who loved officers too well. She was a woman who, after fleeing a bad marriage, managed to reinvent herself, whose ambition and talent took her to the top and contributed to her downfall.

# FOUR

# Crusading Ladies

## Anne Hutchinson
### 1591–1643

*A woman of a haughty fierce carriage, a nimble wit and an active spirit,
and has a very voluble tongue, more bold than a man.*

—JOHN WINTHROP ON ANNE HUTCHINSON

On a chilly November day in 1637, the meetinghouse in Cambridge, Massachusetts, was packed as Anne Hutchinson, declared Public Enemy No. 1 by the founders of the colony, was led into the dimly lit room to stand trial. At the time, Anne was forty-six, the mother of twelve living children, a grandmother, and pregnant with her fifteenth child. She was well known in the community, as a midwife and nurse.

In the three years since her arrival in the Massachusetts Bay Colony, Anne had managed to piss off a lot of powerful people, specifically the clergy. Her "crime" was holding weekly meetings at her home to discuss scriptures and theology. At first her meetings were only attended by women, who couldn't wait to hear her unique take on the latest Sunday sermon. Ironically Anne had been chastised for not joining in at these meetings when she first arrived in the colony.* To the women, Anne was like Oprah and Billy Graham wrapped up in one package. She was witty and genuinely wanted to help other women, whether by medical care or by spiritual counseling. Her gift to them was her surety about her faith and salvation.

The women soon convinced their husbands to attend her meetings. The meetings became so popular that she had to add an additional day to accommodate the demand, and they began attracting powerful men, such as Sir Harry Vane, soon to be governor. Vane was the son of one of Charles I's Privy Council, sent to the colony for "seasoning."† Her stand against the war with the Pequot Indians influenced her male followers not to fight.

Anne's chief nemesis was the most powerful man in the colony, five times governor John Winthrop. He described her in his journal as "a woman of a haughty fierce carriage, a nimble wit and an active spirit and has a very voluble tongue, more bold than a man." And those were the nice things. He also called her "an instrument of Satan," "enemy of the chosen people," and "this American Jezebel." John Winthrop had been keeping an eye on her both figuratively and spiritually since the Hutchinson family got

---

* "Gossipings," as they were called, were the only accepted way for women in the colony to talk about spiritual matters while doing embroidery and quilting. Like a coffee klatch for God.

† Sir Harry Vane became a moderate in the English Parliament after his return in August 1637. He led the Independent Party with Oliver Cromwell but later broke with him over the execution of Charles I. Vane argued for religious tolerance and a constitutional monarchy. Although he was for the restoration of the monarch, in 1662 he was convicted of high treason and executed.

off the boat in 1634. He conveniently lived across the street from them in Boston, where he had a bird's-eye view of the comings and goings at the Hutchinson house. Winthrop began making a long laundry list of what he considered to be her "errors." It eventually came to one hundred items.

It was a crucial moment in the fledgling colony. Having fled England to escape religious intolerance, the Puritans then proceeded to impose religious uniformity on others. Like Abraham Lincoln 230 years later, Winthrop believed that a house divided against itself could not stand. Dissension had to be stopped before it destroyed Winthrop's "holy city on the hill." Roger Williams* and Anne's own brother-in-law John Wheelwright had already been exiled for their unorthodox beliefs. The bickering got so bad that Harry Vane resigned as governor of the colony (which opened the door for Winthrop's return to power), claiming he had to return to England for "personal reasons." The division also came down along class lines. Winthrop's supporters were those who had been landed gentry in England and conservative. Anne's supporters were the merchants and other professionals, the rising middle class.

Anne came by her opinionated nature honestly. Her father, Francis Marbury, spent the first three years of her life under house arrest by the church on a charge of heresy,† the same charge that would be brought against Anne. A Cambridge-educated clergyman, he was jailed only a few months into his first post. Marbury

---

* Roger Williams went on to found the Providence Plantation, where he welcomed Anne after her banishment from Massachusetts.

† After his third imprisonment, Francis Marbury decided it would be prudent to keep his mouth shut, something Anne never learned. He was rewarded with a London parish near St. Paul's, where he died in 1611, no doubt from the strain of not speaking his mind.

had repeatedly challenged the Anglican Church authorities on religious truth. Although Anne wasn't formally educated, her father taught her and her siblings, using his trial transcriptions, the Bible, and a book of martyrs. Arguing about scripture passed for leisure time in the Marbury household.

The colony magistrates passed a series of resolutions that were aimed at curbing dissidence, including a direct condemnation of meetings with more than sixty people. Anne had more than that on a slow day. They were also annoyed that when she began questioning whether certain ministers had the "seal of the spirit," her followers began to heckle some of these ministers at their sermons. This was considered "traducing the ministers and the ministry" and it was a big no-no.

Anne was summoned before the General Court with Winthrop presiding. He told her that she was "called as one of those that have troubled the peace of the commonwealth." Anne refused to meekly submit, pointing out that she hadn't actually been charged with anything. Despite her advanced pregnancy, she was forced to stand for several days as they tried desperately to get her to admit to blasphemy. Not exactly Christian behavior! She and Winthrop sparred back and forth like prizefighters, Anne bobbing and weaving as she matched him scripture for scripture. Winthrop accused her of breaking the fifth commandment of honoring thy father and mother, which to Winthrop included all authority figures, including him. When she was told this, Anne replied, "Put the case, sir, that I do fear the Lord and my parents. May not I entertain them that fear the Lord, because my parents will not give me leave?"

When Winthrop tried to prove that her meetings were public rather than private, Anne insisted that since women had no public role, her thoughts were private and not subject to censure. If she decided to have some friends over to her house for some cider and a little religious talk, that was her business, no one else's. Anne even cited the apostle Paul's letter to Titus, which called for "the elder women to instruct the younger." Winthrop then accused her of keeping the women from getting their husbands' dinner on time. Time and again, Anne had Winthrop against the ropes, sweating, until Winthrop finally snapped, "We do not mean to discourse with those of your sex." Kind of hard not to do when the person on trial is a woman.

But it wasn't just the meetings that riled them up. It was Anne's unique take on scripture that disturbed the Puritan leaders. Like the Puritans, Anne believed in God's free grace, which was a covenant between God and man, where God drew the soul to salvation. Where Anne and the Puritans were at loggerheads was on the need to prepare oneself by doing good deeds. Anne thought that this smacked of buying your way into heaven.

She was ahead of her time in her belief that everyone could be saved, even nonbelievers. This didn't sit well with the Puritans, who believed that they were God's chosen people. And then there was the matter of her belief that God placed the Holy Spirit direction within those he saved, and guided their actions like some sort of cosmic GPS. She was also a bit picky about which ministers she felt had a direct line to God. Only her brother-in-law and the Reverend John Cotton, who had also left England not long before, having upset the church authorities, met her high standards. And then there was her belief that one could have a personal relationship with God cutting out the middle man of clerical authority. This threatened the very foundation on which the Puritans had built their state, their church, and their lives. They even came up with a special name for her beliefs called Antinomianism, which is Latin for "against the law." Winthrop and his buddies of course were on the right side of the law.

When Anne's spiritual guru and best friend, John Cotton, was called as a witness for her defense, things got really interesting. Cotton was caught between a rock (Anne Hutchinson) and a hard place (John Winthrop). He considered Anne to be his spiritual collaborator, writing that she was "the apple of our eye." But the pupil had surpassed the master. And he'd already gotten into a heap of trouble back in the old country for his beliefs, so he was walking a fine line. Cotton managed to defend Anne, sort of. He wouldn't admit that Anne had talked trash about the other ministers in his favor, although he made certain to point out that he was distressed at the idea. With Cotton's testimony, Anne would have defeated the charges against her.

But Anne couldn't keep her mouth shut. Having an audience was just too good to resist. She was like the smartest girl in class who can't help showing off how smart she is. Winthrop, being the gentleman that he was, let her hang herself. He must have been rubbing his hands with glee, though. Anne started off talking about her journey of faith, how she remained unsettled by the quality of the preaching in the Church of England.

That would have been fine if she had just stuck to that topic, but then she dug a hole for herself that was deeper. She continued on about how the spirit of the Lord opened the Bible and thrust certain passages in her mind. She then revealed that "the Lord did give me to see that those who did not teach the New Covenant had the spirit of the Antichrist."

Oh, no, she didn't! The judges were flabbergasted. It was one thing for a man to consider revelation through scripture, but the idea that a woman should claim such a thing was crazy talk. However, Anne was not done. Not only did she claim to hear the voices of Moses, God, and John the Baptist but she then pulled out the big guns. Comparing herself to Daniel in the lion's den, she told them that she knew she was going to be persecuted in New England and that their lies would bring a "curse on upon you and your posterity and this whole state." Yeah, nothing like telling the people who hold the power of life and death over you that they are going to be cursed for punishing you. With these revelations, even Cotton had to back off.

The judges ruled that Anne would be jailed under house arrest until the spring, when she would be dealt with by the church. They weren't so kind to her supporters, who were disenfranchised for signing a petition in support of her. The others were disarmed just in case they decided they had a divine revelation to kill the judges. Many of the petitioners recanted and were allowed to keep their guns.

Anne's actions had the Puritan godfathers running so scared that, to minimize Hutchinson's threat, they decided to get started on building the college they'd been planning. After her trial, they finally got cracking on it. Harvard graduates everywhere can thank Anne Hutchinson for the fact that their school was founded to stop smart-alecky female fanatics from getting the better of the law in court and convincing other females that they had a right to their own opinions. Modeled after Winthrop's alma mater, Cambridge, the new college was named after John Harvard, a recent immigrant to the colony, who had bequeathed half his estate and his library to the college before his premature death at the age of thirty.

In March 1638, Anne was accused of heresy and also of "lewd and lascivious conduct" for having men and women in her house at the same time during her meetings like they were having a spiritual orgy. She was found guilty and excommunicated by the Boston church. It had the opposite effect on her than it would have on most people. Instead of being "oh, woe is me!" Anne was ecstatic, claiming that "it was the greatest happiness, next to Christ that had befallen her." Winthrop claimed that actually it was the churches in the colony that should be happy, as "the poor souls who have been seduced by her had settled again in the truth." In other words, "Hooray for our team!"

No one knows what her husband, Will Hutchinson, thought about having to uproot his family once again. No doubt after over twenty years of marriage, he was used to his wife's convictions. His only recorded words about Anne are, "I am more nearly tied to my wife than to the church. I do think her to be a dear saint and servant of God." Winthrop called him "a man of a very mild temper and weak parts and wholly guided by his wife." After leaving the colony with her family, Anne ended up on the island of Aquidneck on Narragansett Bay. Thirty families voluntarily followed her into banishment. The men signed the Portsmouth Compact, creating the new settlement of Rhode Island. Anne gave birth with great difficulty in the summer of 1638, to a hydatidiform mole, a cluster of cysts that develops in place of an embryo. The Puritan fathers patted themselves on the back and broke out the cigars when they heard the news of the "monstrous birth." To them it just proved the point that she was evil and they were wise to kick her out.

Will Hutchinson died in 1642, having served as governor of the new colony. When it looked as if the Massachusetts Bay Colony was going to annex the Rhode Island colony, Anne decided to move with some of her children to the New Netherlands. The last thing she wanted was to be under the yoke of John Winthrop and his friends again. Anne and her family settled a farmstead on a meadow in Pelham Bay, near what is now the Split Rock golf course in the Bronx.

A year later, Siwanoy Indians scalped Anne and six of her children and burned down their house. Only her daughter Susan survived. Anne had been warned about a possible Indian attack, but she ignored it because of her long history of good relations with the Natives. Instead of arming herself, or abandoning her home, Anne did what she had always done: put her faith in the will of God. The Siwanoy chief Wampage renamed himself Ann-Hoeck after his most famous victim. Nine-year-old Susan was adopted by the Siwanoy and lived with them until she was eighteen, when she returned reluctantly to her family in Boston. The river near where Anne was killed is now known as the Hutchinson River.

Anne Hutchinson was an American visionary, a pioneer who became the poster girl for religious freedom and tolerance. Long before the Constitution guaranteed the right of free speech, Anne was defending hers. In 1987, Governor Michael Dukakis pardoned Anne, 350 years after John Winthrop "banished [her] from out of our jurisdiction as being a woman not fit for our society." A bronze statue of Anne stands proudly on the front lawn of the Massachusetts State House, calling her a "courageous exponent of civil liberty and religious toleration." Ironically, her statue looks toward the cemetery, steps away from where her old nemesis John Winthrop now rests.

# Mary Wollstonecraft

## 1759–1797

*I am going to be the first of a new genus, the peculiar bent of my nature pushes me on.*

—MARY WOLLSTONECRAFT

Mary Wollstonecraft wrote her masterwork, *A Vindication of the Rights of Woman*, in a frenzy in six weeks, distilling thirty years of anger. Published in 1792, it was an immediate success, attracting admirers that included future First Lady Abigail Adams. It was a ferocious rejection of the traditional ideas of femininity. She was not writing to please; she wrote about what she felt was real. In this landmark work she argued that women were not naturally inferior to men, but appeared to be only because they lacked an education.

She suggested that both men and women should be treated as rational beings and imagined a social order founded on reason.

From the moment of her birth in 1759, Mary had a chip on her shoulder. She felt unloved and unappreciated by her parents, who preferred her older brother, Ned, to her. And as each new baby was born in the family, Mary got lost in the shuffle. When her paternal grandfather died, his will divided his estate between her father, her brother, and her aunt. Nothing was left to her and her sisters, a slight that she never forgot. It was her first hint of the injustices that were meted out to women.

With his inherited money, Mary's father decided to pursue the life of a country squire, moving the family out of London to near Epping Forest in Essex. While he was good at spending, he had no skill at farming. As the years passed, the family slowly slid down the social ladder. They moved from Epping to Yorkshire and then back to London again. Her father began to drink heavily as his fortunes dwindled. His only talent was for beating his wife. Mary tried as much as possible to protect her mother, sometimes even sleeping outside their room. Despite her intervention, Mary was not loved for it. From that point on, Mary began to despise her father and pity her mother.

Even as a young girl, Mary wore her heart on her sleeve. She was a woman of tempestuous emotions, given to self-pity and depression, huge resentments, and a habit of impulsive and sometimes imprudent attachments. "I will have the first place in your heart or none," she told a female friend at the age of fourteen. She suffered from what they called "an excess of sensibility"; in other words, she was a bit intense. Although it was the fashion to conceal emotion, Mary rejected that notion completely. She never hid behind a mask of polite indifference or protected herself from getting hurt. She threw herself wholeheartedly into her friendships and love affairs and couldn't understand when the feelings were not returned with equal fervor.

She had decided against marriage at the age of fifteen, seeing how trapped her mother was, and she had no dowry even if she had been so inclined. Nothing she had seen of men had endeared

them to her. Not her brother, Ned; her father; or her brother-in-
law Meredith Bishop. But she also doubted her ability to attract a
husband. Handsome rather than beautiful, Mary cared nothing
for fashion, and while she was tall, with lovely fair hair and hazel
eyes, she also had a sharp tongue. Mary's own courage and determination often made her impatient and short with those who
lacked her drive and energy.

Mary's feelings about marriage seemed to be confirmed when
she was summoned by her brother-in-law to help her younger
sister, Eliza, after she gave birth. Eliza, who was probably suffering
from a bad case of postpartum depression, convinced Mary—or
was it the other way around?—that her only chance to get better
was to leave her husband. Worried for her sister's sanity, and appalled by her brother-in-law's unsympathetic attitude, Mary decided to rescue her, making all of the arrangements for them to
flee. When Eliza, missing her child, began to waver, Mary made
her stand firm. Her actions not only deprived Eliza of her child,
who died before she was a year old, but with no support from her
husband, she now had no choice but to work for a living, leaving
her resentful and bitter of Mary's later success.

In order to make a living, Mary, her sisters, and her best friend
Fanny Blood set up a school together in Newington Green. Despite her lack of formal education, Mary had developed radical
ideas about teaching. She believed that children shouldn't learn by
rote or be disciplined by the rod. The residents of the town were
Dissenters,* Jews, and others who had supported the Americans
in the recent Revolutionary War, including the Reverend Richard

---

* Dissenters were Quakers, Baptists, Methodists, and Unitarians, basically anyone who
  wasn't Church of England. Barred from universities and many professions, they
  started their own schools.

Price. Although not a Unitarian, Mary went to hear his sermons, finding that his ideals appealed to her. This was the beginning of her political education. Mary found the Dissenters that she met hardworking, humane, critical but not cynical, and respectful toward women; they proved kinder than her own family.

Initially a success, the school failed after Mary left to go to Lisbon in 1785 to nurse Fanny, who had married and was expecting her first child, but she didn't survive. Depressed and distraught over her friend's death in childbirth and the closure of the school, Mary took a job in Ireland working for the Viscount Kingsborough and his wife and their brood of children. Her inability to hide her emotions would get her into trouble during the year that she worked for the Kingsborough family as a governess. She found it hard to hide her contempt for the useless lives of the aristocracy, and the family alternated between treating her like an equal or like a servant, depending on their whims. She ended up in a power struggle with Caroline, Lady Kingsborough, over the affections of her daughters and she made the mistake of starting a flirtation with George Ogle, whom Caroline had marked out for her own. While traveling in England, Mary was fired by Lady Kingsborough.

With no money and no references, Mary had few options. She was saved by Joseph Johnson, a publisher she had become acquainted with when she lived in Newington Green. He had agreed to put out her first book, *Thoughts on the Education of Daughters*, for ten guineas before she left for Ireland. Now she made the impetuous move to make her living solely by her pen. This was a radical and daring choice since few women, or men, for that matter, could support themselves solely by writing.

Johnson put her up in a house and hired her to edit and write reviews for several of his publications, primarily the *Analytical*

*Review*. He became much more than a friend; Mary described him in her letters as a father and a brother. He also agreed to publish her novel, entitled simply *Mary: A Fiction*, encompassing her experiences in a thinly fictionalized version of her life, and set her up in rented lodgings. She taught herself French and German and translated texts. Johnson asked her to attempt Italian but it gave her a headache. Mary soon began writing a monthly column in which she criticized, with humor and disdain, novels that she felt had weak female characters. She tartly dismissed one work, calling it "Much ado about Nothing": "We place this work without any reservations, at the bottom of the second class." She wrote to a friend that she was soon making almost two hundred pounds a year by her writing. She was finally able to pay her debts and to help her sisters financially.

In between all her other work, Mary found the time to write *A Vindication of the Rights of Woman*. In it she demanded "Justice for one half of the human race." Mary did no special research for the book. She didn't need to; she lived it. Mary had experienced firsthand the plight of poor, respectable women who were forced to earn a living. She advocated training single women for adequate employment and was the first to call marriage "legal prostitution." Mary deplored the relegation of women to a state of ignorance and dependence. She was the first to propose that women were taught to be superficial and simpering; they weren't born that way. In her book, she wrote that men and women were human beings before sexual beings, that psychologically they were both the same. She courted controversy by encouraging parents to teach their children about sex and promoted the idea of coeducational schools.

The book was published in England, America, Germany, and

France and made Mary famous. Although it only sold three thousand copies in its first five years, it was the first treatise of its kind published in Britain and America to enter the mainstream. Aaron Burr used the book as a guide to teaching his daughter Theodosia. Amid the hosannas were a few sour notes. There was a cry to burn Mary in effigy. Horace Walpole famously called Mary "a hyena in petticoats."

Mary left for Paris in December 1792, joining a circle of expatriates then in the city. In the stimulating intellectual atmosphere of the French Revolution she met and fell passionately in love with Gilbert Imlay, an American writer and adventurer. While Mary had taken a prim attitude toward sex in her book, Imlay awakened her passions. He was thirty-nine, handsome, charming, and easygoing. He told Mary that he considered marriage a corrupt institution, which she wasn't savvy enough to know meant he was keeping his options open. Like a lot of women, Mary built up an image in her head of Imlay that had nothing to do with reality. Imlay, on his part, must have been flattered to have this famous woman so into him, but he had no idea what he was letting himself in for. As Virginia Woolf wrote, "Tickling minnows, he had hooked a dolphin."

As the political situation grew worse, Imlay registered Mary as his wife in 1793, giving her the protection of his American citizenship, even though they were not married. To Mary this was proof of his commitment to her. "My friend," she told Imlay, "I feel my fate united to yours by the most sacred principles of my soul." She soon became pregnant, and while waiting to give birth at Le Havre, Mary spent her time writing *An Historical and Moral View of the French Revolution*, which was published in December 1794. On May 14, 1794, attended by a midwife, she gave birth without complications to her first child, Fanny, naming her after her late friend.

Mary reveled in motherhood, and the pleasures of breast-feeding. She wrote to her friend Ruth Barlow, "My little Girl begins to suck so MANFULLY that her father reckons saucily on her writing the second part of the Rights of Woman." Refusing to let Fanny be swaddled, she dressed her in loose, light clothing, allowing her plenty of fresh air, which scandalized the women of Le Havre who called her the "raven mother," considering her unfit to be a mother.

Imlay became tired of the maternal Mary and eventually left her. She attempted suicide twice, first by an overdose of laudanum, the second time by trying to drown herself in the Thames. Mary considered her suicide attempts completely rational, writing after her second attempt, "I have only to lament, that, when the bitterness of death was past, I was inhumanly brought back to life and misery." In a last-ditch attempt to win Imlay back, she agreed to help him recover cargo stolen by a Norwegian captain. With only her infant daughter and a teenage nursemaid as her companions, Mary spent four months battling seasickness, traipsing over fjords, and haggling with officials all to save her lover's bacon to no avail. Her reward was to discover on her return that Imlay had taken up with another woman. She did get a bestseller out of the deal, publishing her account of her travels as *Letters Written During a Short Residence in Sweden, Norway, and Denmark in 1796*. William Godwin later wrote these prophetic words in his memoir of Mary's life: "If ever there was a book calculated to make a man in love with its author, this appears to me to be the book."

Calling herself Mrs. Imlay in order to bestow legitimacy to Fanny, she returned to London. In April 1796, Mary presented herself at Godwin's lodgings. The first time they had met, they disliked each other. Godwin had come to Joseph Johnson's house to hear Thomas Paine, but, to his annoyance, Mary wouldn't shut up. They had become reacquainted in January, before her second suicide attempt. Just friends at first, they soon became lovers. It was a tempestuous relationship. Mary was still gun-shy after Imlay, and Godwin, at forty, had gotten used to the life of a bachelor. By December, however, she was pregnant. They married in March 1797. Mary wasn't about to have another illegitimate child, and after some reluctance, Godwin agreed.

Despite their marriage, they both still prized their independence. "I wish you for my soul, to be riveted in my heart, but I do not desire to have you always at my elbow," she told Godwin. So Godwin rented separate quarters to work. They communicated by letter, several times a day, and each spent evenings, as before, with separate friends. However, their happiness was short-lived. On August 30, Mary went into labor. Infection set in, and nine days after giving birth to a daughter, named Mary, Wollstonecraft expired.

Godwin was devastated; he wrote to his friend Thomas Holcroft, "I firmly believe there does not exist her equal in the world. I know from experience we were formed to make each other happy. I have not the least expectation that I can now ever know happiness again." In January 1798, Godwin published his *Memoirs of the Author of A Vindication of the Rights of Woman*. In his grief, Godwin wrote a warts-and-all memoir that did a great deal of damage to Mary's reputation. Godwin turned Mary into a tragic heroine, and readers were appalled that he would reveal intimate details about her love affairs and suicide attempts. The book also portrayed Mary as a woman deeply invested in feeling, who was balanced by his reason and as more of a religious skeptic than she actually was. Mary's reputation wasn't restored until one hundred years after her death when Millicent Garrett Fawcett, a suffragist, wrote an introduction to the centenary edition of *Vindication*. In the two-hundred-plus years since her death, Mary has become one of the most discussed, admired, demonized, reviled, and criticized feminists in history. Her life was full of contradictions that confound modern feminists—she shunned marriage, yet married; she admired the ideas of the French Revolution, but hated the bloodshed. However, her unconventional ideas lived on in her daughter Mary Shelley.

# Rose O'Neal Greenhow
## 1813?–1864

*I am a Southern woman, born with revolutionary blood in my veins.*
—ROSE O'NEAL GREENHOW

In July 1861 at the height of the Civil War, a young woman managed to deliver vital information about Union troop movements to General Pierre Beauregard of the Confederate army, stationed near a little town called Manassas in Virginia. She kept the small piece of paper, containing a combination of numbers written in ink, hidden in a black silk bag no bigger than a silver dollar tucked in the heavy coil of her dark hair. Where had she gotten the information from? Rose O'Neal Greenhow, a Washington matron, Southern sympathizer, and Confederate spy. When Rose heard of the subsequent Confederate victory at the First Battle of Bull Run, she always believed that it was her information that made the difference.

Born Rose O'Neale, her family lived on a small plantation in Montgomery County,* Maryland. The middle child of five daughters, she was high-spirited, with dark eyes and a will of iron. When Rose was four years old, her father was found dead by the side of the road, after spending the afternoon and night drinking in a tavern. His favorite slave, Jacob, was tried and convicted for killing his master in a drunken rage. Rose's mother was given four hundred dollars' compensation for losing her slave to the gallows.

Her mother tried to keep the family together and to save the farm, but after a few years, everything was auctioned off to pay the remaining debts. Rose and her sister Ellen were sent to live with an aunt and uncle who ran a boardinghouse in Washington, DC, that served as a temporary home to lawmakers while Congress was in session. The young women were introduced into Washington society through the connections they made while living at the boardinghouse. Rose's wit was sharp, her manner dynamic, and the politicians were soon calling her "Wild Rose."

Their days were filled making social calls or spending time in the visitors' gallery watching the debates on the Senate floor, which was a popular pastime. These were the days when great orators such as Daniel Webster, Henry Clay, and John C. Calhoun

---

* She was born either in 1813 or 1814; her birth was not recorded, and no one is sure exactly when she was born. The family later dropped the *e* from their last name.

took the floor. Women swooned over their favorite orators. Rose became particularly fond of Calhoun, who became a father figure to her, and she often sought his advice. He and Rose became very close; her thoughts about slavery and the South were formed by the time she spent with him. She once wrote about him, "My first crude ideas on State and Federal matters received consistency and shape from the best and wisest man of this century." Rose's sisters made socially advantageous marriages, which helped bring her more into society. The next step for Rose was to also make a good marriage.

Robert Greenhow was one of the most eligible bachelors in the capital. From a fine Virginia family, Greenhow was cultured; he'd lived abroad, spoke several languages, and was working for the State Department as a translator and librarian. They were married in 1835. Rose was gregarious and social, while Robert was more comfortable with his books and maps, but they shared an interest in learning. Rose was passionate about preserving the Southern way of life, including slavery. She adamantly opposed the abolitionist movement, believing that blacks were inferior to whites. And she wasn't hesitant to express her views.

Since Robert was not terribly ambitious, Rose was ambitious enough for the both of them. They socialized two or three times a week, and Rose learned to throw glittering dinner parties. Modeling herself after her idol, Dolley Madison, Rose became an effective and knowledgeable hostess. By the 1840s, Rose was an ardent proslavery expansionist. Over the next two decades she came to know all the movers and shakers in Washington society.

Widowed in 1854, while they were living in California, Rose received a small settlement in regard to her husband's accidental death, but the money quickly ran out. Moving back to Washington, DC, Rose had to improvise, moving to smaller and smaller residences. The charming widow wore black clothing that she made herself, which emphasized her dramatic coloring. Easing herself back into the social whirl, she soon had several beaux who were quite smitten with her but Rose wasn't interested in remarrying. She persuaded her old friend James Buchanan to run for president, working tirelessly for his campaign.

When Buchanan was elected, Rose once again was close to the seat of power. She was described by the *New York Herald* as a "bright shining light" in the social life of the new administration. Rose threw popular dinner parties, entertaining both Northerners and Southerners, but tensions ran high in the capital. At a dinner party, Charles Francis Adams's wife expressed sympathy for the radical abolitionist John Brown. Rose snapped, "I have no sympathy for John Brown. He was a traitor and met a traitor's doom." These were strong words from a woman who prided herself on being the epitome of a gracious hostess. When Lincoln was elected president, the world that Rose knew came to an end.

With the Southern states seceding from the Union, Rose was eager to help any way that she could. She was recruited by Captain Thomas Jordan of the Confederacy, who taught her basic cryptography, which she diligently practiced. Although she was no longer in the inner circle, Rose still had connections in Washington, which she used to get information to send to the Confederate army stationed in Virginia under Beauregard. Using her feminine wiles, she cajoled military secrets from Union sympathizers who were so blinded by her charms, they loosened their tongues without even realizing what they were doing. Rose didn't limit herself to powerful men but also their clerks and aides as well.

Rose, not being a trained spy, was a little careless. She kept copies of information that she had sent and didn't completely destroy information that she had received. Her neighbors became suspicious of her and one of them reported her to Thomas Scott, who was the new assistant secretary of war. Thomas Scott hired Allan Pinkerton, founder of the Pinkerton Detective Agency, and put him on the case. Pinkerton was in Washington under an assumed name, Major E. J. Allen, working on counterintelligence as part of the fledgling U.S. Secret Service. He had set up a network of informants in the South who were sympathetic to ending the Civil War.

In August 1861, Rose was arrested on the doorstep outside her house just as she popped a note in her mouth and swallowed. The detectives put her and her youngest daughter, little Rose, under house arrest after they ransacked the house searching for evidence. Although they found a large number of documents and maps, including the ones that Rose had sewn into her dress, they missed others that she was able to destroy. A prisoner in her own home, she was watched constantly, even at night; she had to sleep with her door open. Anyone who tried to visit her was arrested. Soon other prisoners were brought to her house to join her. Rose was outraged that lower-class women "of bad character" were placed in her home.

Rose made things difficult for her guards as well as herself. She complained that her rights were being trampled on, that the food was inedible, that she had no privacy. Lincoln had suspended habeas corpus shortly after the war started. Although she was under arrest, Rose still managed to get information to her string of informants. Some of her messages didn't go through and were added to the pile of evidence against her. Rose wrote a letter to Secretary of State William H. Seward protesting her imprisonment. "The iron heel or power may keep down, but it cannot crush out, the spirit of resistance, armed for the defense of their rights: and I tell you now, sir, that you are standing over a crater, whose smothered fires in a moment may burst forth." A copy found its way to the *Richmond Whig*. The newspaper called it the "most graphic sketch yet given to the world of the cruel and dastardly tyranny" of the Yankee government. Rose's imprisonment made her a martyr in the eyes of the South. The evil Yankees who could imprison a mother and child were grist for the propaganda mill.

After several months under house arrest, Rose and her daughter were moved to her former childhood home, her aunt's boardinghouse, which had been turned into a Union prison. The room they were confined in would have been familiar to Rose; it was the same one where she had nursed her dying hero, Senator Calhoun in 1850, treasuring his last words. Rose complained about having to share the prison with Negro prisoners. The room was filled with vermin, so Rose would use a lit candle to burn them off the wall. She tucked clothes underneath the mattress to make it more comfortable for her little daughter. Somehow she even managed to smuggle in a pistol even though she had no ammunition.

After almost eight months in prison, Rose was finally brought up on charges of espionage. Rose was feisty and defiant to the members of the commission. Without counsel, she demanded to know what evidence they had against her, and she complained that her rights were being trampled. When they presented their evidence, including a letter Rose wrote that gave details of the Union army's movements, Rose brazened it out, giving them no satisfaction. Although her actions were treasonable, Lincoln was reluctant to have her stand trial. Treason was a hanging offense but Lincoln had no stomach for hanging a woman. Something had to be done, though; Rose was considered too dangerous. She was given a choice: either swear allegiance to the Union or be deported to the Confederacy. Rose agreed to be deported to the South.

On May 31, 1862, after almost ten months in prison, four

months on house arrest, and five months in the Capitol prison, Rose was escorted out of the city that had been her home for more than thirty years. Did she feel a pang as the wagon passed through the streets of the city where she had met her husband, given birth to her children and buried them, the avenues where she had strolled with her beaux and her sisters? Rose would never see the city again.

Before Rose was allowed to set foot on Confederate soil, she had to sign a statement as a condition of her parole that she would never set foot in the North again while the war continued. In Richmond, Rose was welcomed with open arms. She was hailed as a heroine, a true daughter of Dixie who defied the North. At a welcoming lunch, Rose cheekily raised her glass and toasted the president of the Confederacy, Jefferson Davis. Davis granted her twenty-five hundred dollars for her services to the Confederacy. After her arrival, Rose was sent by Davis to Europe to drum up support for the South's cause. Despite the fact that she suffered greatly from seasickness, Rose was eager to go.

She went to France to plead with Emperor Napoleon III and to England to do the same with Queen Victoria. Although privately people were sympathetic, Rose could not get anyone in Parliament or Napoleon III to publicly come out in support of the South or to recognize the Confederate states. In her first two months abroad, she wrote her memoir, *My Imprisonment and the First Year of Abolition Rule at Washington*, which sold well in Britain. She dedicated the work to "the brave soldiers who have fought and bled in this glorious struggle for freedom." The book is a valuable record of Southern sentiment that led up to the Civil War.

Rose drowned off the coast of North Carolina on October 1, 1864, when the ship in which she was returning to America ran aground at the mouth of Cape Fear, chased by a Union gunboat.

Although the captain advised that everyone stay on board, Rose was frightened of being captured by the Yankees again. She was on her way to shore when her rowboat was overturned by a large wave. Her body was found washed up onshore a few days later. She had been weighed down by gold sewn into her clothing. Searchers also found a copy of her book, *Imprisonment*, hidden on her person.

She was given a full military burial, wrapped in the Confederate flag, in Oakdale Cemetery, near Wilmington, North Carolina. The *Wilmington Sentinel* wrote that her funeral "was a solemn and imposing spectacle . . . the tide of visitors, women and children with streaming eyes, and soldiers with bent heads and hushed stares standing by, paying the last tribute of respect to their departed heroine." Her grave bears the inscription "Mrs. Rose O'N. Greenhow. A Bearer of Dispatches to the Confederate Government." Every year on the anniversary of her death, a ceremony is held to honor her contributions to the Confederate cause.

Rose O'Neal Greenhow was not to be admired for her views about slavery. But her devotion to the Confederacy and her ability to further her cause through her charm and determination certainly made her one of the most dangerous and formidable women in the country. Although her spying career was brief, and there is doubt among historians about the value of the information she was able to pass on, Rose proved that even through traditional means, women could be effective instruments of war.

# Ida B. Wells-Barnett
## 1862–1931

*It was through journalism that I found the real me.*

—IDA B. WELLS-BARNETT

Long before Rosa Parks refused to give up her seat on the bus, a young schoolteacher refused to move from the ladies' car on the train on the Chesapeake and Ohio Railroad. When she was removed from the train she sued—and she won, proving that a woman of color could make her voice heard. Although the decision was later overturned, Ida B. Wells-Barnett kept raising her voice, educating Americans and Europeans about the horrors of lynching and other social injustices that were being heaped on African Americans in the nineteenth century. Ida appeared at a time when the previous generation of black leaders who had led the fight for slavery was now too old to head a new battle to protect the freedoms promised by the Emancipation Proclamation. A new generation was needed and Ida was one who stepped into the breach. In her heyday, she was praised as the Joan of Arc of her people in the black press.

Ida wasn't one to back down or compromise. She was tough and argumentative, and she clashed with several prominent African American leaders of the time for compromising instead of standing firm. She also clashed with various whites, including temperance advocate Frances Willard. "Temper . . . has always been my besetting sin," she conceded. She owned newspapers and wrote articles at a time when most women were relegated to writing what was known then as the "women's page." She hyphenated her name at a time when most women automatically took their husband's name. Living in Chicago, she started the first kindergarten for black children. Although she lost a race for the Illinois State Senate, just the fact that she ran, ten years after women won the vote, is a testament to her courage and ambition.

Ida B. Wells was the eldest of eight children, born in 1862 in Holly Springs, Mississippi, to James Wells, a carpenter, and Elizabeth "Lizzie Bell" Warrenton Wells, who were slaves on the Bolling plantation. Although the Emancipation Proclamation of 1863 freed slaves held in the Confederate states, Holly Springs, where the family lived, changed hands between the Union and the Confederacy more than fifty times during the war. It wasn't until the end of the Civil War that the entire Wells family was free.

When Ida was sixteen, yellow fever struck Mississippi, killing Ida's parents and one of her siblings. Despite tongues wagging at the idea, Ida rose to the challenge of taking care of her remaining siblings and keeping the family together. She took the teacher certification exam and passed with flying colors. Despite the difficulties of raising her six siblings while teaching, Ida still managed to keep up her education, working her way through Shaw University during the summers. Ida knew that education was power, a way out of the backbreaking work of sharecropping and poverty. In 1881, however, she was expelled from Shaw. She never talked about what occurred, but she apparently did something that angered W. W. Hooper, the white president of the college. Ida refused to back down or apologize.

She decided to move to Memphis to live with her father's stepsister along with several of her siblings. While living in Memphis, Ida availed herself of the social life that was available, taking in lectures, going to the theater, shopping at Menken's Palatial Emporium, which boasted "Thirty Stores Under One Roof." She was a regular customer at William's bookstore, and whenever possible, she attended classes at Fisk University. She enjoyed going to church, not just the black churches but also the white ones, where she would sit in the segregated galleries to hear the sermon.

She started teaching at a country school in northern Mississippi just across the state line from the city. The Federal Civil Rights Act of 1875 that had banned discrimination on the basis of race, creed, or color had just been declared unconstitutional, which led several railroad companies to start practicing segregation. Every day Ida rode the train to work but she never knew from one day to the next whether or not she would be ill-treated, until the day that the Chesapeake and Ohio Railroad Company tried to force her to sit in the smoking car when she had paid for a first-class pass. Ida later wrote in her autobiography, "I refused, saying that the forward car closest to the locomotive was a smoker, and as I was in the ladies' car, I proposed to stay. . . . The conductor tried to drag me out of the seat, but the moment he caught hold of my arm I fastened my teeth in the back of his hand. I had braced my feet against the seat in front and was holding to the back, and as he had already been badly bitten he didn't try it again by himself. He went forward and got the baggage man and another man to help him and of course they succeeded in dragging me out."

White passengers cheered the conductor as he removed Ida from the train. Black newspapers throughout the country reprinted her first article about her railroad court case. With the help of a second lawyer (she was suspicious that her first lawyer had taken money to throw the case) Ida won her lawsuit and was awarded five hundred dollars in damages. However, in 1887, the railroad company appealed the decision to the Tennessee Supreme

Court and won, reversing the court's decision. Ida was required to return the money and to pay two hundred dollars in damages to the railroad.

Ida's teaching in Memphis schools led her to write articles for the *Evening Star*, a black-owned newspaper, about the inequalities between the separated black and white schools. She began writing for another local black newspaper, the *Memphis Free Speech*, where she eventually would become a co-owner and editor. In her editorials, Ida took on the violence against blacks, disfranchisement, the poor school system, and the failure of blacks to fight for their rights. She traveled the country getting subscribers. After she became a co-owner, Ida started printing the paper on pink paper so it would stand out.

She was elected secretary of the Colored Press Association, where she received the nickname "the Princess of the Press." Her writing style was simple and direct because, as she said in her autobiography, *The Crusade for Justice*, she "needed to help people with little or no schooling deal with problems in a simple, helpful way." Eventually fired from her teaching job for writing about the inequalities between black and white schools, Ida became a full-time journalist.

In 1892, a longtime friend, Tom Moss, a respected black store owner, was lynched along with two of his friends after he defended his store against an attack by whites. Wells was outraged, particularly since nothing was done to bring the culprits to justice. She wrote a scathing series of editorials, encouraging black residents of Memphis to leave town and attacking the practice of lynching. She also encouraged those blacks who remained to boycott white-owned businesses.

"Lynch's Law," which became corrupted to "lynch law" and

then "lynching," originated during the American Revolution when Charles Lynch, a Virginia justice of the peace, ordered punishment against those who supported the Tory cause. After the Civil War, lynching became a form of terrorism practiced by white mobs against mostly innocent blacks. Instead of waiting for due process of law, organized mobs would take the law into their own hands. Many of the victims, while being hung, were set on fire or shot.

Lynching was the preferred method to control the African American male population, to keep him in his place, basically poor and illiterate. Between 1880 and 1930, more than three thousand African Americans and some thirteen hundred whites were lynched in the United States. Nine times out of ten, the accused were arrested with no evidence, or what evidence there was turned out to be extremely circumstantial. Confessions were obtained under coercion. Many others were lynched for trivial offenses such as not paying a debt, disrespecting whites, or public drunkenness.

Ida wrote pamphlets exposing the horrors of lynching and defending the victims. She believed that lynching was the central issue facing blacks in the South. Although she wasn't the first African American to speak out against lynching, she was the first to grain a broad audience. Ida realized that as long as lynching was seen as a way to protect white women's virtue, black leaders couldn't address it without sounding defensive or self-interested. However, black women could give effective testimony on the evils of lynching in the name of chivalry.

While Ida was in New York, the office of the *Free Speech* was destroyed by a mob and she was warned never to return to Memphis. Trying to avoid bloodshed, Ida did not return home, once she heard that black men had vowed to protect her. Instead she moved to Chicago, where she met Ferdinand Barnett, a prominent attorney and widower, whom she eventually married at the relatively advanced age of thirty-three. She also wrote for his newspaper, the *Chicago Conservator*. After their marriage she became owner and editor.

In 1895, she wrote "The Red Record: Tabulated Statistics and Alleged Causes of Lynching in the United States: 1892, 1893, and 1894," which included all her research of the past few years. She started traveling the country asking for support in putting a stop to lynching. People began to ask her to speak at organization meetings and functions. She would spend the rest of her life writing and giving speeches throughout the country and in Europe.

Ida undertook two lecture tours of England at the request of British Quaker Catherine Impey. The goal was to convince the English of the horrors of lynching, since the United States and England had a special relationship. If England spoke out against lynching, perhaps politicians in America would take notice. While in England, Ida launched the London Anti-Lynching Committee. Ida's tours were a great success, although it led to a rupture between her and one of her sponsors, when she refused to condemn the decision of a woman who fell in love with a man outside her race. She wrote about her tour for the *Daily Inter-Ocean* in Chicago, becoming the first black woman to be paid as a correspondent for a major white newspaper.

After the birth of her four children, Ida continued to lecture, taking her children with her, asking for babysitters at every stop on her lecture tour. Eventually the demands of motherhood kept Ida in Chicago but she continued to write and speak out about injustice. She refused to walk in the back in women's suffrage parades because she was black and she fell out with Susan B. Anthony because she dared to get married and start a family instead of devoting herself solely to the cause of suffrage and the establishment of antilynching law.

Although busy raising her four children and her two stepchildren, she found the time to serve as secretary of the National Afro-American Council and she was part of a delegation to President William McKinley to seek justice after the lynching in South Carolina of a black postman. Unfortunately McKinley was too preoccupied by the Spanish-American War and its aftermath to give the matter much attention.

Ida remained active and militant for the rest of her life. She was a founding member of the NAACP, but she later withdrew her membership because she considered the organization not militant enough. In her writing and lectures, she often criticized middle-class blacks for not being active enough in helping the poor in the black community. Her militancy placed her out of sync with more moderate black leaders, such as Booker T. Washington, who were more willing to compromise with whites. Deciding to stick to local issues in the Chicago area, she worked with social reformer Jane Addams to defeat an attempt to segregate Chicago's public school system. Ida became interested in the settlement movement, in particular the work that Jane Addams had done with Hull House, the first of its kind in the United States. Hull House was essentially a neighborhood center that catered to the recent immigrants in its neighborhoods.

In 1910, she helped found and became president of the Negro Fellowship League, which established a settlement house in Chicago to serve the many African Americans newly arrived from the South. It offered lectures and classes, as well as a kindergarten, a summer day camp, and a meeting place for black women's clubs and community organizations. To help support the settlement house, she worked for the city as a probation officer, donating most of her salary to the organization. Unfortunately, due to competition from other groups and her own poor health, the league closed its doors in 1920.

Ida started to write her autobiography, *The Crusade for Justice*, after meeting a young woman who admitted not knowing why Ida was important. Most of Ida's antilynching work had taken place in the 1890s, before the current generation was born. The newer generation cared less about the struggle. Unfortunately Ida died of uremia poisoning in 1931, at the age of sixty-eight, before the book was finished. In fact she left off not in the middle of a sentence but a word. Edited by her daughter Alfreda Duster, who had saved all her mother's papers, the book languished for years unable to find a publisher. It was finally published in 1970, helped by the burgeoning interest in African American and women's history. Ida and her husband's headstone is engraved with the phrase "Crusaders for Justice."

During her lifetime, Ida constantly struggled between her militancy and her need to be perceived as a "lady." Her inability to work successfully with groups meant that she was alienated from movements she founded and she failed to get appropriate credit for her work during her lifetime. For decades after her death, her achievements went largely unsung. It is only in the last forty years that she has gotten the recognition she deserves. In 1990, a U.S. postage stamp was issued, and her work is now studied and taught in high schools and colleges. In 2005, her work was lauded on the floor of the U.S. Congress.

# Carry Nation
### 1846–1911

*Truly does the saloon make a woman bare of all things.*

—Carry Nation

Both repellent and fascinating, this hatchet-swinging, Bible-thumping, God-appointed vigilante swung through Midwestern saloons, smashing glass with shrieks of triumph, like an early-twentieth-century "Dirty Harriet." This self-proclaimed "bull-dog running along at the feet of Jesus" objected not just to drink but also to smoking, the Masons, risqué art, and ostentatious fashion. She took particular delight in assailing people and institutions; not even the office of the President was safe from Carry Nation. Her detrac-

tors considered her to be a puritanical killjoy, while her supporters considered her to be a second John Brown. "Savage" and "unsexed" were just some of the words used to describe this grandmotherly woman who stood almost six feet tall. But for Carry Nation, the crusade was intensely personal. She'd seen up close the damage that drink could do.

Carry was born Carrie

Amelia Moore in 1846 in Kentucky to a prosperous family. Her mother, frequently ill from constant pregnancies and the strain of taking care of her four older stepchildren, alternated between violent antipathy toward her and smothering her with affection. As a child Carry slept in the slave quarters rather than in the big house with her parents. It was there she found the affection that was lacking from her mother. Young Carry was fascinated by the slaves' attitude toward religion, their songs and shoutings, and their belief in spirit possession. She kept the secret of their slave meetings, and they rarely tattled on her for her childhood indiscretions.

Carry was a semi-invalid through most of her childhood, suffering from chlorosis, an iron deficiency that manifested a greenish skin color. Biographer Fran Grace believes that Carry's invalidism might also have been her way of rebelling against being forced to give up her tomboyish ways to conform to society and her mother's expectations of appropriate female behavior. Being sick kept her from having to assume any responsibility around the house.

The Moore fortunes declined and Carry and her family moved several times, from Kentucky to Missouri and then to Texas. When the Civil War broke out, they had to leave their slaves behind in Texas, while they moved to Independence, Missouri. With no slaves and her mother sick, Carry was forced to take over the household.

When she was eighteen, she met Dr. Charles Gloyd, a Civil War vet who was boarding with her family. Starved of affection, Carry was susceptible to his attentions. Totally innocent, when he kissed her for the first time, she thought she was ruined. But her parents disapproved; not only couldn't he support her, but they also figured out he was a drunk. Forbidden to speak, Carry and he exchanged letters by hiding them in a volume of Shakespeare.

Eventually her parents relented. Even on their wedding day, the groom couldn't stay sober, swaying at the altar as he said his vows.

The marriage was a failure; Gloyd preferred drinking with his buddies to spending time with his wife. Carry would often stand outside the Masonic Hall pleading for him to come home. After six months, Carry's family persuaded her to leave Gloyd and come home. Carry begged Gloyd to sign the temperance pledge but he refused. Their daughter, Charlien, was born in the fall of 1868. When Carry came to retrieve her belongings, Gloyd begged her to stay, predicting his death if she didn't. He drank himself to death a few months later. Carry was now a widow at twenty-two, with a baby to support. She regretted for the rest of her life that she had left him, believing that she could have saved him if she'd stayed.

Devastated, Carry decided to strike out on her own. She sold her husband's books and medical equipment and moved to Holden, Missouri. There she lived with her child and mother-in-law. Earning a teaching certificate, she taught for four years until she got into a dispute with a school board official. With no way to support herself, Carry decided her only other option was to marry again. Her second choice was no better than her first. David Nation was an old acquaintance, a lawyer, journalist, and part-time preacher. He was also a recent widower nineteen years her senior with five children. They married three months after his first wife's death. It was a marriage of convenience; his kids needed a mother, and she was jobless and broke. Three years after the marriage, they moved to Texas to grow cotton, with little success. While her husband struggled to establish himself, Carry became increasingly independent over the years, running two hotels and finally acquiring a degree in osteopathic medicine.

A deeply religious woman, Carry began to have visions and

dreams during this period. She felt that she was baptized with the Holy Spirit. In church, she began to break in on the sermons, bursting into prayer or song, and she took to contradicting the preacher when he spoke. Like Anne Hutchinson, she came into conflict with church elders who were dismayed that a woman could suggest that it was possible to have a direct line to God. She was eventually expelled from the church. Although as a child she'd been baptized in the Christian church (Disciples of Christ), she no longer subscribed to one particular creed. Her religious fervor came from a grab bag of influences that she stitched together like a patchwork quilt. It encompassed slave religion, Roman Catholicism, and a few tenets from the Baptist and Methodist churches.

Living in Medicine Lodge, Kansas, Carry became active in the Woman's Christian Temperance Union (WCTU) and served as a "jail evangelist" to drunks in jail to try to show them a new way. What stuck in her craw was that many saloons in Kansas sold liquor in violation of the state's prohibition law,* and oftentimes legislators and law enforcement officers looked the other way or participated in the illegal activity themselves.

In 1900, she became president of the county WCTU. Realizing that writing letters to legislators wasn't doing any good in getting the prohibition law enforced, Carry decided to take matters into her own hands. Carry called on the governor's mansion and reamed him out big-time for not enforcing the law in his own state. She prayed to God for direction and claimed a vision came to her that told her to go to the town of Kiowa. So she took her horse and buggy and headed to Kiowa, armed with bricks to de-

---

* Kansas had passed a prohibition amendment to the state constitution in 1880, only the second state after Maine to do so.

stroy the saloons there. Soon she switched to a hatchet, which was more practical.

Alone or accompanied by hymn-singing women from the WCTU, she would march into a bar and, singing and praying, smash up the bar fixtures and stock. Early on, saloons hired plants and undercover policemen to try to infiltrate the meetings of the "Nation Brigade." To get around this, brigade members used special code words for entry and wore white ribbons. Moving on to Wichita, she wrecked the bar at the Carey Hotel, one of the most luxurious in the Midwest, causing three thousand dollars' worth of damages. She spent two weeks in jail but was undeterred. Soon Topeka and Kansas City also felt the fury of her hatchet.

Although Nation believed that her mission was from God, it was still dangerous. She was pushed down, threatened with a gun, beaten and whipped by prostitutes, pelted with rocks and raw eggs. One saloon owner's wife punched her in the face. Over the course of her career, she was jailed over thirty times, from California to Maine. Even in jail, she was subject to abuse. In Wichita, the judge issued quarantine in the jail, and she was thrown into solitary confinement for days at a time. On more than one occasion, Nation was pursued by a lynch mob. Carry, however, was fully prepared to be a martyr to the cause. In 1901, the state temperance league awarded her a gold medal and the title of "bravest woman in Kansas."

Carry's antics, or "hatchetation," as she liked to call it, made her a nationally known figure. Newspapers eagerly covered her day-to-day activities. Nation was soon receiving two hundred letters a week. Meanwhile her husband divorced her for cruelty and desertion. After the decree came through she said, "Had I married a man I could love, God could never have used me." Although a divorce tarnished her reputation as a "defender of the home," Nation now decided that social reform demanded that women see the world as their home. Along the lines of the Salvation Army, Nation organized the Home Defenders Army, creating hatchet brigades. She even tried to reach out to children and teenagers. Despite her reputation as a harridan with a hatchet, Carry was generous to a fault. She collected clothes for the poor and invited them to her house for Thanksgiving and Christmas.

In response to her crusade, saloon owners began to offer "Carry Nation" cocktails while the Senate Bar in Topeka, after reopening, offered a relic from its smashing with every drink. Business boomed so much that the bar had to hire four more bartenders. "All Nations Welcome but Carry" became a popular slogan in bars. After a merchant gave her some pewter hatchet pins left over from Washington's birthday to sell to pay her legal fees, Nation had her own emblazoned with "Carry Nation Joint Smasher." They became collector's items; people who didn't even believe in her crusade had to have one. Media savvy, she also hawked autographed photos, buttons, her autobiography, and even special water bottles.

In 1903, she had her name legally changed to Carry A. Nation since she believed that was what God had chosen her to do. Carry took her message to the state capitols, not waiting for an invitation to the legislatures of Kansas and California. She once caused the U.S. Senate to grind to a halt while she was forcibly removed from the public galleries for having shouted out her opinions. She started several short-lived magazines with catchy titles like *The Smasher's Mail* and *The Hatchet*. All the money that she made went to serve her causes, the magazines, and homes for the families left behind in poverty by alcoholism.

For the next several years until her death, Carry Nation traveled nationally and internationally, from lecture halls and college campuses to the vaudeville stage. Carry believed that God had called her to take her message to the stage, to reach the masses. "I am fishing. I go where the fish are, for they do not come to me. I found the theaters stocked with the boys of our country. They are not found in churches."

People either liked her or didn't but no one was indifferent to her. She made no apologies for her religious fervor, declaring, "I like to go just as far as the farthest. I like my religion like my oysters and beefsteak, piping hot." Carry Nation appeared at the crossroads between the old world order and the new. She represented old-fashioned moral values of home, hearth, and religion as well as the emergence of the new woman who rejected traditional roles. She both threatened and reassured people at the same time. Even the WCTU both embraced her and kept its distance, applauding her successes yet deploring her methods.

By 1910, Carry had worn out her welcome. After one last speaking tour, she moved to Eureka Springs, Arkansas, buying several homes including one she called Hatchet Hall, a unique woman-centered community for the wives and children of alcoholics, like her daughter Charlien, whose husband turned out to be an emotionally and physically abusive alcoholic. In 1911, she collapsed giving a speech in Eureka Springs Park and was taken to a hospital in Leavenworth, Kansas. She died of a nervous seizure five months later on June 9 and was buried in Belton, Missouri, near her mother. The WCTU later erected a stone inscribed "Faithful to the Cause of Prohibition, She Hath Done What She Could."

For the short years of her career, Carry Nation was the public face of the temperance movement. Although her tactics could be melodramatic, she influenced lawmakers. As a result of her actions, Kansas at last tried to adhere to its own state laws, and her work eventually led to the Eighteenth Amendment prohibiting alcohol in 1919. Yet during national prohibition, which she had done so much to bring about, and which was abolished in 1933, her grim, iron-jawed figure became a symbol not of reform but of intolerance.

Although Carry died almost a hundred years ago, one can still hear echoes of her message in the moral crusaders who fight what they see as the moral laxity in today's society, calling for warning labels on DVDs and CDs, supporting antismoking ads, and promoting chastity. No doubt Carry would feel right at home, protesting and swinging her ax at the drive-through liquor stores.

# FIVE

# Wild Women of the West

## Mary Ellen Pleasant
### 1814?–1904

*I am a whole theater in myself.*

—MARY ELLEN PLEASANT

During the late nineteenth century, she was the most gossiped-about woman in California. They called her "Mammy" Pleasant but she was no one's mammy, thank you very much, although she wasn't above playing the role if it benefited her. For more than a century, Mary Ellen Pleasant's name has gone down in history as a voodoo queen, sorceress, and murderer who had unnatural powers over others. In the process her remarkable achievements as a savvy businesswoman and civil rights activist have been obscured.

Mary Ellen Pleasant's birth, like many aspects of her life, is shrouded in mystery. She claimed to be born in Philadelphia, and that her father was a native of Hawaii and her mother a freed slave from Louisiana. What is known is that at the age of six, she was sent to live with the Husseys, a Quaker family on Nantucket, and when she was old enough she began working in their shop. It was here that Mary Ellen learned the business skills that she would use effectively in later years.

Mary Ellen only had a rudimentary education, learning to read and write. It was something that bothered her until her death. In her autobiography, published in 1902, she wrote, "I often wonder what I would have been like with an education." In her early twenties, Mary Ellen left the island for Boston, where she met her first husband, James W. Smith, a successful contractor and foreman. He was also an abolitionist who introduced his new bride to New England's antislavery society. Mary Ellen may have already been involved in abolitionist activity on Nantucket, which had a small but thriving black population.

Mary Ellen was soon a widow, but a wealthy one. When her husband died, he left her fifteen thousand dollars, which was practically a fortune in nineteenth-century America, particularly for African Americans. She wasn't lonely for long. Soon she was being courted by another mulatto gentleman, by the name of John James Pleasant, a waiter and cook from New Bedford. They were married in 1847 and lived together on and off until his death, his work as a ship's cook keeping them apart for months at a time. Their only child, a daughter named Elizabeth, was born in 1851.

In 1852, Mary Ellen and her husband, like thousands of others, decided to try their luck in California, lured by talk of opportunities that seemed limitless. Unlike most free African Americans, they had the money to pay for the passage. San Francisco was still the wild Barbary Coast. The boundaries of race and capitalism hadn't yet been set in stone. This gave Mary Ellen the opportunity to get in on the ground floor.

Although she had a sizable inheritance, she wasn't afraid of hard work. Most of the jobs available to blacks were menial but they paid better than they did back East. Taking advantage of the stereotype that blacks were great cooks, Mary Ellen managed to auction off her services to the highest bidder, an investment firm, for five hundred dollars a month and she didn't have to do dishes! She was so amazingly persuasive, her income was twice what other cooks were making.

Keeping her eyes and ears open, Mary Ellen began looking for investment opportunities. Using the investment tips that came her way through her jobs as a housekeeper and cook for some of San Francisco's most elite families, she began speculating on commodities like gold and silver. Soon she was able to open up three laundries, taking advantage of the demand, and employed newly arrived African Americans. In only three years, Mary Ellen had become one of the most successful businesswomen on the West Coast.

With her accountant, Mary Ellen opened her first boarding-house, which was actually a refuge for runaway slaves. She also put up the money for several legal battles, most notably the effort to free an eighteen-year-old fugitive slave named Atchy Lee in 1858. Although California was admitted as a free state, it still allowed slave owners to bring their slaves to the state until the Civil War. Mary Ellen lent her support to the black-owned newspaper *Mirror of the Times*, the first African American newspaper west of the Rockies. Historian Sue Bailey Thurman has said that it was Mary Ellen's money and leadership that led to the repeal of the law banning black testimony in court.

Mary Ellen and her husband left California in 1858 and moved clear across the continent to Ontario to work with abolitionists there, smuggling slaves into Canada. She would later claim that not only did she financially aid John Brown's raid on Harpers Ferry but that she also traveled through Virginia, dressed like a man, in advance, like an African American female Paul Revere, warning the slaves. There is no proof of her claims, although years later she requested that inscribed on her tombstone would be the words, "She was a friend of John Brown."

After her return to California, Mary Ellen went to work as a housekeeper for a wealthy merchant named Selim Woodworth. Now she really made her mark in San Francisco. Although she owned her own carriage, Mary Ellen decided to help focus attention on the discriminatory policies of the San Francisco streetcars that refused to stop for blacks. These policies hurt African American women the most, as domestics; they relied on the streetcars to get to work. She had already dropped one suit against one company when it appeared that it had changed its policies.

However, her lawsuit against the North Beach and Mission Railway Company went ahead. Pleasant won her case before a jury and was awarded five hundred dollars in damages. Her trump card was having a white witness confirm her story that the streetcar refused to stop for her. And not just any witness but a well-respected society matron, Lisette Woodworth, the wife of her employer. It was the first time a white had testified on behalf of a black person, male or female. Mrs. Woodworth's testimony lent legitimacy to Mary Ellen's case. Her case brought a great deal of publicity and affirmed the right of African Americans to ride the streetcars.

For the rest of her life, Mary Ellen decided to focus on her business activities. Despite her success as a businesswoman, housekeeping was still one of the few occupations open to a black woman, and it had the added benefit of putting her in a position near those with political and financial clout. She purchased another boardinghouse, at 920 Washington Street, this one catering to white businessmen downtown. It was known for its "fine food and wines, and its lavishly furnished upstairs rooms which were set up as a combined private dining and bedroom." Her boardinghouses—she eventually came to own three—were among the most expensive and exclusive in the city, catering to some of the city's most successful white businessmen and politicians.

When one of her former borders, Newton Booth, was elected governor, Mary Ellen threw an elaborate postelection gala at her house, telling guests, "This is Governor Booth who has been elected from my house." At some point, she began to cultivate a devoted following of young marriageable white women whom she matched up with white males she met through her boardinghouses. This led to the later accusations and rumors that her boardinghouses were in reality houses of ill repute.

At some point Mary Ellen met Thomas Bell, one of the eventual cofounders of the Bank of California. No one knows exactly how they met or the exact nature of their business partnership. One of the rumors surrounding Mary Ellen was that she provided some of the seed money for Bell's success. Bell was a bachelor when they met, and Pleasant introduced him to Teresa Percy, whom he married. In 1877, she moved to a thirty-room mansion on the corner of Octavia and Bush. The mansion, built and decorated according to her specifications, was worth one hundred thousand dollars and was one of the largest black-owned residences in the nation. Thomas Bell, his wife, Teresa, and their two children soon moved in as well. Many people were under the impression that Mary Ellen was the housekeeper, which she did nothing to correct. But she was clearly more than just a housekeeper, although she did hire and fire servants and order the groceries. She acted as a mediator between Teresa and Thomas Bell. In fact she controlled all aspects of Teresa Bell's life, including choosing her clothes and friends. She later told a judge, "Mr. Bell knew what I was there for, and I knew what I was there for."

By the 1880s, Mary Ellen owned property in San Francisco and Oakland, as well as mining stock, and was worth an estimated three hundred thousand dollars. Still she cultivated the air of a servant, always dressed in a modest dark dress and apron—albeit one who drove around in a carriage with a liveried footman. Mary Ellen's husband and child didn't live to share in her bounty; her daughter died in 1878 and her husband sometime before that.

In 1884 the city of San Francisco was titillated by the scandal of Sharon vs. Sharon. Twenty-four-year-old Sarah Hill filed for divorce, claiming that she was the wife of former Nevada senator William Sharon, having married him secretly in 1880. At stake was thirty million dollars. During the trial it was revealed that it was Mary Ellen who had supplied the cash to pay for Sarah's suit. Under oath, she reluctantly admitted to providing five thousand to Sarah's cause, but in reality she may have actually spent thousands more in legal fees. The trial lasted a year and became one of the most publicized cases in the nation. It had all the ingredients of a Victorian melodrama—voodoo, sex, a secret marriage, and, in the thick of it, a mysterious elderly African American woman. Soon Mary Ellen became the one on trial, not the plaintiff or the defendant.

Sharon's lawyers claimed that Pleasant was a ruthless madam who used voodoo and blackmail to control Sarah Hill, while Hill's lawyers portrayed Pleasant as the stereotypical "Mammy" figure who had tried to protect the innocent and naive Sarah from being exploited by wealthy white men. The case exposed Mary Ellen as not just another black servant but someone who had become the holder of secrets, which she'd gleaned from years of watching and listening to her powerful employers to make her a force to be reckoned with and feared. Suddenly Mary Ellen Pleasant became "the most discussed woman in San Francisco." The Sharon trial earned Mary Ellen a reputation as a sinister black woman preying on vulnerable whites.

On October 15, 1892, at half past ten in the evening, the servants at the Bell mansion heard the cries of Thomas Bell and a dull thud as his body fell over the stair railing twenty feet to the basement. Only Mary Ellen and Fred Bell, the Bells' eldest son, were at home. Teresa Bell was at a ranch house in Sonoma that Mary Ellen later claimed to own. Fred Bell ran for the nearest doctor while Mary Ellen went for pillows and blankets, but Bell was dead. At the inquest, Mary Ellen stated that Thomas Bell had been ill, and then when he woke up in the night, he must have gotten disoriented. The press dubbed the Bell mansion "Mystery House."

Things began to unravel after Bell's death. While his will was tied up in probate, Teresa and Mary Ellen continued living together at the mansion. But Mary Ellen had dangerously overextended herself buying property and made some bad investments and had to declare insolvency. She was in great need of liquid capital as creditors began to swarm like vultures. In her eighties, Mary Ellen was no longer at the top of her game and suffering from ill health. Teresa Bell, who it turned out was one taco short of a combination platter, threw Pleasant out. Mary Ellen moved into a small six-room apartment and launched a counterattack, insisting that every last dime including the jewelry Teresa wore belonged not to Teresa Bell but to her.

The question of just who owned what occupied the courts for years. Deeds changed hands from Mary Ellen to Teresa and back again. Without Thomas Bell to stand behind, Mary Ellen was vulnerable. There were plenty of people willing to believe that a black woman could only be successful by blackmail, murder, and witch-craft. Her life became a cautionary tale of "uppity" black women not knowing their place.

Mary Ellen Pleasant breathed her last on January 11, 1904, taking her secrets with her to the grave. Legend has it that she was once offered a small fortune to spill the beans about San Francisco society. She regarded the man with disdain and told him, "I have never needed money bad enough to betray anyone."

Mary Ellen hit a lot of societal hot buttons in post–Civil War California. Not only was she a black woman who had amassed a great deal of money and property but many influential white men had confided their secrets to her, giving her a great deal of power. She challenged society's norms not just for women in general but for black women specifically. In her own lifetime she became legendary as a black woman who devised her own way to power. People who knew her described her as a formidable and terrifying presence. Others said that "if she had been white and a man, she would have been president."

# Sarah Winnemucca
## 1844–1891

*I, only an Indian Woman, went and saved my father and his people.*

—Sarah Winnemucca

Pocahontas, Sacajawea, Sarah Winnemucca. "Wait, Sarah Win-newho?" would be most people's reaction when they heard that last name. Thanks to the Disney cartoon, every schoolkid knows the story of Pocahontas saving the life of John Smith. More people have mispronounced Sacajawea's name than know that she was the guide during the Lewis and Clark expedition mapping the Oregon Trail. But Sarah's name should be on everyone's lips. She spent her life trying to establish a peaceful coexistence between her people and the white settlers. She fought corrupt government agents, who tried to blacken her reputation, calling her a whore and a drunk. And when the government ignored her, she took the story of her people to the American public through her lectures and books. Only after her death would she be recognized for her work as a peacemaker between the two races.

Sarah Winnemucca was born sometime in 1844 near Humboldt Lake, in what is now Nevada, to the chief of the Paiute Indian tribe. She was named Thocmetony, which means "shell flower" in the Paiute language. In just a few short years, she would witness the destruction of a way of life her people had known for centuries. Already the "white owls," as they were called by the Northern Paiutes* because of their beards and faces, were striking fear in the hearts of the Native tribes. "They came like a lion," she later wrote, "yes, like a roaring lion and have continued to do so ever since."

Her grandfather believed that his people needed to learn and understand the ways of the white man in order to survive. He had guided John C. Frémont and his men during his mapmaking expedition across the Great Basin into California and fought in the Mexican-American War. Sarah's father, Chief Winnemucca, was not as convinced; he distrusted most whites, preferring to keep his distance.

---

* The Northern Paiutes' territory encompassed southwest Oregon, western Nevada, and northeast California. They shared a name but little else with the Southern Paiutes, who had different customs and language.

To prepare her for the future, her grandfather sent her and her sister Elma to live with a stagecoach agent's family in Utah Territory; it was they who gave her the name Sarah. There she learned to speak and write English and Spanish. It was her first prolonged exposure to the white world, and Sarah found much to admire. But when hostilities broke out between the white settlers and the Paiutes, Sarah and her sister were sent home. After her grandfather's death, she and Elma spent three weeks at a convent school in California but were expelled when the parents of the other students objected to their presence. It was the end of Sarah's formal education, but she became determined to continue to learn on her own.

When gold and silver were discovered near Pyramid Lake, the trickle of white settlers became a flood. By 1866, the Paiutes began to submit to the policy of the Bureau of Indian Affairs to resettle on a reservation. Determined to help her people, Sarah moved to the reservation, only to find that there they were exploited by corrupt or incompetent Indian agents who left them starving and destitute. Because Washington was so far away, government orders were ignored or disobeyed. The few good agents who were concerned about the Indians and treated them well were quickly removed and sent elsewhere. Sarah became an outspoken critic concerning the injustices she saw meted out to her people. She was used to speaking up. In Paiute culture, women were permitted to voice their opinions and participate in the decision making.

Since Sarah could speak English as well as several Indian languages, she was hired as a scout and an interpreter at Camp McDermit for the Bureau of Indian Affairs. Proud of her new job, she began dressing in tailored suits like a white woman. In July of 1868, five hundred of the Paiutes relocated to Camp McDermit rather than starve. Sarah wrote a letter to Major Henry Douglass, who was assigned as Indian superintendent to Nevada. He was so impressed that he passed it along to the Commissioner of Indian Affairs in Washington, DC. In her letter she wrote, "If this is the kind of civilization awaiting us on the reserves, God grant that we may never be compelled to go on one, as it is preferable to live in the mountains and drag out an existence in our native manner."

Any hope that Sarah had for her people was smashed when President Grant declared them wards of the government and consigned them to reservation land. In 1872, Sarah was invited to work as an interpreter at the Malheur reservation in southwestern Oregon. The agent there, Samuel Parrish, was the only agent Sarah ever trusted. She became his interpreter, and she taught alongside his sister-in-law at the school on the reservation. Parrish treated the Indians fairly for the work they did, encouraging them to work the land. The idyll couldn't last. Parrish was replaced by William V. Rinehart, who was far from being filled with Christian charity. Rinehart was a bigot who thought that the only good Indian was a dead one. He soon became a thorn in Sarah's side and one of the worst things to happen to the Paiutes. The Indians were now told that everything they produced belonged to the government but they would be paid a small fee. However, after expenses were deducted, the Indians were left with nothing. Rinehart clashed with Sarah, claiming that she stirred up trouble among the Paiutes. After she complained about him to his superiors, he had her banished from the reservation. Sarah moved to Canyon City, Oregon, where she did housework for a woman who lived on the John Day River.

The Bannocks, an Idaho tribe on a reservation near Fort Hall, were sick and tired of their mistreatment at the hands of oppressive Indian agents and ready to fight. Sarah's father refused to join the uprising. In retaliation, the Bannocks held him and several other members of the Paiutes hostage. When Sarah found out, she offered her services as a scout and interpreter to General Howard, who was the commander of the army during the Bannock war. But Sarah decided to go one step further and rescue her father and the other prisoners. It was an insane undertaking involving miles of treacherous rocky terrain. Nearing the Bannock camp, Sarah and her brother Lee dismounted and crawled on their hands and knees up the mountain. While the Bannocks were slaughtering cattle for the evening meal, they stealthily made their way through enemy lines and rescued seventy-five people.

Sarah continued to serve as a scout and interpreter, slipping out to the Bannock camps, stealing plans, and aiding in the capture of prisoners. "That was the hardest work I ever did for the government in all my life," she wrote. For her pains Sarah earned the sum of five hundred dollars. Despite her heroism there were some among the Indian tribes who saw Sarah as a traitor for working with the army, but she felt that the army at least had always treated the Indians decently and could be trusted, as opposed to the civilian Indian agents.

By the end of the summer of 1878 the war was over. The Paiutes assumed that because they hadn't joined the Bannock war they would be able to stay at the Malheur reservation, but the army instead considered all Indians prisoners of war, regardless of their tribe. Instead they were forced to march three hundred miles north to the Yakima reservation in what is now Washington State. The Paiutes were poorly housed and fed, many of them dying before spring came. The Paiutes were assured that wagonloads of warm clothing were on their way. However, the promised goods turned out to be twenty-eight shawls and a handful of fabrics. The Yakimas resented the newcomers and stole their horses. The agent in charge did nothing to foster good relations between the tribes.

Deciding that she had to do more to raise awareness about the injustices being done to her people, Sarah turned to the lecture stage. This was not her first time on the stage. In 1864, when she was twenty, Sarah had acted in a series of *tableaux vivants* that conformed to Indian stereotypes, including "The War Dance," "The Indian Camp," and "Scalping the Prisoner," in Nevada and San Francisco with her grandfather and her sister Elma. The shows were to raise money for the Paiutes, who had no other source of income for their basic needs. After each scene, Old Winnemucca had given a speech, which Sarah had interpreted for the audience. Although their appeals were ignored by the audiences, the experience gave Sarah confidence to speak in front of whites.

She launched her new career in San Francisco. Taking the stage before a standing-room-only crowd, she wore a buckskin dress embellished with fringe, scarlet leggings, and an eagle feather crowning her long, dark hair. Within minutes Sarah had the audience spellbound as she began to speak, surprising them with her fluency in English. Speaking without notes, she told stories of her people, about her grandfather and the ill-treatment of the Paiutes. She wasn't afraid to name names of the unscrupulous agents. So it wasn't all doom and gloom, she told humorous anecdotes and performed impressions of people she knew. At the end, instead of hitting them up for money, as was expected, Sarah asked for books and teachers for her people. "Educated Indians would quickly become good citizens of the United States."

Called the "Paiute Princess" by the press, Sarah was now a celebrity of sorts after her exploits during the Bannock war. Local and regional newspapers covered the speeches, and several, including the *San Francisco Chronicle*, the *San Francisco Call*, and the Nevada *Daily Silver State*, ran feature stories about her. It was the first public relations campaign by a Native American woman.

The publicity garnered by her lectures led to an invitation to Washington to voice her complaints. Accompanied by her father, brothers, and an escort from the Bureau of Indian Affairs, Sarah discovered after her arrival that she was confined to a strict schedule. Her only appointments were with government officials, interspersed with lots of sightseeing. Sarah soon realized that the trip was less about helping her people than it was damage control after all the publicity generated by her lectures. The Bureau of Indian Affairs was trying to save face. Still Sarah was optimistic.

As a placating gesture, Secretary of the Interior Carl Schurz gave her a letter that stated that the Paiutes could go back to Malheur, along with an allotment of one hundred tents and much-needed supplies. When he heard that she was hoping to lecture, he admonished her not to, telling her it would be bad form since the government invited her and then paid her way. If she hadn't been sure before that they were trying to keep her quiet, it was clear to her now. Even her brief meeting with President Hayes seemed designed more as a photo op than a real opportunity. What she didn't know was that her old nemesis William Rinehart undermined her efforts by sending a barrage of letters to government officials, calling her a prostitute and a drunk.

Sarah waited for two weeks at the delivery point for tents and supplies, but they never came. Sarah was ridiculed for once again believing in the empty promises of the whites. Though she had an order authorizing the Paiutes' return to Oregon, the move was never funded, and the Yakima agent James Wilbur refused to free the Paiutes from the reservation. Instead he tried to get her to keep quiet by offering her a job as an interpreter. When she refused the job, Wilbur sent a letter to Schurz, claiming that Sarah had misrepresented the Paiutes and been banned from the reservation. It was another blow to both Sarah and her people. Her failures led them to question her loyalty. She left the reservation with a broken heart to work as an interpreter and teacher at Fort Vancouver.

At the end of 1881 in San Francisco, Sarah married a handsome dandy named Lewis Hopkins. This was her second marriage to a white man, and no better than the first. For an intelligent woman, Sarah had the worst taste in men. Like her first husband, Hopkins was another charming soldier who stole from her and left her heartbroken. Even before they left the city, he'd gambled away five hundred dollars of her money. Since Hopkins preferred a life of leisure to actually holding a job, the couple moved to a reservation.

Sarah hoped that another lecture tour of the East would not only help the Paiutes but restore her good name, which had been tarnished after the debacle with Schurz. In Boston, Sarah met Elizabeth Palmer Peabody and her sister Mary Peabody Mann, who became her most ardent supporters. Meeting them was the break Sarah needed. Elizabeth Peabody, considered the first woman publisher in the country, owned a bookstore frequented by the literati of Boston. The two women encouraged Sarah to write a book about the history of the Paiutes. The result was *Life Among the Paiutes: Their Wrongs and Claims*, the first book published by an Indian woman. A subscription was taken up to publish the book for six hundred dollars. An appendix with affidavits attesting to Sarah's character was added to the book to counter attacks by Rinehart.

With Elizabeth Peabody's help, Sarah gave three hundred lectures from New York to Baltimore and Washington. Peabody was impressed by her protégée. Sarah didn't use notes when she spoke, but somehow she never repeated or contradicted herself, trusting that the right words would come. The only fly in the ointment was her husband; apparently their joint bank account was a temptation that couldn't be resisted. He not only gambled away her money but also passed bad checks. When Sarah found out, he skipped town, leaving her holding the bag. Sarah repaid the money from sales of her autobiography and her lecture fees, the money that she had earmarked to help her people. It was yet another stain on her reputation.

In 1884, Sarah spoke before the Senate Subcommittee on Indian Affairs. She proposed that Camp McDermit be established as a reservation for the Paiutes, and that the heads of family be allotted land of their own. More important, she requested that the goods and money be administered not by the Bureau of Indian Affairs but by the army. Although the House of Representatives passed the bill in 1884, the Senate refused to pass it as it currently stood. When the bill later passed, it affirmed Bureau of Indian Affairs control and condemned the Paiutes to Pyramid Lake, in Nevada.

When railroad magnate Leland Stanford gave her brother an undeveloped ranch in Lovelock, Nevada, Sarah opened a school for Indians called the Peabody Institute. She had long believed that education would make the difference, eradicating the distance between the two races. In an article in the *Daily Silver State*, she wrote, "It seems strange that the Government has not found out that education is the key to the Indian problem. Much money and precious lives would have been saved if the American people had fought my people with books instead of Power and lead." Ill with rheumatism, she managed to run the school for three years until the money ran out. Although Mary Mann had left a small bequest to the school, it was not enough. The U.S. government denied Sarah additional funds, preferring to support schools like Carlisle in Pennsylvania that forced Indians to conform completely to white ways. In 1886, her estranged husband, Lewis Hopkins, died of tuberculosis. With the closing of the school, Sarah went to live with her sister Elma in Monida, Montana, where she died in 1891, possibly of tuberculosis, at the age of forty-six.

For most of her life Sarah was caught between two worlds, yet she worked tirelessly to preserve the traditions of her Indian culture. She fought against gigantic odds for the welfare of her people. While some saw her as a heroine, others considered her to be a sellout for advocating peace and for encouraging the Native tribes to try to understand whites. For her pains, she was distrusted at times by her own people and reviled and hated by those white men who were alarmed at the idea of an Indian woman challenging the establishment.

# Calamity Jane
## 1856–1903

*I'm Calamity Jane. Get to hell out of here and let me alone.*

—CALAMITY JANE

By the time Calamity Jane came riding into Deadwood, South Dakota, at the side of Wild Bill Hickok in 1876, she was already well on her way to becoming notorious in the West. Barely out of her teens, she had acquired a reputation as a wild woman who drank and shagged with abandon. By the time of her death at the age of forty-seven she'd added gun-toting hellion who rode with Custer, Indian Scout, Pony Express mail carrier, and lover of Wild Bill Hickok to her list of accomplishments. The only trouble is that none of the above is true. Even over a hundred years after her death, it is still hard to separate fact from fiction. How did a foul-mouthed, illiterate, drunken camp follower and dance hall girl become an icon of the Old West?

Born Martha Canary in 1856 in Princeton, Missouri, she was the oldest of Robert and Charlotte Canary's children.* While her father was remembered as an inept farmer, her mother, Charlotte, was as notorious in Princeton as her daughter was in the boom-towns of the Old West. Her unconventional behavior marked her as different from the other frontier wives. Red-haired Charlotte wore eye-catching clothes in bright colors, swore in public, smoked cigars, and drank. Rumor

had it that she met Robert in a bawdy house. Like mother, like daughter, as a child, Martha's misbehavior and swearing got her into trouble. Although she went to school, none of it seemed to have stuck, since she was barely literate.

In 1862, the family left Princeton under a cloud, moving to Virginia City, Montana, where her father hoped to try his luck mining, but times

---

* Although Martha's birth year has been given as 1852 in some biographies, James D. McLaird writes in his definitive biography *Calamity Jane: The Woman and the Legend* that 1860 census records for Mercer County, Missouri, state that she was born in 1856.

were tough. An expert rider, Martha later claimed to have spent much of the trip "at all times with the men when there was excitement and adventures to be had." But by the time Martha was twelve, both her parents were dead. Martha's siblings were taken in by Mormon families in Salt Lake City, but Martha's unruly behavior forced her out on her own. Orphaned, adrift, without the civilizing influence of a female role model, Martha added two years to her age and headed to Fort Bridger in Wyoming. She got a job tending children for a time but she soon began drinking and hanging out with the soldiers, which got her canned. Before long she was working as a dance hall girl and prostitute.

No one knows for sure how she acquired her nickname Calamity Jane.* In her colorful but inaccurate memoirs she claims that during the Nez Perce outbreak in 1873, she rescued Captain James Egan when he was wounded by ambushing Indians. When he recovered, Egan gave her the name "Calamity Jane, the heroine of the plains."

Although she claimed in her memoirs to have been an Indian scout for Custer in Arizona, Calamity was little more than a camp follower. Crazy for adventure, dressed in an army uniform, she would join the troops as they went scouting. She generally seems to have joined them when they were far enough from civilization that it would have been cruel to send her back. The men liked her, treating her like a mascot. Calamity enjoyed the camaraderie of the men, who accepted her at face value. She cooked for them, nursed them when they were ill, and darned their clothes.

Calamity often ended up in the paper for her exploits, and not

---

* Martha was not the only one to carry the nickname Calamity Jane. Several other women, including Mattie Young, Annie Fillmore, and Mrs. Opie, were also known as Calamity Jane. Ironically all three women were alcoholic and prostitutes and known for their eccentric behavior.

the heroic kind, such as the time she was arrested for stealing the clothes of two local women. She pleaded not guilty and was jailed in Cheyenne. When she was acquitted, Calamity paraded down the street wearing a dress lent to her by the wife of one of the sheriff's staff. Continuing her celebration, she got drunk and then rented a wagon to drive the thirty miles to Fort Russell, only she was so out of it that she misjudged the distance and ended up passing it and arriving at Fort Laramie instead, which was ninety miles away.

Calamity owes her reputation as an icon to two men, Horatio N. Maguire and Edward L. Wheeler. Calamity's local notoriety had captured the attention of Maguire, who was writing a promotional pamphlet on the Black Hills. A largely fictional portrait, he first introduced the idea that Calamity had been a scout in an Indian campaign. His fanciful description of her was picked up by several newspapers in the East where it came to the attention of Edward L. Wheeler.* Wheeler used Calamity as a character in a series of dime novels set in the Black Hills called *Deadwood Dick*. Deadwood Dick was sort of a Robin Hood of the Dakotas, with Calamity as his Maid Marian. Wheeler's Calamity is beautiful, with flashing eyes, an able frontierswoman and strong horsewoman, comfortable wearing both buckskin and a dress. In the series, Calamity saves Dick's life repeatedly while having improbable adventures.

---

* Born in New York, Edward L. Wheeler (1855–1885?) wrote over one hundred dime novels during his short career, including thirty-three in the Deadwood Dick series. He started his career in 1877 with his first novel, *Hurricane Nell*. At the height of his career, he was making $950 a year. His other series included titles with colorful names like Rosebud Bob, Sierra Sam, and Kangaroo Kit. Like Calamity Jane, Wheeler's heroines defied society's conventions by smoking, drinking, dressing, and cussing like men. Unlike Calamity, they became submissive when it came to relationships with men.

The books sold thousands of copies, transforming plain Martha Canary to national heroine Calamity Jane. Because she was utilized as a character alongside such other larger-than-life heroes like Buffalo Bill Cody, Wild Bill Hickok, and Kit Carson, it was assumed that she had to be equally accomplished. A few months after Calamity's appearance in Edward Wheeler's dime novels, she was the central character in T. M. Newson's play *Drama of Life in the Black Hills*. He, too, used the description of Calamity from Maguire's pamphlet. In less than a year, she was a nationally known heroine. Calamity was in the right place at the right time. People back East were entranced with the romance of the West. During a five-year period from 1876 to 1881, from the massacre at Little Big Horn to the OK Corral shoot-out, the entire country couldn't get enough of tales of the frontier.

Calamity's life is a study in the fine art of mythmaking. Minor episodes in her life were blown up into epic adventures, and generic tales were tailored to fit her life until there was no semblance to reality. Take for example her relationship with Wild Bill. Calamity had only met him six weeks before they arrived together in Deadwood. She'd joined his expedition of gold seekers to the Black Hills, making herself useful as a cook and bushwhacker. Most eyewitnesses state that they were no more than casual friends, that Bill had no real use for Calamity although he loaned her twenty dollars to buy a dress. It wasn't until later on that stories sprang up tying the two icons of Deadwood together, going so far as to claim that they were married.

Locals in Deadwood and other towns enjoyed repeating the tall tales of her exploits to gullible tourists. When it was reported that a woman was seen with a gang of outlaws, everyone claimed that it was Calamity. Stories were written that she had killed forty Indians and seventeen white men, that she had been with Custer at

Little Big Horn. Others claimed that Calamity Jane tried to warn Custer of the danger he faced but she was held back by bad weather and pneumonia. While readers back East may have been entranced with the mythical Calamity Jane, journalists in the West were less sanguine. They seemed to delight in reporting her various drunken escapades and brushes with the law.

Calamity Jane became an icon not because of who she really was but because of what she represented. Both the mythical Calamity Jane and the real woman challenged society's standards of behavior for women. By temperament, the real Calamity was easygoing, loyal to her friends, and full of sympathy for those who were sick or in trouble. In 1876, a smallpox epidemic swept through Deadwood. Hundreds of people fell ill, and most of the town was afraid to help because the disease was highly contagious. Dr. Babcock, the only doctor in town, recalled that Calamity risked her life to care for the dying miners.

Calamity just didn't conform to the image of Victorian womanhood. She did what she wanted when she wanted. She smoked in public, wore men's clothes, cussed, and drank in saloons where no respectable woman would dare be seen. "Lots of us knew the better side of Calamity," remembered a man named Charles Haas. "She would go to these bawdy houses and dance halls, and it was 'whoopee' and soon she was drunk and then, well things sort of went haywire with old Calamity!" Local journalists recorded her comings and goings with barely disguised glee. But the realities of Calamity's actual life, the drunkenness, the poverty, set her apart from her fictional counterpart.

Calamity led a nomadic life, following the railroad from one boomtown to the next, searching for excitement in Montana and Wyoming. She stayed just long enough in each town to make her presence known before moving on. Over a period of ten years, she made her way from Billings, Miles City, and Livingston in Montana to Rawlins and Lander in Wyoming. When she was sober, she worked a series of jobs as a cook, dance hall girl, or laundress. She had several "husbands" over the years, and gave birth to two children, a boy who died young and a little girl named Jessie.* Local newspapers were filled with "Calamity sightings" during these years, usually detailing some brawl or drunken escapade that she'd gotten into.

Although Calamity claimed to hate the dime novels and journalists whom she constantly accused of printing lies about her, she wasn't above spinning a few yarns herself, giving herself a bigger role in events that she was on the periphery of, especially when she was in her cups. One of her more interesting claims was that she went after Wild Bill Hickok's murderer Jack McCall† with a meat cleaver when she heard the news of his death. Another story she told was the time that she rescued a stagecoach besieged by Indians, driving it to Deadwood. While the story of the stagecoach was true, Calamity had nothing to do with it. Deciding to cash in on her notoriety, she had photographs taken of her in her buckskin suit and peddled them to tourists. In 1896, she wrote her autobiography to coincide with her brief stint as the star attraction in a traveling dime museum. Her notoriety came in handy when she

---

\* Years later, a woman named Jane Hickok claimed to be the illegitimate daughter of Calamity and Wild Bill. As evidence, she said that she had letters that Calamity had written to her. Despite the fact that Calamity was illiterate, many people believed that the evidence was legitimate, adding yet another note to the legend of Calamity Jane. To add to the mystery, Calamity's real daughter claimed at first that Calamity was her grandmother and then that her real mother was the outlaw Belle Starr, whom she claimed was Calamity's sister.

† McCall shot Wild Bill during a card game.

fell ill and ended up in the poorhouse. Her plight made the news-papers and money came pouring in to help the notorious Calamity Jane. While she was peeved at having her plight publicized, she wasn't too embarrassed to take the money, which she spent in the nearest saloon as soon as she was able.

Calamity's downfall was booze. Her favorite libation was whiskey but she'd settle for beer in a pinch. Calamity would try to stay off the hooch, and for a while she would succeed, but inevi-tably she would fall off the wagon. When she was sober, her de-portment was no different from other women of her class. When she was drunk it was a different story: she fired her guns, cursed at the top of her voice, howled like a coyote, and was willing to fight anyone who tried to stop her. Although her friends were aware that booze was killing her, instead of helping her they just enabled her by drinking with her.

In 1901, a wealthy easterner named Josephine Brake heard about Calamity's most recent arrest and illness. She claimed that she wanted to take Calamity back East to take care of her. How-ever, when they arrived in Buffalo, Calamity realized she'd been hoodwinked. Brake wanted Calamity to help her publicize her writing at the Pan-American Exposition. Calamity, not one to be used, went to work instead for Colonel Frederic T. Cummins's Indian Congress show. She managed to stay off the booze for a while, but it didn't last. Calamity drank her way back West.

As if sensing that her time was coming to an end, in the last two years of her life, Calamity made a pilgrimage of sorts to the places of her youth. But the boomtowns were now respectable and Calamity's antics were not welcome anymore. By spring of 1902, she was suffering from a lingering illness and once again was com-mitted to a Montana poorhouse. Leaving Montana behind, Calamity headed back to Deadwood. She finally passed away on August 1, 1903, from an inflammation of the bowels. She was buried near Wild Bill Hickok in the Mount Moriah Cemetery. No doubt the leading citizens realized what a draw it would be to have two of Deadwood's most famous citizens lying near each other.

On the surface, Calamity Jane's life seems tragic: poverty, drunkenness, lack of family. But Calamity was also an independent woman trying to make her way in the American West, which was rapidly changing from a lawless frontier to more respectable society. Calamity tried to settle down, to be a wife and mother, but she was just too restless to stay in one place for long.

In the years since her death, Calamity Jane has been depicted in films, novels, and history books as everything from a gun-toting, rowdy wildcat to a romantic tomboy warbling about her secret love for Wild Bill to the revisionist depiction of her as a sad-eyed drunken cross-dresser waiting to die, having outlived the notion of the Old West. Despite historians' attempts to debunk the myths surrounding Calamity Jane, the image of a lively, rambunctious hellcat continues.

But the real Martha Canary is the story of a young orphan girl who refused to conform, who was as wild and stubborn as the Black Hills. In her forty-seven years, Martha Canary witnessed firsthand the most dramatic period in the American West. Her story gives voice to the poor, the ones who came out West hoping to make their fortune, a part of western history that is often forgotten.

# Elizabeth "Baby Doe" Tabor
## 1854–1935

*I have only this one legacy of my great love. It is my mission and my life.*
—BABY DOE ABOUT THE MATCHLESS MINE

On March 7, 1935, Sue Bonnie noticed that there was no smoke coming from the chimney of her neighbor Baby Doe Tabor's cabin near the Matchless mine in Leadville, Colorado. Worried about the frail elderly woman who seemed to have no family, Sue Bonnie and a friend dug their way through six feet of snow up to the cabin. When they peered through a window they saw her partially clothed body frozen on the floor of the cabin, although there was firewood left. The one remnant of Baby Doe's legendary beauty was her hair, which contained no gray.

In her obituaries, she was called "the Wallis Simpson of the American Empire." She lived one of the most amazing and dramatic lives ever in American history. "Abject Poverty. Fabulous Riches," screamed the headline in *True Story* magazine after her death. She was a Rocky Mountain Cinderella who went from rags to riches and back again. Her so-called sins were many: gold digging, husband stealing, and lousy mothering. Like many women of the Old West, myth and reality have become so intertwined that the legendary Baby Doe has superseded the real woman.

Baby Doe had enjoyed tremendous wealth as the pampered second wife of "Silver King" Horace Tabor. After his bankruptcy and subsequent death, she lived on for over thirty years in poverty but rumors abounded that she maintained a massive stash of silver. She became a public spectacle in her last years, dressed in baggy clothing, wearing a large crucifix, feet wrapped in rags. When they heard the news of her death, scavengers came running to see the madwoman's home, destroying it to search for silver. All they found were scraps of paper, the ravings of a madwoman. The silver was long gone.

She was born Elizabeth Blonduel McCourt in 1854 in Oshkosh, Wisconsin. By the time she was sixteen, there were eight McCourt children, and they were moderately comfortable. Her parents owned a clothing store, McCourt and Cameron, that was patronized by those who had made money in the booming lumber industry. By her midteens, Elizabeth was known as "the Belle of Oshkosh." As pretty as a Dresden doll, she couldn't help but attract attention with her striking blue eyes, reddish blond hair, and a come-hither manner. Her frantic social life consisted of dances, the theater, buggy rides, and yachting parties on Lake Winnebago.

Elizabeth wasn't willing to settle for just any old husband. She was looking not just for a great match, but also for love. She thought she had found it in Harvey Doe, the son of a former mayor. Harvey seemed perfect; he had a fine singing voice and played the piano well, not to mention his family was wealthy. Here was the man who would be her knight in shining armor. Harvey's mother was not happy at her son's choice. As far as she was concerned, Elizabeth was nothing but an Irish Catholic tramp that wasn't good enough for her son. Still, the two sweethearts were married.

The newlyweds headed for Colorado, where Harvey's father owned the Fourth of July, a silver mine in Center City. The West still represented opportunity for anyone willing to work hard. For Elizabeth, it meant freedom from gossiping women. The town was noticeably lacking in women, which meant that she was the center of attention. Although she was married, men were drawn to her flashy figure and friendly manner. It was here that she acquired the nickname Baby Doe, whether for her striking doelike eyes or as a sign of affection, no one knows for sure.

Unfortunately for the newly christened Baby Doe, her husband was allergic to hard work. Although his father had promised him the profits from the mine, Harvey had to dig for it first. That wasn't their only problem. Gold had been king but it was being challenged by silver as currency, and most mines were now owned by large corporations that could afford to hire experienced miners to work a claim. Baby Doe proved herself a willing wife when she donned men's clothing to help supervise the workers. The *Town Talk* newspaper wrote, "The young lady manages one half of the property while her liege lord manages the other. This is the first instance where a lady, and such she is, has managed a mining property."

Their bad luck held when they ran out of money to pay their workers. Harvey became a day laborer in the nearby town of Black Hawk. Soon they had to move from their modest cottage to a rented room above a store. This was not what Baby Doe had signed up for. The few women in Black Hawk didn't throw out the welcome wagon for her, so she and Harvey made friends with Jake Sands, the proprietor of a clothing store. Soon there was speculation that she and Jake were more than just friends. Baby Doe wrote in her diary, "He kissed me three times and oh! How he loved me and does now!" Whether it was just a romantic friendship or a real physical love affair, both parties took the answer to their grave.

Depressed over his failures, Harvey left Elizabeth and went back to Wisconsin, leaving her alone and pregnant. The baby boy was stillborn in July 1879. Baby Doe began to spend more and more time with Jake Sands, who lent a sympathetic ear and lavish gifts. She decided to end her marriage, a relatively easy matter out West, which had the highest divorce rates in the country. When she had caught Harvey entering a brothel it gave her grounds for divorce. Harvey pleaded innocence, claiming he was meeting a business acquaintance. They divorced in 1880, the grounds modified to nonsupport. Baby Doe was given a small settlement by Harvey's parents.

To make a fresh start, she moved to Leadville, Colorado, the second-largest city in the state. While Sands would have been happy to marry Baby Doe, marriage to a clothing merchant like her father was not exactly appealing. Baby Doe was still looking for her prince, a strong, self-confident man. She was sure she would find him in Leadville. She didn't have far to look. The name Horace Tabor was everywhere in Leadville, including the Tabor Grand Opera House, which had recently welcomed Oscar Wilde. All of Leadville knew the story of the dumb luck that had led to Horace's success. Running a supply store, Horace gave two miners sixty-five dollars' worth of groceries in exchange for a one-third share in the Little Pittsburg mine. The miners found a rich vein of silver, and soon Horace had five hundred thousand dollars. By the time he met Baby Doe, he had parlayed that into millions by buying into other stakes that came through. Tabor had been mayor of Leadville and lieutenant governor of Colorado, parlaying his wealth into political power. The whiff of success must have been a powerful aphrodisiac to Baby Doe. Later, she confessed that she had been half in love with Horace, or at least his legend, before she met him.

Horace met Baby Doe one evening at the Saddle Rock Café, where she was dining alone on oysters. He took one look at her blue eyes and luscious figure, so different from his sour-faced wife, and invited her to join him. Horace was a frisky fifty years old, and Baby Doe at twenty-six was at the height of her beauty when they met. They talked all night, Baby Doe confiding in him about her troubles, finding his a sympathetic ear. Horace told her about his marriage, how his wife didn't understand him. His wife, Augusta, reminded him of the past when he was poor, but Baby Doe was his future. By morning, Horace had paid all her debts and they were a couple. Over the next two years, their affair would be covered in detail by all the major newspapers, shattering their reputations.

Horace moved Baby Doe into a lavish suite at the Clarendon Hotel. Local gossips called her "the hussy in a veil," for her penchant for wearing one whenever she and Horace ventured out into public. Baby Doe knew their affair was wrong but she didn't care. At last she'd found a real man, although grizzled around the edges. She knew it was just a matter of time before she was Mrs. Horace Tabor. Baby Doe was his confidante, listening to his troubles as he rested his head on her bosom. She encouraged his grandiose ambitions to turn Denver into "the Paris of the West." Horace told her, "You're so gay and laughing and yet you're so brave. Augusta is damned brave too but she's powerful disagreeable about it." But after two years, Baby Doe wasn't feeling so agreeable. She wanted to be made an honest woman. Finally she put her dainty foot down, informing Horace that as a good Irish Catholic girl she was risking her immortal soul by sleeping with a married man.

Augusta wasn't prepared to let go of her husband without a fight. When he asked for a divorce, she refused. Instead she sued him for fifty thousand dollars for lack of support. Horace was sneaky, though. With Baby Doe's encouragement, he decided to file for divorce in Durango, where he owned a mine. He managed to obtain the divorce from an unscrupulous judge who owed him a favor. The happy couple celebrated by getting secretly hitched in St. Louis. Baby Doe wasn't happy about keeping it a secret but at least she had a marriage certificate. Finally, Augusta finally agreed to an official divorce but as she told the judge, "Not willingly, oh God, not willingly." She made out okay, receiving $250,000, the mansion in Denver, an apartment block, and mining stock.

Horace's actions cost him a chance to replace the retiring senator who had been appointed to President Chester A. Arthur's cabinet.* Instead, as a consolation prize, he was allowed to serve out the final thirty days until a new senator was appointed. Horace accepted. He and Baby Doe headed to Washington, where he gave her a wedding that was talked about for decades. Sparing no expense to make his darling happy, the wedding took place at the Willard Hotel in March 1883. Baby Doe wore a seven-thousand-dollar white satin brocaded gown trimmed with marabou, a seventy-five-thousand-dollar diamond necklace around her neck. The decorations included a massive wedding bell made of white roses, topped with a floral cupid's bow made of violets, and a canopy of flowers covered the ceiling. Although the wedding

---

* At the time, senators were appointed by state legislatures, not elected.

guests included the president, senators, congressmen, and cabinet members, their wives shunned the ceremony out of sympathy for Tabor's ex-wife.

Before the ink was dry on the marriage certificate, the Catholic priest who married them was furious to find out that he'd been duped into marrying a divorced couple. And the revelation of their earlier secret wedding hit the headlines. Baby Doe would never win the acceptance she craved from Denver society matrons, who refused to accept the former mistress of a married man as one of them. She wasn't even repentant; she just turned her dainty nose in the air. To save face, she once told a newspaper reporter that although she had been "flooded with invitations from the very best people to attend all sorts of affairs, I have decided not to accept them so as not to create jealousy among the society leaders of Denver."

One respectable and esteemed lady did pay a social call on Baby Doe: her husband's ex-wife, Augusta. Although she claimed that she hoped for Horace's sake that if she called, Denver society would follow, her later comments to the newspapers showed that her visit was anything but altruistic. "She is blonde and paints her face," she told a Denver reporter months later. No doubt she just wanted to get an up close look at the woman who had taken her place.

Horace built Baby Doe a pretentious fifty-four-thousand-dollar Italianate mansion that occupied a whole block as a consolation prize. Set on three acres, it had the finest furnishings and art, including five paintings of Baby Doe, a staff of five, and a hundred peacocks, but few people ever set foot inside their showplace. While Denverites acknowledged Baby Doe when she appeared in public—in a series of carriages that matched her outfits—they still shunned her socially. Instead, Baby Doe spent her days cutting inspirational articles out of newspapers and magazines. Despite this, Baby Doe kept her sense of humor. When neighbors criticized the naked statues in the Tabors' yard, she ordered her dressmaker to drape them in chiffon and satin costumes. And she defiantly breast-fed her children while driving through the streets of Denver.

Their two daughters, Lillie and Silver, kept her busy. She spoiled them, lavishing them with expensive toys and clothes. For her christening, Lillie wore a fifteen-thousand-dollar lace and velvet gown and diamond-studded diaper pins. A sketch of the baby by Thomas Nast graced the cover of *Harper's Bazaar*. She was also featured in articles with titles like "The Little Silver Dollar Princess" in magazines across the country and in Europe. Baby Doe was so devoted to her children that she refused to leave them to travel with Horace.

Horace had opened the Tabor Grand Opera House in Denver in 1881, which cost eight hundred thousand dollars and rivaled the opera houses of Europe. It was the opera house performers who treated Baby with the respect and deference she craved. In gratitude, she threw them lavish dinners at the mansion. Excluded from the social clubs and associations in Denver, Baby Doe gave generously to Catholic charities and colleges. On Christmas Eve she distributed toys, food, and clothes in the Denver slums. She even set aside two offices, rent free, in the block that Tabor owned for the use of Colorado's women's suffrage leaders. Although excluded from Denver society, Horace and Baby Doe were still welcomed in the mining towns and in New York, where money had begun to matter more than pedigree.

But the high life didn't last long. After about ten years Horace began hemorrhaging money when the government stopped using silver as the monetary standard. He'd also plowed a ton of cash into speculative ventures that hadn't panned out. Horace had continued to rely on luck instead of applying himself to following the market. Baby fended off creditors as best she could while Horace was out of town in Mexico working on his mines there. But by 1896, the opera house and the mansion had been seized by creditors.

Many thought that Baby Doe would dump Horace for greener pastures now that he was broke. Even his ex-wife, Augusta, had prophesied that she would "hang onto him as long as he's got a nickel." But Baby Doe was no fair-weather wife, although plenty of men were lining up, eager to take Horace's place. No, she stubbornly believed that Horace would make a comeback. Even when Horace, like her first husband, Harvey, had to take a job as a day laborer in a mine, Baby Doe followed him into cheap lodgings, doing all the domestic chores herself.

But the best Horace could do was a job as postmaster of Denver. It paid $3,500 a year, and he was able to rent them a comfortable suite at a hotel. It looked like things might be turning around but a little over a year later, Horace died of appendicitis, leaving Baby Doe and their two daughters destitute. Legend has it that his final words were, "Hold on to the Matchless Mine . . . it will make millions when silver comes back."

Although still beautiful, Baby Doe was now forty-five years old. Instead of moving back to Wisconsin to her family, she moved her daughters into a tenement, begging money from Horace's old business acquaintances to reopen the Matchless mine. Finally Baby Doe moved back to Leadville, which had become a ghost town, to work the Matchless mine herself. In 1902, her daughter Lillie moved to Chicago to live with relatives. Although she and her mother continued to write, they rarely saw each other over the years. As she became increasingly religious, Baby Doe considered it scandalous when Lillie married her first cousin, particularly when she discovered it was a shotgun wedding.

Silver, on the other hand, had a wild streak like her mother but not her strength. She worked for a time as a journalist in Denver and wrote an unsuccessful novel called *Star of Blood*. Telling her mother she was going to join a convent, she, too, moved to Chicago, where she worked as a stripper, ending up hooked on drugs and alcohol. She died in a flophouse in 1925 under suspicious circumstances. When reporters came to Baby Doe for a comment, she insisted that it wasn't her daughter, that she was in a convent.

Increasingly religious, she seemed to be doing penance for her past sins. Baby Doe exchanged her low-cut dresses for miner's boots, an old black dress, and a huge black crucifix. She wandered the hills carrying an old sack. When hungry, she lived on stale loaves of bread that she bought twelve at a time, and scraps of beef. When her shoes were worn, she wrapped her feet in gunnysacks tied with twine. When she was ill, she dosed herself with vinegar and turpentine. She refused to accept charity unless she believed it was sincerely meant. She would return baskets of food left at her front door.

After her death, seventeen trunks were discovered in a Denver warehouse and also in the basement of St. Vincent Hospital in Leadville. In them were scrapbooks, a china tea set, bolts of expensive cloth, and the gold watch fob that Horace had been given by the citizens of Denver when the opera house opened. The items were auctioned off; most reside in the Colorado History Museum. Baby Doe and Horace are now buried together in Mount Olivet Cemetery in Denver.

Ironically, Baby Doe's death brought her the acceptance that she had yearned for all her life. No longer was she the home-wrecking gold digger, but the noble widow who endured poverty and heartache, devoted to her husband's last wishes. The *Denver Post* wrote, "Society, which had been quick to judge her as a frivolous coquette when she divorced her first husband and married Tabor, had learned in thirty-six years to wonder at and admire the quality of courage that held her to the old mine and its stark poverty."

# Margaret Tobin Brown
## 1867–1932

*I don't care what the newspapers say about me just so long as they say something.*

—Margaret Tobin Brown

On her third night at sea Margaret Tobin Brown was settling down in her brass bed with a good book in her luxurious stateroom at the forward end of Deck B of the *Titanic*, when the massive ship experienced a jolt. Startled, Margaret decided to investigate. The engines of the luxury liner on its maiden voyage were eerily silent. "I saw a man whose face was blanched, his eyes protruding, wearing the look of a haunted creature," she later wrote. "He was gasping for breath, and in an undertone he gasped, 'Get your life-saver!'" Rushing back to her room, she grabbed whatever warm clothing she could find: a black velvet two-piece suit, seven pairs of stockings, and a sable stole. Before she left her room, she grabbed five hundred dollars from the wall safe and strapped on her life jacket.

Up on deck, Margaret calmly helped other women and children into the lifeboats, reassuring them that everything was going to be okay. She saw no reason to panic; she had dealt with the rough-and-tumble, male-dominated world of Leadville, Colorado, and not just survived but thrived. This was nothing in comparison. Suddenly she was picked up and unceremoniously dropped into a lifeboat along with two dozen other passengers. Quickly grabbing the oars at quartermaster Robert Hichens's command, she helped to maneuver the lifeboat around just in time to see the ship break into two and sink into the ocean, disappearing under the ice-laden surface. It was an image that was seared on Margaret's memory forever. She wanted to go back and look for survivors but Hichens ordered them to row. He thought they were doomed and said so repeatedly. Margaret admonished him, "Keep it to yourself if you feel that way. We have a smooth sea and a fighting chance!" Margaret encouraged the other passengers to help row. When she saw that one of the passengers in lifeboat sixteen, which was tethered to theirs, was only wearing pajamas, she wrapped her fur stole around his legs. She was later credited with keeping the passengers from freezing to death.

Margaret was later immortalized in the Broadway and movie musical *The Unsinkable Molly Brown*. That Molly is a coarse, crude woman with a heart of gold. Unfortunately this portrait of Molly is a combination of myth and caricature. For one thing she was never called Molly. Her name was Margaret, or Mrs. J. J. Brown, if you please. The true story of Margaret Tobin Brown is more interesting and complex than the simpleton portrayed in the musical. Hers is the quintessential rags-to-riches tale. Her parents were hardworking Irish immigrants. Margaret was born in Hannibal, Missouri, in 1867, two years after the Civil War ended.

Margaret and her siblings attended a local neighborhood school until they were old enough to go to work, making her far from the illiterate character in her fictional representations. When she was seventeen, she moved to Leadville, Colorado, to keep house for her brother Daniel. Bored, she took a job working in a local department store. Margaret was full-figured, red-haired, and vivacious. Since men outnumbered women, she undoubtedly got plenty of attention.

When she was eighteen, she met James Joseph Brown, a foreman in a silver mine, at a church picnic. He was thirteen years her senior, intelligent, gregarious, and ambitious. Despite the fact that Margaret had planned on marrying rich, she married "J.J." for love. "I thought about how I wanted comfort for my father and how I had determined to stay single until a man presented himself who could give the tired old man the things I longed for him. . . . Finally, I decided that I'd be better off with a poor man whom I loved than with a wealthy one whose money had attracted me." They were married in Leadville's Annunciation Church soon after she turned nineteen, in September 1886. The Browns soon added two children, Lawrence and Helen, to their family.

It took eight years of hard work before the Browns became rich. For years, J.J. had risen through the ranks of the Leadville silver mines. Just as silver prices collapsed, J.J. found gold in the

Little Jonny mine, which was owned by the Ibex Mining Company. When his engineering efforts proved successful in the mining of the gold, the company gave him almost thirteen thousand shares of stock and a seat on the board. The most famous and enduring myth about Margaret is that after they became rich, J.J. accidentally burned three hundred thousand dollars she had hidden in a potbellied stove. (When a relative asked why she didn't correct the story, she replied, "It's a damn good story.")

The Browns headed to Denver, where they purchased a thirty-thousand-dollar mansion in the upscale Capitol Hill district and a country home they named Avoca. Margaret soon became part of the social life of the city, cutting a dashing figure, always dressed in the latest fashions, with huge hats and a walking stick decorated with flowers. "Mrs. Brown's vivacity and merry disposition is a refreshing trait in a society woman of her position," wrote the *Denver Times*, "for in the smart set any disposition to be natural and animated is quite frowned upon."

Part of the Molly Brown legend is that social leaders of Denver shunned her for being too much, too Irish, too Catholic, and too loud. Polly Pry, a local gossip columnist, went out of her way to bash Margaret for her lack of good breeding and for trying too hard to be accepted. But while Margaret and J.J. were not members of the "Sacred Thirty-six," Denver's answer to Mrs. Astor's Four Hundred, they were very much a part of Denver society. As her biographer Kristen Iversen points out, "From 1894 to the early 1920s, the Browns took up more space in Denver's society pages than nearly any other Denver family and were regularly listed on the Social Register. Margaret and J.J. were not ostracized by Denver society—they *were* Denver society."

But it wasn't all party, party, party for Margaret; she had a social conscience as well. In Denver, she continued to be an out-spoken advocate for the causes she believed in, often putting her money where her mouth was. She became a charter member of the Denver Women's Club and a supporter of Judge Ben Lindsey, who helped to establish the juvenile court system in the United States. "The juveniles have no better friend than Mrs. Brown," wrote a local paper. Like Robin Hood, she loved squeezing the rich to give to the poor. She also wasn't afraid to bite the hand that fed her. In 1914, she took on the titans of Colorado's mining industry, after militiamen fired on innocent women and children during the Ludlow coal strike. Organizing relief efforts, she demanded that working conditions improve.

She lobbied to have women in the military; one of her more eccentric propositions was that the United States send female troops to Mexico if there was a war. Her idea was scorned by men and women. Fascinated with Colorado's multicultural heritage, she created a version of the 1893 Chicago World's Fair in Denver and invited the local Native tribes as well as the African Americans living in Denver to participate.

Margaret continued to work on improving herself after her marriage. She attended the Carnegie Institute, now Carnegie Mellon, in Pittsburgh for a year. She learned French, German, and Russian, and to yodel, a skill she later used to entertain guests at parties. "Perhaps no man in society has ever spent more time or money becoming 'civilized' than has Mrs. Brown," wrote the *Denver Post*. Margaret traveled widely, particularly in France, which she loved. As well as New York and Denver, Margaret also had a forty-three-room "cottage" in Newport, Rhode Island, where she became friends with Alva Vanderbilt Belmont and the Astors.

It was love of travel and her use of the media to promote her causes that caused her marriage to end in separation. J.J. wasn't happy to see his hard-earned money go to causes that he didn't particularly care for. He also thought that a woman's place was in the home. Margaret had her own complaints. She wasn't happy about the rumors of his philandering, either. In 1909, he was sued by a Denver man for seducing his much younger wife. After twenty-three years of marriage, the Browns formally separated. Margaret got to keep the mansion and seven hundred dollars a month in support. Although they never reconciled, they remained fond of each other. After J.J. passed away in 1922, Margaret declared that he was the best man in the world, and she would never remarry.

Margaret's most famous adventure, on the *Titanic*, almost didn't happen. She was in Paris with her daughter, Helen, when she received word that her first grandson was ill. While Helen went off to London, Margaret booked passage on the first ship that she could. After the disaster, when her lifeboat was rescued by the *Carpathia*, she tried to help others by getting the word out via telegraph to their families. Unfortunately the telegraph office was so backed up the messages were never sent. Margaret organized a drive and raised ten thousand dollars to help the immigrant survivors who had lost everything.

While grieving for the friends she'd lost, Margaret spent days caring for the survivors in New York. For her work, she was hailed as a heroine. She also wasn't afraid to tell the media exactly who she blamed for the disaster. She blamed the White Star Line, owners of the *Titanic*, for the lack of lifeboats. She also had a bee in her bonnet about what she considered the antiquated notion that women and children should go first, believing it separated families unnecessarily. It was her old nemesis columnist Polly Pry who first nicknamed her Molly and called her "Unsinkable" after her adventures on the *Titanic*.

Middle age did not slow her down. "I suppose there are some persons who would like me to sit down to devote the rest of my life to bridge," she said. "Times have changed and there's no reason why I should, like, my mother at forty, put on my glasses and do little but read." Margaret ran for Congress in 1909 and for the Senate in 1914, but World War I intervened, and her sister's marriage to a German baron led Margaret to believe her campaign would not be successful. Instead she lectured across the country about her experiences on the *Titanic* and other subjects, such as women's rights. During the war, she helped to create a military hospital in France and provided money for an ambulance corps. For her efforts, she was awarded the French Legion of Honor medal. Margaret Tobin Brown died at the age of sixty-five from an undiagnosed brain tumor. She was buried in Westbury, New York, next to her husband, J.J. Given their love of Colorado, it is ironic that they are buried so far from the state they adored.

The burnishing of Margaret's myth happened soon after her death. Flamboyant and theatrical, Margaret Tobin Brown was the closest thing to royalty Denver had ever seen. Heck, she even hobnobbed with real royalty, being presented at court in England and befriending a member of Russia's Romanov family. Gene Fowler, a newspaper reporter, wrote a chapter on Margaret in his novel *Timber Line*, depicting her as a crude, cussing, pistol-packing eccentric. He repeated the made-up stories of Margaret surviving a flood as an infant and added new ones, particularly the idea that Margaret was an inspiration for Mark Twain.

Margaret Tobin Brown lives on to this day as "the Unsinkable"

Molly Brown. She is as much a part of the myth of the Old West as Wild Bill Hickok and Calamity Jane. Margaret was a woman of action, compassion, and conviction. She preferred to think of herself as a "daughter of adventure. This means I never experience a dull moment and must be prepared for any eventuality."

# SIX

# Amorous Artists

## Camille Claudel
### 1864–1943

*All that has happened to me is more than a novel, it is an epic, an Iliad
or Odyssey, but it would need a Homer to recount it.*

—CAMILLE CLAUDEL

Camille Claudel was only seventeen years old when she met Auguste Rodin in 1882. She and her family had just moved to Paris from the Champagne region where she was born so that she could attend the Académie Colarossi. She was determined to establish herself in Paris and earn her living as a sculptor. Her brother, Paul (who was a little biased), wrote that she was "this superb young woman in the full bloom of her beauty and talent."

Camille was obsessed at an early age with the wonders and possibilities of clay. She roped in whoever she could—siblings and servants—to act as assistants and models. When other children grew up to move on to other things, Camille did not. By chance, her work attracted the notice of sculptor Alfred Boucher, who gave her some constructive criticism of her work and encouraged the family to move to Paris. When Boucher moved to Florence, after winning the Grand Prix de Salon, he asked his friend Rodin to take his place in guiding his protégée. Auguste Rodin was twenty-four years older than Camille and was finally experiencing the success that had eluded him for so many years of grinding poverty.

Camille was soon hired to work at Rodin's atelier at rue d'Université along with her friend Jessie Lipscomb. They were the only women, acting as chaperones for each other. Sculpture was not for the faint of heart; it was messy, strenuous, and expensive. It was not a pretty, feminine art like painting. It was manual labor, requiring women to hike up their long, bustled dresses to climb ladders, carrying heavy materials.

Rodin was immediately attracted to the vibrant young sculptor with the wavy chestnut hair and vivid blue eyes, and he noticed her talent as well. He was struck by her originality and her fierce ambition. Rodin himself said about Camille, "I showed her where to find gold, but the gold she finds is truly hers." Camille quickly became a source of inspiration to Rodin, his model, and his confidante. He soon entrusted Camille with the task of modeling the hands and feet for *The Burghers of Calais*. Camille's friend and first biographer, Mathias Morhardt, wrote that from the beginning Camille was Rodin's equal, not his disciple. "Right away, Rodin recognized Mademoiselle's prodigious gifts. Right away, he realized that she had in her own nature, an admirable and incomparable temperament."

Before long Rodin fell passionately in love and pursued her relentlessly. He followed her to England where she was visiting

Jessie Lipscomb, and he regularly used Jessie as a go-between when Camille was in one of her unreceptive moods. His letters are far from being those of a sophisticated lover; they are more like those of a teenager in the throes of first love.* "You did not come last night and could not bring our dear stubborn one: we love her so much and it is she, I do believe, who leads us," he wrote to Jessie. From the beginning, Camille blew hot and cold, leaving Rodin in torment. She wasn't just playing hard to get. While attracted to Rodin, she was worried about being consumed by him, losing her independence, and being forever in the shadow of a great man, her work neglected. She was already giving up so much of herself to Rodin artistically, with her energy, her modeling for him, and working as his assistant.

When she did embark on a relationship with him, she hated sharing him with Rose Beuret, his mistress of over twenty years. They had a son, Auguste, although Rodin refused to legally acknowledge paternity. Rose grudgingly turned a blind eye to Rodin's affairs, as long as it didn't interfere with her role as primary mistress. Barely literate, Rose couldn't compete with a woman like Camille on an intellectual or artistic level. Still she was devoted to him, and Rodin felt a certain loyalty to her; she had been with him since the beginning, sharing the poverty and the worry, modeling for him, and taking care of the little details, leaving him free to work.

Camille and Rodin had a private contract drawn up between them, in regard to their relationship, which wasn't discovered until 1987 among Rodin's papers. In the contract Rodin promised to

---

* Letters between Camille and Rodin, donated by their mutual friend Mathias Morhardt, are missing from the Rodin Museum. There is speculation that some well-meaning person destroyed them.

arrange for her to be photographed in her best dress by the celebrated photographer Carjat and to take her to Italy for six months
if he won the Grand Prix de Salon. She also wanted him to refuse
to take on other female students. In exchange, she agreed to receive
him four times a month at her studio. But the most important
promise was of "a permanent relationship or liaison, to the effect
that Mademoiselle Camille shall be my wife." None of these promises were kept.

When her family discovered the truth about her relationship
with Rodin, she was forced to move out into an apartment of her
own. Her relationship with her mother and sister had always been
difficult, and now they refused to see her. Her brother, Paul, hated
Rodin for seducing his sister. Since Rodin paid the annual rent on
her apartment, she was now officially a "kept" woman. Rodin
found a new atelier near her apartment on the boulevard d'Italie
that had a romantic and mysterious past. George Sand and her
lover playwright Alfred de Musset were said to have used it for
their trysts. Rodin and Camille worked side by side every day, but
at the end of each day Rodin returned to the home that he shared
with Rose. During the summer, they holidayed together, secretly
staying at the Château d'Islette, in the Loire Valley.

For Rodin, their relationship was one of the great joys of his
life. Her face and body haunted his work. He modeled several of
the damned souls in *The Gates of Hell* on her. For Camille, it was
more complicated. In one of the few letters that remain between
the two of them, she writes a racy little love note: "I go to bed
naked to make myself believe you're here, completely naked, but
when I wake it's no longer the same." But the postscript states:
"Above all, don't deceive me again with other women." Models in
Paris were like groupies for rock stars: ready, willing, and able.
And there were stories of ugly confrontations between Rose and

Camille as if the two women were dogs fighting over a particularly meaty bone.

Camille's fears regarding her work proved well founded. Rodin used his influence with journalists and art critics to promote Camille's career but it wasn't translating into commissions. And when she exhibited her work, critics focused on Rodin's influence on her work, and not enough on her own originality. Those critics who did support her work tempered their praise with comments about how amazing it was that she, a mere woman, could create works of art. The novelist and art critic Octave Mirbeau described her as "a revolt against nature: a woman genius."

Although her early work showed Rodin's influence, her pieces were also daring and shocking, particularly in *The Waltz* (1893), a piece that depicts two barely clothed lovers in a sensual embrace. It was a work of such stunning eroticism that critics considered it improper. "The couple seems to want to lie down and finish the dance by making love," Jules Renard wrote in his diary. While other female artists, such as Mary Cassatt and Berthe Morisot, were stuck painting pictures of domestic scenes, mothers and children, Camille created sexually daring sculptures that flew in the face of propriety. The only way that Camille could get a state commission for the piece was to compromise and alter her work, clothing the lovers.

In 1892, after an abortion, Camille ended both her professional and her personal relationship with Rodin. It was clear that he was never going to leave Rose. She was also tired of being treated as just Rodin's student, as if she had no identity of her own as an artist. Rodin had hoped that they could stay friends but Camille made it clear that she didn't want to see or talk to him. With him out of the picture, her relationship with her family improved, especially with her brother.

Eventually, after two years, a tentative friendship between Camille and Rodin sprang up. Despite the break, Rodin still intervened on her behalf with influential people whenever he could. In 1895, he asked the scholar Schiel Mourney to "do something for this genius of a woman (no exaggeration) whom I love so much." He even paid for her assistant when Camille was short of money. The next ten years were the most prolific in her career, as she worked relentlessly. She was determined to make a name for herself and to find her own voice. "You can see that it isn't Rodin's anymore, not in any way at all," she wrote to her brother about one piece. While her earlier work had been made up of large pieces, now she deliberately worked on a smaller scale. She was on her way to creating a new genre of narrative sculpture with pieces like *The Gossips*, which anticipated pop art. She began to use materials that were difficult to carve, such as onyx.

However, she became increasingly isolated. And since she was no longer working out of Rodin's atelier, she began to run out of money. Her decision to become something of a recluse, as well as increasing ill health, made taking on pupils or working in another artist's atelier out of the question. Suspicious and distrustful of women, Camille didn't socialize with other female artists.

*The Age of Maturity* is a powerful depiction of her break with Rodin. The sculpture consists of three figures: an old hag leading a middle-aged man off as a young woman is seen imploring him. When Rodin saw the sculpture, he was upset that she would make his private life so public. He used his influence to have a commission for a bronze of the statue canceled. The tenuous threads of friendship were now broken and Rodin stopped supporting her work.

From that moment on, Camille became convinced that Rodin was out to get her. She began to feel that Rodin had fed on her genius like a leech, that all her vital energies had been sapped. In 1905, she had her first retrospective of thirteen pieces at a gallery but it was not well received. She soon began a slow descent into full-blown paranoia. Destroying many of her statues, she disappeared for long periods of time. She directed all her disappointment and anger at Rodin, accusing him of stealing her ideas and of leading a conspiracy to kill her, along with the Protestants, Jews, and Freemasons.

Moving to the Île St.-Louis, she lived alone in a ground-floor flat, surrounded by cats. Desperate for affection, Camille began inviting homeless people to parties whenever she had money; for these she would dress in extravagant outfits and serve champagne. Convinced that Rodin was trying to poison her, she began scrounging in garbage cans for food. After a visit to her studio, her brother, Paul, wrote in his journal: "In Paris, Camille mad. Wallpaper ripped in long strips, the only armchair broken and torn, horrible filth. Camille huge, with a dirty face, speaking ceaselessly in a monotonous and metallic voice."

Her father tried to help her and supported her financially. But when he died in 1913, no one in her family bothered to tell her. With his death Camille lost her only protector in the family. One week later, on the initiative of her brother, she was admitted to the psychiatric hospital of Ville-Évrard. Although the form read that she had been "voluntarily" committed, Camille was forcibly removed from her ground-floor apartment through a window. She later wrote of "the disagreeable surprise of seeing two tough wardens enter my studio, fully armed and helmeted, booted, menacing. A sad surprise for an artist, instead of being rewarded, this is what I got!" Rodin was shaken by the news of her committal; he tried to visit her but was refused admittance. The Claudels had requested that Camille be sequestered completely after her cousin had brought her plight to the newspapers causing a scandal. She was allowed no communication, correspondence, or visitors apart from her immediate family. Rodin wrote to their mutual friend Mathias Morhardt offering to help by sending her money.

Over the years, as her condition improved, her doctors regularly proposed that Camille be released, but her mother adamantly refused each time, blaming Camille for bringing scandal into their lives. She wouldn't even countenance a move to an institution near Paris, even when Camille suggested that it would save money. As the years passed, Camille gave up hope of ever being released and became resigned to her incarceration. She died in 1943, after having lived thirty years in the asylum without a single visit from her mother. No one from the family and only a few members from the hospital staff attended the funeral. Her body was never claimed by her family, although her brother, Paul, paid ten thousand francs for Mass to be said for her. After Paul's death, his son Pierre inquired about removing her body to the family plot, but was told that her remains were buried in a communal grave.

Only ninety statues, sketches, and drawings survive to give any evidence of Camille's talent. In 1951, Paul organized an exhibition at the Rodin Museum, which was not successful, and she slid into obscurity. That all changed in 1984, when a major exhibition of her work was again shown at the Rodin Museum in Paris, which continues to display her sculptures. It was the first step toward reclaiming her from the dustbin. But it was the 1988 film *Camille Claudel*, starring Isabelle Adjani as Camille and Gérard Depardieu as Rodin, that brought her story to a wider audience.

It is easy to see why filmmakers were attracted to her story. A beautiful, talented artist falls for one of the greatest sculptors of the nineteenth century and becomes consumed by him to the detriment of her own career, finally succumbing to madness and ending her days in a mental institution. But her story is more complex than that. It is the story of the struggle of women artists in the nineteenth century, trying to overcome the limitations imposed on them by the conservative male establishment.

---

## Isadora Duncan
### 1878–1927

*I am an expressionist of beauty. I use my body as my medium just as a writer uses words.*

—ISADORA DUNCAN

Isadora Duncan claimed that she was born to dance. "If people ask me when I began to dance, I reply, 'In my mother's womb, probably as a result of oysters and champagne.'" Isadora's dancing, her spellbinding influence over audiences, her lovers, and her revolutionary politics made her one of the most notorious artists of her era. Rodin sketched her, Eleanora Duse was her friend, and Stanislavsky went into raptures over her. Audiences were bowled over by her in London, Paris, Berlin, Vienna, Budapest, Moscow, and Athens. Only her native country was immune to her charms and talent.

Isadora danced to classical music before it became the norm in ballet. Eschewing the usual elaborate sets, Isadora danced before simple dark blue curtains, setting a new fashion. Her costumes were as daring as her dancing. Abandoning corsets and stockings, Isadora wore a brief tunic, scandalizing audiences with glimpses of her bare arms and legs. Her dances were never set in stone, the choreography changing as her response to the music changed over the years.

A typical Gemini, Isadora's life emphasized her dual nature. She lived out of a suitcase, but never lost her taste for luxury. From the lovely auburn-haired sylph of her youth, in middle age she became a fat, lazy hedonist who spent less and less time onstage. Isadora was a woman who dared to live and love. Her lovers were varied: millionaires, actors, musicians, designers, and countless nameless others. "Isadora could no more live without human love than she could do without food or music," her close friend Mary Desti wrote. "They were as necessary to her as the breath of life."

She was born in San Francisco when Venus was in the ascendant, blessing her with beauty and charm, according to astrological interpretation. Her father, Joseph Duncan, was a poet, journalist, and deadbeat dad who left his family soon after Isadora was born. After the divorce her mother, Dora, gave piano lessons to make ends meet. They moved from lodgings to lodgings, leaving debts behind, a pattern Isadora would repeat her entire life. Despite the lack of material goods, Isadora's mother instilled in her children a love of art, reading to them from Shakespeare, Byron, and Isadora's personal hero, Walt Whitman. The children did whatever they pleased without worry of being disciplined.

Isadora always claimed that she absorbed her first impression of movement from the rhythms of ocean waves. By the time she was six, she was teaching the other children to wave their arms to music. By the time she was ten, she had dropped out of school, convinced that there was nothing that conventional education could teach her. While she had little formal training, she knew the popular dances of her day, and she studied the theories of François Delsarte, although she didn't like to admit it. The French musician and teacher believed that natural movements were the most genuine and could be used to interpret music. Her dancing incorporated only those movements that were natural to the body, which led her to reject ballet, which she considered abnormal. Dance at the time wasn't really considered an art. Isadora wanted to change that, to place dance alongside music, sculpture, and painting.

At eighteen, Isadora was convinced that San Francisco was too provincial to understand her art. The family moved to Chicago with only a small trunk, twenty-five dollars, and some jewelry. Isadora auditioned in her cute little white tunic for various producers but there were no takers. After months of no work, Isadora got an audition at the Masonic Temple Roof Garden. The manager, however, told her that she could perform her original dances if she also performed what they called a "skirt-dance" number. Isadora lasted three weeks before she quit, disgusted at having to "amuse the public with something which was against my ideals."

Next stop was New York. If she could make it there, she could make it anywhere. After two years touring with Augustin Daly's theater company, she met a young composer with whom she gave five solo concerts at Carnegie Hall. Things began to turn around when Isadora was taken up as a sort of pet by wealthy society matrons who invited her to dance in Newport and at their mansions on Fifth Avenue. High society applauded, but it didn't pay the rent. The final straw for the family occurred when the hotel where they were living burned, along with all their possessions. It was time to make her mark in Europe, where she was convinced her art would be appreciated. With only three hundred dollars, the family had to cross the ocean on a cattle boat. Isadora's mother cooked for the crew to help pay for their passage.

London and Paris proved to be more hospitable. She made her Paris debut, and audiences adored her. It was in Paris that Isadora developed the idea of dancing from the solar plexus, whereas classical ballet emphasized dancing from the spine. Soon she went off on a tour of Hungary and Germany; in Berlin, the audience mobbed the stage and refused to leave. Newspapers were filled with interviews with "Holy Isadora." One night she improvised to Johann Strauss's "Blue Danube" waltz, which was a huge hit. Wagner's son invited her to dance at Bayreuth in *Tannhäuser*, but her new style clashed with the ballet dancers hired to dance the Bacchanal with her. In Greece, Isadora danced among the ruins.

Isadora not only influenced the future and evolution of modern dance but also the first modern ballet company, the Ballets Russes. Both impresario Sergei Diaghilev and the choreographer Michel Fokine were taken by her on trips to St. Petersburg in 1905 and 1907. Diaghilev thought she gave an irreparable jolt to classical ballet in imperial Russia. Fokine wrote that "she reproduced in her dancing the whole range of human emotion."

She founded her first school, in Grünwald, Germany, to teach not just dance but also what she called "the school of life." "Let us teach little children to breathe, to vibrate, to feel and to become one with the general harmony and movement of nature. Let us first produce a beautiful human being, a dancing child." While Isadora was inspirational, she wasn't great at communicating her techniques. That was left to her sister Elizabeth, who taught at the school for years until it closed. It was the first of many schools that Isadora would found in her lifetime. The school gave rise to her most celebrated troupe of pupils, dubbed the Isadorables, who eventually took her surname and later performed both with Duncan and independently.

But artists cannot live by acclaim alone. Who would finally initiate her into the delights of Aphrodite? For such a free spirit, Isadora was still a virgin at twenty-five. In Hungary, she was finally introduced to the pleasures of the flesh when she met the actor Oscar Beregi, whom she immortalized as Romeo in her autobiography. They met at a party in her honor. Beregi was twenty-six, tall, dark, and handsome. Soon he was declaiming poetry from Ovid and Horace, backed by a chorus, in between her dances. Isadora was in love but Beregi expected her to give up her career to support his. Isadora was determined to stay free. Still, all her life she would be torn between love and her art.

The great love of her life was probably the stage designer Edward Gordon Craig. Gordon Craig was a creative genius as well as a misogynistic bastard. The father of eight, he'd already abandoned a wife and a mistress and was now living with his common-law wife. Introduced after one of Isadora's shows, he soon invited her up to see his etchings and she stayed for four days. She fell madly in love with him. "A flame meets flame; we burned in one bright fire." Isadora abandoned her art for a time, lost in passion. She bore him a child, Deirdre, in 1906. The relationship eventually crashed and burned over their fierce jealousies of each other.

The longest and most enduring relationship of her life was with

Paris Singer, the sewing machine heir. Named after the city of his birth, Singer was tall, blond, bearded, and looked like a Nordic god. She called him Lohengrin in her biography, after Wagner's hero, and later claimed that he was the only man she'd ever loved. He was rich, worldly, and a generous patron of the arts. He brought luxury and devotion into her life. Once again, her career took second place to her new love as she spent time sailing on his yacht or at his villa. "I had discovered that love might be a pastime as well as a tragedy. I gave myself to it with pagan innocence." She gave birth to their son, Patrick, in 1911.

On April 19, 1913, Deirdre and Patrick drowned when the car they were riding in accidentally rolled into the Seine. Isadora's life could now be divided into two parts: before and after the tragedy. She never spoke of her children again, and for years afterward the sight of a blond child moved her to tears. Following the accident she went to Corfu with her brother and sister to grieve and then sought solace with her friend Eleanora Duse at her villa in Viareggio, Italy. Isadora didn't dance for two years. When she returned to the stage, Europe was at war, and Isadora infused her dancing with her grief, channeling the sorrows of the world. She added an impassioned rendition of "La Marseillaise" to her repertoire.

She broke with Singer, who was turned off by her habit of making public scenes. The final blowup came after he booked Madison Square Garden for a performance by her school. When Isadora heard the news, she sarcastically replied, "What do you think I am? A circus? I suppose you want me to advertise prize fights with my dancing?" Singer was livid; he got up and walked out. Isadora was sure that he would be back but it was over. He cut off her funds and refused to see or speak to her for a long time.

Professionally, Isadora's pupils caused her both pride and anguish. The Isadorables were subject to ongoing hectoring from Duncan over their willingness to perform commercially. Where once she claimed not to be jealous of the dancers, she now considered them to be her rivals and envied their success. Only Irma Duncan (no relation) would be the most faithful of her acolytes, following her to Russia in 1921, where she taught in Moscow for seven years. Returning to the States, Irma continued to teach Duncan's techniques until her death in 1977.

America had never embraced her with open arms the way Europe had. Her atheism, love affairs, illegitimate children, and lack of embarrassment were a little out-there for early-twentieth-century America. During the war, she moved herself and her students to safety in New York, where she hoped to open a school, but she was too outspoken about America intervening in World War I and about free love, and she flouted the puritanical codes of the country. Even her native city, San Francisco, gave her the cold shoulder. Isadora became convinced that Americans had little appreciation for art and beauty, or at least her version of them.

By the end of her life, Duncan's performing career had dwindled and she became more notorious for her financial woes, and all-too-frequent public drunkenness, than for her dancing. There was an ill-fated attempt to start a school in Soviet Russia and a disastrous marriage to Sergei Esenin, a mentally unstable poet seventeen years her junior, which ended with his suicide. Her espousal of communism made her persona non grata in the United States. She had lived long enough to see her style and technique be considered old-fashioned and perhaps a little bit out of touch. Barefoot dancing was no longer new and innovative. She spent her final years moving between Paris and the Mediterranean, running

up debts at hotels. By the time she sat down to write her autobiography, she hadn't danced in three years. Her love of luxury
eventually led to her death, in Nice. Settling into her seat as a passenger in the Bugatti she was thinking of buying, with a handsome
French-Italian mechanic, her long, embroidered Chinese red scarf
became entangled around one of the vehicle's open-spoked wheels
and rear axle. When the car sprang forward, the scarf tightened,
snapping her neck. Her last words had been *"Adieu, mes amis, Je
vais à la gloire."* ("Good-bye, my friends, I go to glory.")

After lying in state in Nice and Paris, her funeral was sched-
uled on what was the tenth anniversary of America's entry into
World War I. The American press, who had never understood her,
wrote that her funeral cortege was barely noticed as the American
Legion parade wended its way down the Champs-Élysées. There
was no report of the ten thousand people who gathered at the
cemetery or the one thousand who crowded the crematorium as
her favorite music played. Her ashes were placed next to those of
her beloved children at Père Lachaise Cemetery in Paris.

There is no film of Isadora dancing, which is perhaps as she
would prefer. Isadora claimed that she preferred to be remembered as a legend. She died before the advent of sound recording,
which would have allowed the cameras to capture her performance with the music that inspired it. One can only get a sense of
the glory and passion of her art from still photos, the dancers that
she inspired, and the reviews and memories of those who saw her
dance. While her schools in Europe did not survive for long, her
work can be felt in the many dancers and choreographers that she
influenced.

# Josephine Baker
## 1906–1975

*What a wonderful Revenge for an Ugly Duckling!*

—JOSEPHINE BAKER

On the night of October 2, 1925, audiences had no idea what to expect when the curtain rose at 9:30 p.m. at the Théâtre des Champs-Élysées, on a new show from America called La Revue Nègre. Then Josephine Baker burst onto the stage, letting rip with a fast and loose Charleston. At the end of the show, she reappeared naked except for beads and a belt of pink flamingo feathers between her legs, carried upside down in a split, by her partner, bringing a little bit of Africa to France. It was the event of the season. Critics in Paris thumbed through their thesauruses trying to outdo themselves with animal metaphors and exotic imagery to describe her performance.

Overnight Josephine Baker's life had become something like out of the fairy tales that she had absorbed as a child.

Born illegitimate in the slums of East St. Louis, from childhood she was made to feel like an outsider in her own family because she was lighter skinned, while her mother and half siblings were dark. A poor student, she began making funny faces as a defense mechanism. What began as a way of coping later turned into a way for Josephine to make a living. By the age of twelve, she had dropped out of school, living on the streets, scrounging for food in garbage cans. A natural dancer, she learned all the latest steps in the streets of St. Louis. "I was cold and I danced to keep warm, that's my childhood," she later wrote. Dancing on the street corner to make money brought Josephine her first success. Soon she was playing vaudeville houses, working behind the scenes as a dresser. By the age of fifteen, she had married and discarded two husbands. It was her second husband who gave her the last name she would use for the rest of her career.

Rejected after she auditioned for a new Broadway musical called *Shuffle Along* because she was too young, too thin, and too dark, Josephine became determined to join the show. When she was offered a job as a dresser, she took it; she learned all the songs and dances, and when a chorus girl took sick, Josephine stepped in. Happy to be onstage, she was a sensation, stealing scenes from more experienced performers. She fed off the energy of the audiences, improvising dance steps, the audience giving her the unconditional love she'd never received at home. Kicking up her heels, Josephine continued to knock 'em dead in the Broadway show *Chocolate Dandies* and performed at the Plantation Club.

In 1925, she was offered the chance to go to Paris and never looked back. She had heard that life was better there for blacks and the two hundred bucks a week didn't hurt. At first Josephine wasn't too keen when she found out she was to perform half naked. It wasn't the glamorous image she was aiming for. She wanted to be seen as a singer, or at least wear a dress. But she soon came around when she realized the alternative was a one-way ticket back home. She was excited, though, when the artist Paul Colin, who later became her lover, used an image of her, rather than the star, Maude de Forest, for the poster advertising La Revue Nègre.

As Josephine shook and shimmied on opening night, her dancing verged on the obscene, titillating some and offending others. Her dancing emphasized her rear end, a part of the human anatomy that had once been hidden by bustles and skirts. She made it an object of desire. One critic called her dancing the "manifestation of the modern spirit." Another wrote, "She is constant motion, her body like a snake." People were so fascinated by her mugging, and how little she wore, that the difficulty of the choreography was often overlooked. Josephine used her press clippings to learn French, amused by the high-flown language used to describe her dancing. She was smart enough to know that it was all hyperbole, that they thought she was from Africa and not the wilds of St. Louis. "The white imagination sure is something," she said, "when it comes to blacks."

Paris was in the grip of "Negromania"; they were crazy for "Le Jazz Hot" and anything African and primitive. Josephine was the living, lusty embodiment of white French racial and sexual fantasies. She was "the Bronze Venus" and "the Black Pearl." Picasso, who painted her, called her "the Modern Nefertiti." They adored her; women bobbed their hair à la Josephine and tanned their skin. Baker wasn't just a success in Paris; she was a hit in Berlin, where the great theater director Max Reinhardt offered to take her under his wing, to help her become a great actress. It was tempting but Josephine went back to Paris to the Folies Bergère. This time she was the featured star, performing the "Danse Sauvage" wearing nothing but a necklace, a skirt made of bananas, and a smile.

Josephine made the most of her new status as a sex symbol, sharing her charms with whoever struck her fancy, from chorus boys to industry titans. She became a notch on the belt of writer Georges Simenon, test-drove the Crown Prince of Sweden, and hobnobbed with the architect Le Corbusier. Because she didn't need a man to support her, she could indulge just for the pleasure. Whether it took ten minutes or an hour, Josephine was always in the driver's seat. She accumulated dozens of marriage proposals and forty thousand love letters in just one year. The ugly duckling had turned into a swan, and now men couldn't tell her enough how beautiful she was. She lapped up their attentions like a starving child.

Josephine quickly became the most successful American entertainer working in Paris. Photographs of her sold like hotcakes, and people bought Josephine Baker dolls, wearing the little banana skirt, by the thousands. She became a poster girl for the Roaring Twenties in Paris. Soon Josephine added movie star to her list of accomplishments, appearing in three films, *Siren of the Tropics* (1927), *Zou Zou* (1934), and *Princess Tam Tam* (1935), which were only successful in Europe. In each one, Josephine played a variation on the noble savage, an exotic creature who sacrifices and loses at love.

But sensing that the city would soon get tired of her shtick, Josephine realized that she would need to reinvent herself if she was going to continue to be a success. She was helped by her manager and lover Giuseppe Abatino, called Pepito, a former stonemason. He played Pygmalion to her Galatea, teaching her how to dress and act in society, training her voice and body, and sculpting her into a highly sophisticated and marketable star. When she moved on from the Folies Bergère to the Casino de Paris she had a whole new act. Descending a grand staircase, wearing a tuxedo, she now sang French torch songs, including her signature number "J'ai Deux Amours." Josephine had reinvented herself from an exotic savage to a sophisticated French chanteuse, becoming "La Bakaire."

She played the role of star to the hilt, adding an accent over the *e* in her last name to appear more French. Josephine wore couture and expensive jewelry and she spent hours after shows signing autographs. At night she was chauffeured from one lavish party to the next in a snakeskin-upholstered limo. She once showed up at a nightclub with her snake Kiki wrapped around her neck. Given a cheetah named Chiquita as a pet, Josephine and the animal, wearing a twenty-thousand-diamond collar, became a familiar sight on the streets of Paris and Deauville. She bought a château fit for a princess, but offstage, Josephine, wearing housedresses, lived a simple life in the country with her menagerie of animals.

Her stunning success did not come without its price. She was often the only black performer onstage surrounded by whites. And the racism she had left America to escape often reared its ugly head. During a tour of Germany and Austria, Nazi protesters tried to bar her from performing. Other performers in France, both white and black, resented her success. Although she became more French than the French, there were barriers that she was never able to overcome. Throughout her life Baker was criticized for turning her back on her people. While some gloried in her success, seeing her triumphs as their own, there were others who felt that Josephine had abandoned her country and her race.

After ten years in France, she decided that it was time for her to return to Broadway. Pepito arranged for her to appear in the 1936 Ziegfeld Follies, making her the first and only black female ever to appear in the show. When the show reached New York, the reviews were devastating. Audiences and critics were used to seeing black performers as either mammies or blues singers; they were not interested in seeing a sophisticated black woman on-stage. To them Josephine was just an uppity colored girl. At the St. Moritz Hotel on Central Park South, where she was stay-ing, she was asked to use the service entrance when she came and went. Josephine blamed Pepito for the whole debacle. He left for Paris and died of cancer before they could make up. Hurt and disillusioned by the experience, Josephine had learned a hard les-son: that America would never look at her without seeing her color.

With Europe on the brink of war in 1939, Josephine was eager to do her part for her adopted country. "It is France which made me what I am," she declared. The Deuxième Bureau, the French military intelligence group, was reluctant at first to use her be-cause of the whole Mata Hari debacle during World War I. Jose-phine convinced them of her sincerity. She would have no official role except that of "honorable correspondent." Because of her fame, Josephine rubbed shoulders with people with high profiles. She was able to attend parties at the Italian embassy and pass on any gossip that might be of use. She also helped the war effort in other ways, by sending Christmas presents to soldiers and helping people in danger obtain visas and passports to leave France.

When France fell to the Germans in 1940, she fled to her Châ-teau des Milandes, gasoline stored in champagne bottles packed in the trunk of her car, with her maid and her dogs. Soon she was joined by Belgian refugees and others who were working for the resistance. Because she was an entertainer, Josephine had an excuse to move around Europe. She smuggled intelligence coded in invisible ink within her sheet music. In 1942, she went to North Africa under the guise of recuperating from pneumonia, but the real reason was to help the resistance. From her base in Morocco, she toured Spain and North Africa, entertaining Allied troops, pinning notes with any information she gathered in her underwear. For her work during the war, Josephine was awarded the Cross of War and the Medal of the Resistance with rosette, and she was made a Chevalier of the Legion of Honor by Charles de Gaulle.

Happily married to her fourth husband, she decided to tour America once again, but this time with her own show. She refused, however, to perform before segregated audiences in Las Vegas and Miami. For her pains she was considered to be politically dangerous, demanding, and difficult. But things got worse after she charged the Stork Club in New York with racism. She had come into the club with two white friends and experienced less than stellar service from an indifferent waitstaff. Used to being treated like a star, Josephine was appalled. She immediately got on the horn to the NAACP to picket the club. Influential columnist Walter Winchell, who was there that night, took her to task in his column. He accused her of being anti-American and a communist sympathizer. Her controversial image now threatened her career. Concerts were canceled and Josephine went back to France.

Unable to have children of her own, Josephine adopted what she called her "Rainbow Tribe." Initially she had planned on adopting only two or three children. However, once Josephine got started, she couldn't stop, eventually adopting twelve children in all, in various hues and nationalities. Living at Château des Milandes, a sprawling three-hundred-acre estate, with her children and an enormous staff, Josephine had to keep touring to pay for the upkeep. Long before Branson or Dollywood, Josephine cooked up the idea of turning her home into a tourist attraction/theme park, complete with a simulated African village, a wax museum, a foie gras factory, a patisserie, a J-shaped swimming pool, and even a nightclub where she would be the star attraction. But by the late 1960s, Josephine was deeply in debt. Creditors seized the property and belongings and sold them at auction. Until the bitter end, like a tigress protecting her young, Josephine tried to hold them off until the gendarmes had to forcibly remove her. Help came from her own fairy godmother, Princess Grace of Monaco, who offered financial assistance and the use of a villa.

But in 1975, at the age of sixty-eight, when most women are collecting social security, Josephine came roaring back with a retrospective revue at the Bobino in Paris, celebrating her fifty years in show biz. She had already conquered Carnegie Hall and the Palace in New York, and was in great demand from spectators including Mick Jagger, Jacqueline Kennedy Onassis, Sophia Loren, and Diana Ross. The revue opened to rave reviews but Baker didn't live to savor her triumph. Four days later, she was discovered lying peacefully in bed, surrounded by her glowing notices. She had fallen into a coma after suffering a cerebral hemorrhage. Her funeral was held at the L'Église de la Madeleine; she was the first American woman to receive full French military honors at her funeral. The streets were thronged with thousands of fans paying homage to La Bakaire one last time.

# Billie Holiday
### 1915–1959

*She whispered a song along the keyboard ... and everyone and I stopped breathing.*

—Frank O'Hara, "The Day Lady Died"

Death. Pain. Sadness. When people think of Billie Holiday, these are the words they invariably use. The 1972 film *Lady Sings the Blues* reinforced the portrait of a childlike woman with no greater ambition than to "sing in a club downtown" who was derailed by drugs but saved by the love of a good man. It's true that in her four decades, she knew more sorrow and tragedy than joy or love. But there was more to Billie Holiday than the portrait of a singer, gardenia tucked behind her ear, clutching the microphone like a lover. She was a musical genius, who pioneered a new way of singing. Although she couldn't read music, Billie only had to hear a song once before she could sing it.

Her voice ranged over little more than an octave, but she used it the way a musician plays an instrument, patterning her phrasing in unexpected ways. Her vocal style, strongly inspired by jazz instrumentalists, manipulated phrasing and tempo. Singing just behind the beat, she would take a song and twist it in unexpected ways. Rarely did she sing a song the same way two nights in a row. "I hate straight singing," she once said. "I have to change a tune to my own way of doing it. That's all I know." Critic John Bush wrote that she "changed the art of American pop vocals forever." Duke Ellington called her "the Essence of Cool." Frank Sinatra claimed that Holiday "was and still remains the greatest single musical influence on me."

It was a long way from Philadelphia, where she was born Eleanora Fagan on April 17, 1915. Her mother, Sadie Fagan, and her father, Clarence Holiday, were barely out of their teens when she was born. Despite what she wrote in her autobiography, her parents never married and Billie didn't see much of her father until she moved to Harlem and started singing in the clubs. She was farmed out to relatives in Baltimore almost from birth, who made her feel unwanted, never giving her the security of a home life. By the time she was eleven, she'd been busted for truancy, sent to reform school, and raped by a neighbor. She had to learn to be tough to survive.

It was at her cleaning job in a brothel in Baltimore that Eleanora first heard jazz being played on the Victrola in the parlor. She nearly wore the record out. Louis Armstrong and Bessie Smith were her first influences. Years later, she would remember, "Sometimes the record would make me so sad I'd cry up a storm. Other times the damn record made me so happy I'd forget about how much hard-earned money the session in the parlor was costing me." In 1929, Eleanora left Baltimore behind for New York

City. Reunited in Harlem, mother and daughter were soon working in a local whorehouse. In 1930, they were both busted but while Sadie got off with a fine, Eleanora was sent to a workhouse for one hundred days. When she got out, Eleanora decided that she "wasn't going to be no damn maid" and she wasn't going back to hooking.

That only left singing as an alternative. Harlem had become not just a haven for African Americans, the promised land of jobs and freedom, but it was also a mecca for jazz, not only at clubs, like the Cotton Club, that catered mainly to white patrons, but also places like Small's Paradise. Eleanora got a job waiting tables and singing for tips at a club called Pod and Jerry's. Most of the girls would pick up their tips by grabbing them between their thighs, but Billie was too dignified for that and refused.

She began to pick up more and more small gigs as word of mouth spread about the talented young singer. At the age of fifteen, she changed her name to Billie after her favorite movie star, Billie Dove, and Holiday after her father. By this time, Clarence Holiday was working with the Fletcher Henderson Orchestra. But the relationship between the two was awkward. Although he was proud of her talent, Holiday didn't like being reminded of his past, or that he was old enough to have an adult daughter.

Billie was eighteen when she was spotted at a club called Monette's by the man who was most important in launching her career. John Hammond, a critic and record producer, came every night for three weeks to hear her sing. "She was the best jazz singer I had ever heard," he later wrote. Before long he had her cutting her first record as part of a studio group led by Benny Goodman, who was then just on the verge of making it big. In 1935, Billie recorded four sides that became hits, including "What a Little Moonlight Can Do," which landed her a recording contract with

Columbia Records. She also made her debut that same year at the Apollo Theater, the mecca of music in Harlem. Despite her stage fright, she made a huge impression on the audience.

Billie's voice wasn't as big as Ella Fitzgerald's or Bessie Smith's, but she made the most of what she had. She mesmerized the audience with the stories she told with her voice. When Holiday came onstage, she sang, and then she left. She didn't entertain the audience between songs with jokes and witty banter. If she felt like it, she gave an encore. Despite the title of her autobiography, *Lady Sings the Blues*, if you had asked her, she would have told you that she was a jazz singer. Her singing style, one writer wrote, was, "as fiercely concentrated as oxyacetylene flame." She would later say that it took about ten years for people to catch on to what she was doing.

Now that she was making money, Billie upped her game, trading her tight, trashy stage costumes for a more elegant, refined image. Her signature look came about by accident. One night before a show, she burned her hair with a curling iron. A gardenia was procured to cover the damage. Liking the look, she kept it.

In a few short years, Billie had gone from singing for tips to touring with Count Basie's orchestra, playing the Apollo, and making a short film with Duke Ellington. She became one of the first black performers to integrate an all-white band when she sang with Artie Shaw. But life on the road was hard. In Detroit, the management of the Fox Theater demanded that she wear darker makeup to blend in better with musicians in Count Basie's band. Billie couldn't stay at the same hotels or eat with her white fellow musicians in restaurants and cafés.

Billie also started to get a reputation for being difficult, complaining about her salary and working conditions. She parted ways with Count Basie when she refused to sing songs she didn't like. Song pluggers were peeved with the liberties she took, saying that she was "too artistic." She fell out with Shaw when she felt that he didn't stick up for her enough with the management of the Lincoln Hotel in New York after the owners insisted that she use the tradesmen's entrance so that customers wouldn't think that blacks were staying there.

In 1939, she became the first black woman to open at an integrated club, Café Society, downtown in Greenwich Village. That same year Barney Josephson, the owner of Café Society, introduced Billie to the Abel Meeropol song "Strange Fruit." Legend has it that Billie at first had no idea what the song was about. Given that black newspapers carried stories of lynching and Billie had toured the Deep South, it's impossible to believe she was that ignorant. At twenty-four, like most blacks in the United States, she knew the sting of racism.

"Strange Fruit" was Billie's contribution to protesting racial violence. It may have been written by a white man, but Billie gave it life. "The first time I sang it, I thought it was a mistake. There wasn't even the patter of applause when I finished. Then a lone person began to clap nervously. Then suddenly everyone was clapping." The song forced the middle-class white audience to confront the reality of racism. Josephson added to the drama by insisting that Billie close her three nightly sets with the song; all service was halted, and the only light was a spotlight that illuminated her face.

Billie's own label, Columbia, wouldn't record the song; the executives were too fearful of antagonizing Southern customers. Hurt and angry, she took it to Milt Gabler, the owner of Commodore Records, a small label that was run out of a record store. Gabler jumped at the chance, paying Billie five hundred dollars for "Strange Fruit" and three other songs; he later paid her an additional thousand dollars. Released on July 22, 1939, "Strange Fruit" rose to number sixteen on the record charts, selling ten thousand copies its first week.

For Billie, "Strange Fruit" changed everything. For the first time, she enjoyed the critical praise from the mainstream press that had eluded her for years. People were beginning to know her name outside of the music world. The song remained a fixture in her repertoire until her death, continuing to have resonance for her, and she never lost her passion for singing it. Once she even walked off the stage at Café Society when she felt the audience wasn't paying sufficient attention to the song, flipping up her dress and flashing her bare behind at them. She had a clause put into her contracts that she could sing it whenever she wanted. Although other singers performed the song before and since, it has her fingerprints all over it. But not everyone was happy at the song's success. John Hammond felt that the song ruined her career, that she began to take herself too seriously, losing her artistry and sparkle.

By the 1940s, Billie was one of the most desired singers in the small clubs on West Fifty-second Street (aka Swing Street), making a thousand dollars a week. She moved to Decca Records, continued to play clubs big and small around the country, and made a film with her idol Louis Armstrong. Vocally she was more assured than ever, refining her sound, with no excess gestures or emotions. But it was also a decade of bad choices and bad men. Billie seemed to be fatally attracted to low-life hustlers who exploited her, stole her money, and supplied her with drugs—men like her first husband, Jimmy Monroe, a sharp, flashy dresser she married in 1941.

Although Holiday had often indulged in marijuana, as did a lot of musicians, and could drink any man under the table, it wasn't until sometime in 1943 that she started to use heroin. It was as prevalent among the musicians she hung out with as reefer. Billie seems to have started for the same reason a lot of people do: for the thrill of it. She had no idea the toll her addiction would take on her life and her career. "I had the white gowns and the white shoes. And every night they'd bring the white gardenias and the white junk." At one point, she claimed that she was spending five hundred dollars a week on her habit. The drugs were giving her a Dr. Jekyll and Ms. Hyde personality. She once went after a naval officer with a broken bottle after he called her a "nigger." She dumped Monroe and took up with Joe Guy, a musician and drug addict who could supply her with the drugs she craved.

After her mother's death in 1945, Billie had fewer people in her life who tried to protect her, the way Sadie had done. Although they had a tense relationship at times, Sadie had always been there for her daughter. With her mother gone, Billie was now an orphan, and she never quite got over her death. Sinking deeper into drink and drugs, she became even more dependent on the men in her life to keep the loneliness at bay. She tried rehab after her agent threatened to drop her but it didn't last.

In 1947 Billie was arrested for narcotics possession after federal agents searched her hotel room in Philadelphia. "It was called 'The United States of America versus Billie Holiday.' And that's just the way it felt," Holiday recalled in her autobiography, *Lady Sings the Blues*. On the idiotic advice of her agent, she pled guilty and waived her right to counsel, probably thinking they would just send her back to rehab. Despite the pleas of the prosecutor, Billie was sentenced to a year and a day and sent to Alderson Federal Prison Camp in West Virginia. She was released seventy-two days early for good behavior. Eleven days after her release, she made her comeback in a sold-out concert at Carnegie Hall.

But because of her conviction, Billie's cabaret license was

revoked, making it difficult for her to get work except in concert halls and theaters. Almost a year later she was arrested again, this time for possession of opium. Her current lover, another thug named John Levy, gave her all his drugs to hold after he got a tip that narcotics agents were coming to arrest him. Before she could do anything, they were both arrested. She beat the charges; the jury acquitted her, deciding that Levy had framed her. But it would not be her last arrest.

There were still some triumphs in her remaining ten years—several new recordings, this time with Verve—but also another abusive marriage, to mob enforcer Louis McKay, who at least tried to get her off the drugs but to no avail. There were missed performances, and some nights Billie clutched the microphone like it was a lifeline. She forgot the lyrics, was inaudible, or fell behind the beat. On other occasions, a miracle would occur, and she would hold it together, producing the magic the way she used to.

In 1954 Billie finally got to go to Europe. She loved touring in Europe. Everywhere she went, she was treated like royalty. But by her second tour, the ravages of the drugs, alcohol, and smoking had taken a toll on her voice. Holiday compensated with a new emotional truth in her singing. Still she was booed in Italy, and the rest of her engagements there were canceled. At the end she was singing in Parisian nightclubs for a percentage of the door.

On May 31, 1959, she was taken to Metropolitan Hospital in New York suffering from liver and heart disease. When a nurse found heroin in her room, she was arrested for drug possession as she lay dying, and her hospital room was raided by authorities. Police officers were stationed at the door to her room. Holiday remained under police guard at the hospital until she died, from cirrhosis of the liver, on July 17, 1959. She died with seventy cents in the bank and $750 on her person.

Her funeral was held at the Church of St. Paul the Apostle on Sixtieth Street and Ninth Avenue. It was a full Catholic Requiem High Mass, with a full choir providing the music. Lady Day was dressed in her favorite pink lace dress and gloves. Three thousand people attended the funeral; five hundred others stood outside the church.

Although she never had a number one hit or was the most popular singer, Billie Holiday probably influenced more musicians than any other singer in the twentieth century. During her career, Holiday collaborated and earned the respect of some of the most noted names in music, a roll call of jazz greats. Her legacy lies not in her story but in the music that she left behind.

# Frida Kahlo
## 1907–1954

*They thought I was a surrealist but I wasn't. I never painted dreams. I painted my own reality.*

—FRIDA KAHLO

Frida Kahlo once wrote that she had suffered "two grave accidents in my life. One in which a streetcar knocked me down . . . The other accident is Diego. And he was by far the worst." Ouch, that's harsh. While there is an element of truth in that statement, it's far more complicated than that. The streetcar accident that Frida suffered at the age of eighteen left her with a lifetime of pain, but it turned her in a new direction. Painting brought her back to life, and in her pain she found one of the most important themes in her work. Diego Rivera was no prize as a husband, chronically unfaithful, but he gave her support both financial and emotional, opened doors for her, and helped to shape her talent.

Frida's parents, Guillermo Kahlo and Matilde Calderón y Gonzalez, were an odd couple from the start. He was a German Jewish atheist widower, with two children, who suffered from epilepsy. Matilde was a devoted Mexican Catholic who never got over the death of her first love, another German, who committed suicide in front of her. Their third daughter, of four, was born Magdalena Carmen Frieda in July 1907 in La Casa Azul (the Blue House), in Coyoacán, a small town on the outskirts of Mexico City. Frida later liked to claim that she was born in 1910, the year of the Mexican Revolution, to emphasize her bond with the rebirth of Mexican culture.

When Frida was six, she contracted polio, keeping her bedridden for nine months. The illness left her with a withered right leg and a limp. Her classmates at school taunted her, calling her Frida *pata de palo* (Peg Leg Frida). For the rest of her life she wore long skirts or pants to hide her leg. Her illness left her with a sense of solitude, but it fired up her imagination. In 1922, she passed the entrance exam for the most prestigious school in Mexico, the Escuela Nacional Preparatoria. Her childhood turned Frida into a tough, rebellious teenager. At school she became involved with leftist politics, cut classes that bored her, tried to get teachers fired that she felt weren't up to the job. By the time she was seventeen, she'd been seduced by both an apprentice engraver who taught her to draw, and a female librarian at the ministry of education. She also became fascinated with Diego Rivera when he was painting a mural in the school's auditorium, sitting quietly watching him work. Later she embellished this version, claiming to have played tricks on him, spying on his liaisons with models. When her friends asked what she saw in him, she claimed that she would have Diego's child when the time was right.

Frida's plans for the future were changed forever when a bus she was riding was hit by an out-of-control streetcar. Frida was impaled by an iron handrail through her abdomen. Somehow her clothes were removed by the collision, and a package of gold powder carried by a worker was scattered across her body. A man at the scene put his knee on her chest and pulled the rail out. Her spine and pelvis were both broken in three places, her right leg in eleven, her collarbone and ribs were broken, and her right foot was dislocated and crushed. The doctors didn't think that she would survive. They had to put her back together in sections like a collage. She would be in and out of hospitals for the rest of her life.

Showing her extraordinary will to live, Frida was up and walking within three months but suffered a relapse within the year. It seems either the surgeons were negligent in not checking out her spine before discharging her or her parents hadn't been able to afford certain procedures. Immobilized in a succession of plastic corsets, Frida decided to devote herself to painting. Her mother installed a four-poster bed in her room, with a mirror attached to the underside of the canopy, and had a special easel made up for her so that she could work while she recovered. Other than attending art classes in school, Frida had no formal training but she had developed a keen eye while working with her father, a photographer, who taught her how to use a camera and, later, how to develop and retouch photos. She began to study art books for hours on end, painting portraits of her sisters and friends, but her greatest Muse was herself. In two years, she had executed over a dozen paintings. What is remarkable is that Frida never painted the accident. Only a single pencil drawing, done in 1926, exists to record the life-changing moment. Years later Frida said that she had wanted to paint the accident, but couldn't; it was too important to reduce to a single image.

The "other accident" occurred when Frida and Diego met again at a party given by a mutual friend, photographer Tina Modotti. Needing to know if she had the goods, Frida took her paintings to Diego to ask him if she had any talent. Soon they were embroiled in a passionate affair. "On a sudden impulse, I stooped to kiss her. As our lips touched, the light nearest us went off and came on again when our lips parted," Diego later wrote. They kissed over and over under different street lamps with the same fascinating results. Diego was enchanted by Frida's fiery personality, her quick, unconventional mind, and her cheekiness, but most of all by her talent.

Frida's family wasn't exactly thrilled with her new love. Although he may have been the most famous artist in Mexico, Diego was nobody's idea of a Latin lover. He was forty-two, weighed over three hundred pounds, was a stranger to personal hygiene, and, more important, was married. But he was also full of humor, vitality, and charm, and he sincerely liked women. When Diego asked her father for permission to marry her, her father told him, "Don't forget that my daughter is ill, and that she will be ill all her life. Think about it." When they eventually married, her family bitterly described it as the union of "an elephant and a dove." There were several unsettling incidents at the wedding that seemed to be an omen of things to come. Only her father showed up to the nuptials. At the reception, Diego's ex-wife, Lupe Marin, turned up and insulted the bride, and Rivera got drunk, drew his pistol, and fired, breaking a man's finger. Frida was so upset; she burst into tears and went home to her parents. She didn't move in with Diego for several days.

From the beginning Frida worshipped Rivera, believing him to be a genius. She painted little during these years, content to be Mrs. Diego Rivera. She used to bring his lunch to him while he worked and even went so far as to befriend his former wife to pick up tips on how to please him. When Diego was expelled from the Communist Party, Frida quit, too, out of solidarity. Knowing his interest in the indigenous Mexican culture, she began to wear the Tehuana clothing that he liked; the ruffled and embroidered blouses, long skirts, and enough gold jewelry to make a rap star jealous became her signature look. For Diego, however, Frida came third in his life, after his art and himself.

Their life together was as much a work of art as their paintings. In the San Ángel district of Mexico City, they had a pair of houses built for them, connected by a walkway; Frida's was sky blue, Diego's bigger and bloodred. The houses expressed Diego's idea of independence between a man and a woman. When Frida was angry, she would close the door on her side of the walkway, forcing Diego to have to go downstairs, cross the yard, and knock on her front door. Their home, filled with pets, became a mecca for the intelligentsia, with writers, artists, and photographers frequently visiting.

When Frida became pregnant she was ecstatic, although Diego was less excited. He was a crap father to the children he already had. After telling her that she would probably never be able to carry a child to term, doctors advised a medical abortion. Frida was devastated. During their marriage, she tried at least three more times to have a child, over Diego's objections. The miscarriage she suffered when they were living in Detroit led to one of her most powerful and intensely personal paintings. With no children of her own, Frida lavished love on her nieces and nephews, as well as a menagerie of animals.

Another torment in Frida's life was Diego's infidelities. A doctor once told Diego that he was biologically incapable of being faithful, which he used as a justification for his rampant womanizing. Although Frida knew of his reputation before they married, no doubt she thought that her love would change him. She bore it stoically, even becoming friends with some of his lovers, but Diego's affair with her sister Cristina finally crossed the line. In his autobiography, Diego wrote, "If I loved a woman, the more I loved her, the more I wanted to hurt her. Frida was only the most obvious victim of this disgusting trait."

Frida expressed her feelings about the affair in *A Few Little Pricks* (1935), depicting a man who has stabbed a woman to death. While the man and woman resemble Diego and her sister, it is really Frida wielding the knife. Kahlo once said, "I paint myself because I am often alone and I am the subject I know best." As a symbol of her new life, Frida cut her hair and stopped wearing the Tehuana clothing that Diego loved.

Her discovery of this affair freed her to assert herself both artistically and sexually. She moved out of their house and into a flat in town. From then on she began to have affairs, with both men and women, seeming to have lost all her inhibitions. Diego's jealousy prevented her from flaunting her affairs in public. When Rivera found out about her affair with the sculptor Isamu Noguchi, he threatened to kill him. She also had an affair with Diego's personal hero, Leon Trotsky, one of the leaders of the Russian Revolution. Kahlo nicknamed him El Viejo (Old Man) and found his vigorous, intellectual personality stimulating. On his birthday, she gave him a painting entitled *Self-Portrait Dedicated to Leon*

*Trotsky* (1937). Frida didn't take the affair seriously; it was just a way of getting back at Diego. Rivera suspected nothing of her affair with Trotsky for over a year. When he eventually found out, he broke all ties with his hero.

On the career front, these were some of her most prolific years. Diego encouraged Frida to show and sell her work, which led to the actor Edward G. Robinson purchasing four of her paintings. Her work expanded beyond the personal. Kahlo was influenced by ex-votos (religious paintings) of the previous century, Goya, pre-Columbian statues, Hieronymus Bosch, and Brueghel. She began to paint monkeys, which, though symbols of lust in Mexican mythology, she portrayed as gentle and caring. She created complex, visual symbols, using a primitive style of bright colors. Frida's art is specific and so personal that it can hurt to look at the images. She bled elements of her life onto the canvas, as though she had opened a vein, tempered by humor and fantasy.

In 1938, an art gallery owner in New York offered her a one-woman show in which she was celebrated as an artist in her own right. She showed twenty-five works and half of them sold. She was now becoming financially independent of Diego although it was he who drew up the guest list for the private showing. Critics were enthusiastic and people began commissioning new work from her. André Breton, the leader of the surrealists, was struck by how similar her work was to the movement despite her never having seen a surrealist painting. He offered her a show in Paris as part of an exhibition called Mexique. And she had a new love in Nickolas Muray, a Hungarian photographer.

While Frida eventually became disillusioned with Breton, she enjoyed meeting other artists. She even inspired designer Elsa Schiaparelli, who was so taken with Frida's Mexican attire that she created the Madame Rivera dress. When Frida returned to the

States it was to discover that not only had Nickolas Muray fallen in love with someone else but that Diego was sleeping with her sister again. It was Diego's idea to seek a divorce. As he put it, he wanted the freedom to sleep with any woman he chose without having to worry that he was hurting Frida. He also wanted Frida to have more independence, which she neither wanted nor needed. Divorced in the fall of 1939, Frida, instead of celebrating, began to drink heavily instead. She couldn't live with Diego but she couldn't live without him, either. "I drank to drown my pain but the damned pain learned how to swim!"

After a year, though, Diego urged her to remarry him and she finally agreed, but under two conditions: she wanted to be financially independent, and she would no longer sleep with him. They were remarried on Diego's birthday in December 1940. Frida moved into Casa Azul, her childhood home, while Diego lived in a flat in San Ángel. Frida now mothered Diego; he was not only husband, friend, lover, but the child that she longed for but could never have, which was fine by Diego. Despite his inability to keep his pants zipped, Frida loved Diego and knew he loved her. A good friend said of the remarriage, "He gave her something solid to lean on."

Frida started teaching at the School of Painting and Sculpture three days a week. Instead of just teaching about technique, she took her students on adventures to the market, to shantytowns, archeological sights, even to bars. She wanted to put them in touch with life. But Frida's body was breaking down, and soon it became impossible for her to stand or sit. The treatments seemed to just make things worse. She had sandbags attached to her feet while being suspended in a vertical position, she had bone grafts, and she spent a year in a Mexico City hospital, but nothing worked. Some biographers speculate that the majority of her operations were unnecessary, that they were a way for Frida to get Diego's attention. To keep up her spirits, Frida would treat her plaster corsets like works of art. In *The Broken Column* (1944), Frida's nude body, encased in a medical corset pierced by nails, is cracked open to show a shattered column, as pale tears pour down her face. Her paintings became a vehicle for channeling and expressing her pain.

In 1953, her friend Lola Álvarez Bravo decided to arrange a one-woman show for Frida at the Galería de Arte Contemporáneo. Although doctors informed her that she was too ill to attend, Frida was not about to miss her moment. Diego arranged for her four-poster bed to be put up in the middle of the gallery. Frida arrived by ambulance like Cleopatra on her barge. She lay in the center, absorbing all the attention, exultant but racked with pain.

Frida fell into a deep depression when her right leg had to be amputated below the knee due to gangrene. She wrote in her diary that she knew the end was near. "I hope the exit is joyful . . . I hope never to come back." She got her wish on the morning of July 13, 1954. It was a few days after her forty-seventh birthday.

While Diego Rivera was more famous during their lifetimes, the tide began to turn posthumously in the 1980s with the rise of neo-Mexicanism. Kahlo has become more prominent as feminists have taken her up as an icon. Fridamania has taken hold as her likeness now appears on everything from mouse pads to tea towels. In 2008, as part of the centennial celebration of her birth, a major exhibition of her work traveled across the United States. Kahlo's legacy as one of the most important and original artists of the twentieth century is assured.

# SEVEN

# Amazing Adventuresses

## Anne Bonny and Mary Read
### 1698?–1782 AND 1695?–1721

Who doesn't love a tale about pirates, swashbuckling stories of adventure on the high seas, where men were men, and women were the naughty figureheads on the ships? Well, among the most notorious pirates of the eighteenth century were two women. If you ride the Pirates of the Caribbean attraction at Disneyland, you'll see portraits of them on the wall: Anne Bonny and Mary Read. Some might call them feminists who chose piracy as a way of rebelling against a male-dominated world. Others might see them as tomboys who just never grew up. Whatever their reasons, Anne Bonny and Mary Read became two of history's most notorious pirates, male or female.

Anne Bonny was probably born in County Cork in about 1698 to a lawyer named William Cormac and his maid, Mary Brennan. Cormac was married and the resulting scandal (apparently Mrs.

Cormac was not of a forgiving nature) led him to flee Ireland with Anne's mother. They settled in South Carolina, where William managed to amass enough money as a lawyer to buy a small plantation, where they lived respectably as husband and wife.

Anne, however, was not interested in the social life of a wealthy planter's daughter. She craved adventure and excitement. From childhood, she was headstrong and determined, with a fierce temper. There is a story that Anne beat the crap out of a man who dared to make unwanted advances toward her, injuring him so badly that he couldn't get out of bed for weeks. She also supposedly once stabbed a kitchen maid with a knife. She was clearly not a woman you wanted to have on your bad side.

Instead of making a good marriage, at the age of sixteen Anne ran off with a small-time pirate named James Bonny, whom she had met in Charleston, a well-known pirate haunt of the day. When her father found out, he was furious and disowned her; he had already planned to marry her off to a medical student. Anne's lack of inheritance was not part of Bonny's plan; it appears that he had only wanted Anne because of her father's estate. She soon found out that not only did James suck as a pirate but he was also spineless. After they settled in New Providence (present-day Nassau in the Bahamas, and at the time an ideal haven for pirates until the British sent in an ex-privateer, Woodes Rogers, to clean it up), James, rather than working for a living, spent his time turning in his fellow pirates in order to collect the "king's pardon" (reward money) from the governor of the island.

Disgusted with her husband's traitorous ways, Anne spent more and more of her time hanging out with the pirates in the local saloons, including one owned by Pierre Bouspeut, aka Pierre the Pansy Pirate. Pierre owned a coffee shop, hair salon, and dressmaking business. Anne may have started her career as a pirate as one of

Pierre's crew. Legend has it that they managed to take hold of a French merchant ship by dressing up an abandoned wreck with a dressmaker's dummy in the bow, suitably done up as a victim. When the French crew got one look at the sight of Anne standing with an ax over the faux bloody corpse, they quickly turned over their cargo without a fight.

Anne soon left James for Calico Jack Rackham.* He was nicknamed Calico Jack because of his flamboyant dress, favoring calico coats and britches. Rackham took Anne the same way he did any ship that he had plundered, with "no time wasted, straight up alongside, every gun brought to play, and the prize boarded." Jack offered to buy Anne (who protested at being treated like a piece of property) in a divorce from James, who refused, taking the matter before Governor Rogers, who declared that Anne should be flogged and returned to James. Then Rogers passed a court order forbidding the two from seeing each other.

Instead the two escaped on Jack's ship, the *Revenge*. Contrary to popular belief Anne didn't disguise herself as a man. Another story has it that when one of the crew members objected to her presence, as it was considered bad luck to have a woman aboard, she stabbed him through the heart. Anne soon found herself pregnant with Jack's child. When he found out, he dropped her off in Cuba to deliver the baby. No one knows what really happened to the child, a baby girl. There is some speculation that she just abandoned her. Others think that she left the baby with a foster family to raise it, or that the baby died at birth.

In any event, when Anne returned to the ship, she met the woman who would soon become coupled with her in infamy, Mary

---

* The design of the skull and crossbones on Rackham's Jolly Roger flag contributed to the popularization of the design and its association with piracy in popular culture.

Read. Local lore has it that Anne became smitten with the new lad on board ship. When she made advances, the "lad" revealed himself to be a woman. (Again, most likely this story is false and Mary didn't disguise her gender.) Since Mary was the only other woman on the ship, the two became fast friends, although there was some speculation that they were lovers as well, or in a ménage à trois with Jack. There is, of course, no way of knowing for sure whether or not they were lovers, since it wasn't exactly like Hogarth was under the bed sketching.*

Mary Read was born in Devon, England, sometime around 1695. Like many of our scandalous women, she had a rough childhood. Her father, who was a sailor, went off to sea soon after she was born, and her half brother, Mark, passed away soon afterward. Mary and her mother waited for years for her father to return but to no avail. In desperation, Mary's mother disguised her as a boy in order to keep her paternal grandmother supporting them. It seems Grandma preferred boys to girls. Mary spent her early childhood pretending to be her dead half brother.

When Mary turned thirteen her grandmother finally passed away. Needing to find work, Mary (still disguised as a boy) managed to find employment as a footboy to a wealthy Frenchwoman who lived in London. After a few months, Mary was bored and left, finding work on a man-of-war. After a few years, she became bored again and joined the army, where she met her future husband, a Flemish soldier whose name is lost to history. After confessing her gender to him, they left the army and opened an inn, called the Three Horseshoes, near Castle Breda in Holland. Unfortunately, Mary's husband died after a few months. Despondent, and

---

* William Hogarth (1697–1764) was a major artist, printmaker, and cartoonist most famous for *A Harlot's Progress* and *A Rake's Progress*.

unable to go back to the army since it was peacetime, Mary joined a Dutch ship on its way to the Caribbean, where it was attacked by Calico Jack. The captured crew was forced to become pirates, a way of life that turned out to suit Mary just fine.

Mary and Anne proved to be more than the equal of any of the men on board ship. Dressed in men's clothing, Anne was often a member of the boarding party when they attacked a ship and, along with Mary, was responsible for the deaths of many sailors, including shipmates who crossed them the wrong way. A washerwoman named Dorothy Thomas who was detained by the pirates testified that the two women wore "men's jackets and long trousers and handkerchiefs wrapped around their heads . . . a machete and pistol in their hands." (When they weren't fighting, they dressed in women's clothing.)

Mary fell in love with one of the crew, a man named Tom Deane. Deane was not a natural pirate; like Mary he had been pressed into service when Calico Jack captured his ship. When he got into a quarrel with a more experienced crew member, Mary, knowing that her lover stood no chance against him in a duel, picked her own quarrel with the older man and challenged him to a duel that would take place prior to her lover's duel. Mary killed the older man, but not before revealing to him her gender.

In October 1720, Captain Barnet, an ex-pirate who was now a commander in the British navy, attacked Rackham's anchored ship. The ship was vulnerable to attack. Almost the entire crew on board was drunk, celebrating a victory, for they had captured a Spanish commercial ship. The fight was short because only Mary and Anne were sober enough to resist. The rest of the crew cowered down in the hold. Read, incensed at their cowardice, shot several rounds into the hole, killing one man.

The crew of the *Revenge* was taken to Port Royal to stand

trial, which was a huge sensation due to the sex of Anne Bonny and Mary Read, who were reviled for daring to step outside the proscriptive bounds for females. The women were tried separately from the men, who testified to their cruelties. They were the only two women ever convicted of piracy during its so-called golden age. During her trial, when Mary Read was asked why she had chosen the life of a pirate, she replied that "as to hanging, it is no great hardship, for were it not for that, every cowardly fellow would turn pirate and so unfit the seas that men of courage must starve."

Mary and Anne obtained stays of execution by claiming they were pregnant. While Anne may have escaped the hangman's noose completely due to the influence of her father, Mary Read died in prison either from fever or in childbirth in 1721. She's buried in St. Catherine Parish in Jamaica. What happened to Anne afterward is a matter of speculation. It's possible that she went back to live with her father on his plantation in South Carolina. However, having had a taste of freedom from the restrictions of being a woman in the eighteenth century, wouldn't she have been more likely to have either gone back to piracy or settled down somewhere on another of the islands?

The *Oxford Dictionary of National Biography* entry on Anne states, "Evidence provided by the descendants of Anne Bonny suggests that her father managed to secure her release from gaol and bring her back to Charles Town, South Carolina, where she gave birth to Rackam's [*sic*] second child. On 21 December 1721 she married a local man, Joseph Burleigh, and they had eight children. She died in South Carolina, a respectable woman, at the age of eighty-four and was buried on 25 April 1782." Calico Jack wasn't so lucky. On the day he was to hang, he asked for special permission to see Anne on his way to the gallows. Anne coldly told him, "I'm sorry to see you here, but had you fought like a man, you need not have been hanged like a dog." Anne Bonny and Mary Read defied convention to live an adventurous life. So next time you're on the Pirates of the Caribbean ride at Disneyland, lift a glass of grog to celebrate the lives of these astonishing women.

# Lady Hester Stanhope
### 1776–1839

*I like traveling of all things; it is a constant change of ideas.*
—LADY HESTER STANHOPE

Born in the Age of Revolution, Lady Hester Stanhope is remembered today as a passionate and intrepid traveler in an age when women were discouraged from being adventurous. She was a woman who thrived at the center of British politics, spent over thirty years in the Middle East dressed like a man, took younger men for lovers, and died destitute and alone in an isolated Lebanese village. The story of her life from drawing room to desert was marked by scandal and intrigue.

Lady Hester was born in 1776 at Chevening in Kent to a distinguished and eccentric family of adventurers and statesmen. Her name, Hester, was a favorite name of her maternal relatives, the Pitts, and a rather unusual and unconventional name for the period. From birth, she was a headstrong and domineering child, determined to have her own way. Raised by a succession of nannies and governesses, she alternately bullied and smothered her younger siblings. A rambunctious tomboy, Hester was a demon on horseback, but had no use for the feminine arts of embroidery and music. At the age of eight, she commandeered a rowboat and tried to make her way to France. She might have made it, too, if her furious governesses hadn't come after her. As a young woman, when her father forbade her to attend the royal review at their neighbor Lord Romney's, where all the gentry of Kent gathered to pay homage to the sovereign, she caused a sensation when she showed up without a chaperone. She charmed George III, who wanted to whisk her off to Windsor much to the queen's chagrin.

Hester was considered to be the favorite of her father's children, when he remembered their existence. Certainly she was the only one of the earl's six children who wasn't afraid of him, for she stood up to him on numerous occasions in her siblings' defense. The third Earl Stanhope was a brilliant but eccentric scientist and inventor who also had strange ideas about education, including for girls, sending Hester to tend turkeys on the common. He also had an unpredictable temper. Father and daughter got along swimmingly until the day he held a knife to her throat.

Fleeing her father's tyranny, she went to live with her uncle William Pitt the Younger.* When he returned to power as prime minister in 1804, Hester was in her element, acting as a political hostess, his unofficial adviser, and a go-between with those who hoped to curry favor with her uncle. This was the happiest period of her life, where she was in the thick of things. Tall and striking,

---

* William Pitt the Younger (1759–1806) became the youngest prime minister in British history in 1783, when he was twenty-four; he held office until 1801 when he resigned over the question of Catholic emancipation. His father, William Pitt the Elder, had also been prime minister and was awarded the title of Earl of Chatham for his services to the crown.

with a bawdy sense of humor, she loved to make off-color jokes that shocked the more staid members of society. Disdaining women as frivolous, Hester was happiest in the company of men who were handsome, intelligent, and slightly in love with her. She had many admirers, including Beau Brummel and her cousin Lord Camelford, but no offers of marriage. Hester was too independent and outspoken for most men to consider her for a wife. Her uncle remarked once that he did not know whether she was an angel or a devil.

When Hester met handsome man-about-town Granville Leveson-Gower, her uncle's protégé, she fell violently in love for the first time. She made her feelings obvious not just to Granville but to everyone in society. Gossip spread, particularly when his visits to 10 Downing Street necessitated an overnight stay. But Granville never had any intention of marrying her; if anything he was more interested in her connection to Pitt than to her. Her uncle decided to take matters in hand, shipping Granville off to Russia as an ambassador. Granville gave the old excuse that he was in love with someone else and decamped. Distraught by his rejection, Hester tried to commit suicide by swallowing poison. Shattered, she wrote to a friend, "My heart points like a compass to the North." Hester retreated to Walmer Castle to lick her wounds while rumors flew that she had a miscarriage.

When Pitt finally expired after years of hard drinking he made sure that Hester was taken care of with a pension of twelve hundred pounds a year, a pitiful sum for an aristocratic woman used to living in high style. It was quite a comedown for Hester, after being so close to the corridors of power. Her status had dropped and it was intolerable. She was suddenly confronted with genteel poverty, caught between two worlds, among other things unable to afford a coach and horses, though walking in London without a maid was something only prostitutes did. "A poor gentlewoman is the worst thing in the world," she declared.

After her brother's death in Spain fighting Napoleon, Hester decided to leave England to travel. Her brother James was due to rejoin his regiment in Cadiz; Hester planned to accompany him and then continue on to Sicily and beyond. She hired a young physician, Charles Meryon, as a medical companion. Wtih her maid, Meryon, and her brother James, Hester used her former position to demand transport from the Royal Navy to Gibraltar. She left England in 1810, not knowing then that she would never see her homeland again. As she drew further away from England, the years of grief dropped away, she looked younger, and her old vitality returned. She cut her hair short, which suited her. In Gibraltar, Hester was feted by polite society. At a dinner party, she met Michael Bruce, who was twelve years younger than her. He was highly educated and charming, with a rich father who'd made his fortune in India. Meryon, who disliked him, conceded that "he was handsome enough to move any lady's head."

They became lovers and travel companions, flouting convention. But Hester wasn't stupid; she knew that one day it would have to end. His father had plans for Michael to have a political career. Not caring a fig about her own reputation but worried about his, she wrote his father a letter stating her intentions toward his son. "At this very moment, while loving him to distraction, I look forward to the period when I must resign him to some thrice happy woman really worthy of him." It wasn't long before news of their affair reached England, and Hester's brother James was shocked, challenging Michael to a duel.

They traveled on to Greece and Turkey; from Constantinople

they planned to head to Cairo in Egypt. She had no purposes for her travels, although at one point she came up with the hare-brained scheme of getting permission to travel to France, where she imagined she would ingratiate herself with Napoleon and study his character in order to report back to the English a way that they could defeat him. Fortunately the French ambassador thought better of issuing her a passport, thereby putting the kibosh on what could have turned out to be an international incident.

While shipwrecked on Rhodes, Hester's party lost all their clothes and had to wear Turkish costumes. Lady Hester found them so comfortable and convenient that she adopted the outfit for the rest of her life. As she traveled in style throughout the Middle East, spending lavishly, rumors spread in the region that she was an English princess. While no one knew who she was, everyone sensed that she must be someone of great importance and must be treated as such. She was received in state by the pasha, Mehmet Ali, in Cairo. She traveled to Jerusalem and Acre and other, lesser-known cities.

When she reached Damascus, Lady Hester refused to wear the veil or change out of her men's clothes to enter the city, despite the warnings she received that it was an anti-Christian community. Instead she rode in unveiled at midday. The people of Damascus didn't know what hit them, but their amazement turned to enthusiasm and she was hailed as a queen. In 1813, she decided to travel to Palmyra, site of Queen Zenobia's ancient kingdom, despite the route going through a desert filled with potentially dangerous Bedouins. Only three Englishmen had attempted the trip before, and all had failed. Dressing as a Bedouin, Hester took with her a caravan of twenty-two camels to carry all her baggage. The local Bedouins were so impressed by her courage that they came to see her. When she arrived in Palmyra, she was crowned in celebration. From then on, she became known as "Queen Hester."

That was the high point of Hester's life. When her lover, Michael Bruce, learning of his father's illness, planned to return to England, he proposed marriage. Hester refused. She had made a promise to his father and she intended to keep it. There was nothing for her back home. In the Middle East she was considered somebody. Although she had high hopes that she and Michael would have a long, loving correspondence as friends, it was not to be. He wrote her only three times over an eighteen-month period after his return. His offer to send her a thousand pounds a year was also another empty promise. Hester was left to live on her pension from the government, which should have gone far in the Middle East but not for a woman who was used to living and traveling in high style.

Part of the problem was that Hester opened her doors to any British traveler who came her way, entertaining them lavishly. She also gave sanctuary to numerous refugees during episodes of civil war in Lebanon. She had no intentions of downsizing just because she had no money. In 1815, Hester decided to mount an expedition to search for buried treasure in the city of Ascalon after discovering clues in an ancient parchment. After receiving permission from the sultan, she requested funds from the British government but was denied. The expedition's only find was a large statue, which Hester destroyed for fear of being accused of smuggling antiquities; this act earned her enmity from generations of archeologists appalled that she would destroy an artifact. The cost of the expedition increased her already burdensome financial problems.

Her faithful maid died in 1828, and Charles Meryon left her finally to return to England in 1831, where he married and started a family of his own. But he returned twice to see her, worried about her health and safety. She'd moved to Djoun, a remote abandoned monastery in the Lebanese mountains. Ruling her household of thirty slaves and servants with a mixture of laxity and an iron fist, she turned more and more to Eastern mysticism and medicine. Her eccentricities increased as she began to lose her grip on reality. She began to believe that the Mahdi, the ruler expected by some Muslims to establish a reign of righteousness throughout the world, was about to appear and make her his bride.

Her pension was finally cut off by the government to pay off her debts. She sent a constant stream of letters to Lord Palmerston, the prime minister, and Queen Victoria herself, but her letters were never answered. She eventually became a recluse, and her servants took the opportunity to steal whatever they could get their hands on to sell to pay their wages. Increasingly she would only see visitors after dark, and then would only let them see her hands and face. After her death, the British consul found thirty-five rooms full of junk and scavenging cats.

She was buried in her garden at Djoun, until her tomb was destroyed during a civil war. Reburied in the garden of the British ambassador's summer residence, she rested there in peace until 2004, when her ashes were scattered over the ruins of her former home. Hester would probably have been forgotten if it hadn't been for the faithful Meryon, who wrote three volumes of memoirs about his travels with her, giving the world a picture of a woman who chose the excitement of travel and adventure into the unknown, mysterious Middle East instead of the constricted life of a spinster in London's regimented society.

# Anna Leonowens
### 1831–1913

*Everyone has the power to make of life a living poem or else a dead letter.*
—ANNA TO HER DAUGHTER AVIS, JUNE 2, 1880

On the ides of March 1862, Anna Leonowens arrived in Bangkok on the little steamer *Chao Phya* along her son, Louis, age six, clinging to her skirts; his ayah; and a large Newfoundland dog named Bessy. The Bangkok air was already thick with humidity that made it hard to breathe. She was thirty years old, widowed, and about to start a new life as the governess at the royal court of Siam. A showy gondola shaped like a dragon and lit by blazing torches drew up alongside the steamer. To her shock, she was greeted by a bare-chested man wearing nothing but a sarong who turned out to be the prime minister. After being questioned incessantly through an interpreter, Anna haughtily demanded to be taken to their accommodations. When she was told that he had no knowledge of the arrangements, she burst into tears of mortification. It was an inauspicious beginning to an amazing adventure.

Anna's story would later be immortalized first by American missionary Margaret Landon and then by the team of Rodgers and Hammerstein in the hit musical *The King and I.** The real-life story of Anna Leonowens is far more fascinating than the romanticized tale of the Victorian governess who showed the King

---

* Anna was not the only one in her family to become famous. Her great-nephew William Henry Pratt took up acting and changed his name to Boris Karloff. Unfortunately they never met.

of Siam how to waltz. From the moment that Anna Leonowens disembarked that day, she reinvented herself, obscuring the origins of her life and inventing a new life for herself as a proper Victorian lady. During the rest of her lifetime, Anna's deception was never discovered. Like many other women who reinvent themselves, Anna actually became the character that she created. The ruse allowed Anna to lead a wildly adventurous and influential life. She remains the only foreigner to spend years inside the royal harem of Siam. She became a travel writer, crossed Russia on her own, immigrated to the United States, where she became a well-known author who hobnobbed with the literary figures of her day, and finally in her seventies settled down in Canada to help raise her eight grandchildren.

Anna Harriette Emma Edwards was born a poor, mixed-raced army brat in 1831 in Ahmadnagar, India. Her father was an enlisted soldier in the Sappers and Miners of the Indian army who died several months before she was born. Her mother, who was of Anglo-Indian heritage, married another enlisted soldier six weeks after Anna's birth. Anna and her half siblings grew up in the army barracks, with only a screen dividing their cramped back corner from the noise of the rest of the soldiers. Although the living and sanitary conditions were poor, it was a vibrant place to grow up. The family moved constantly due to her stepfather's work with the company before they settled permanently in Poona. One gift of her childhood that Anna developed was a lifelong interest in other cultures, which would prove to be her greatest asset.

Anna attended a regiment school, typically a one-room classroom filled with kids of all ages. The schools used what was called the Madras system, where the older kids taught the younger ones. She did well in school, and it left her with a hunger to continue to learn more. As she got older, no doubt Anna was picked to teach the younger children. By the time she was eighteen, she probably had several years of teaching under her belt. As well as English, Anna also spoke Hindi, Persian, and Marathi, and began learning Sanskrit. After a yearlong courtship, at the age of eighteen, she married on Christmas Day in 1849 a young Irishman named Thomas Leon Owens, who worked as a clerk in the commissary general's office.

After the death of their two oldest children, the couple immigrated to Australia to seek a fresh start, which caused a rift with her family. Both of her surviving children, Avis and Louis, were born in Perth. But Australia proved not to be the paradise they had hoped for. Anna had tried to open a school for young ladies but it failed. Instead the little family moved to Penang, Malaysia, where Thomas managed a hotel until he died in 1859 of apoplexy.

After her husband's death, Anna could have repaired the rift with her family and gone back to India. She would have probably found it easy to remarry as her mother and grandmother had done. Anna chose to be independent instead and journeyed to Singapore. It meant she would need to completely reinvent herself as a genteel widowed Englishwoman. The stigma attached to being of mixed heritage was huge. Deciding to become a teacher, Anna knew that no British officer would allow their children to be taught by a mixed-race woman. She created a new background, including just enough true details of her life to make it easy to remember. Singapore's other advantage: no one knew her there and it would be easier to maintain the fiction.

Anna's new story was that she was born in Wales to an army captain, and that she lived with family friends until she was fifteen. Her father was killed by Sikhs during the rebellion in Lahore. Not getting along with her stepfather, she met a reverend and his wife who recognized her aptitude for languages and in 1849 they took her with them on a tour through Egypt and Palestine. Returning to India, she married Tom Owens, who she now claimed was an army major. After the loss of her first two children, she and her husband moved to London for three years, until he was assigned to Singapore. Her husband later died of heatstroke during a tiger hunt.

The chance of a lifetime dropped into her lap when she heard that King Mongkut of Siam was looking for an English governess to teach his children. He had been burned by the wives of the American missionaries he'd hired, who had tried to convert his children to Christianity. It had taken him several years before he decided to try again and he still had not found a suitable replacement. Among the British in Singapore, pickings were slim. And not many Englishwomen were willing to leave the relative safety of the British colony for the wilds of Siam. Anna had a deep and abiding interest in other cultures since her upbringing in India and she was available. After three years, her school was not doing too well, thanks to the inability of British army officers to pay their fees on time, although it cemented her reputation as an educator. The move to Siam seemed to offer respectability and security, and a chance to move away from the prying eyes of Singapore society. Although she asked for 150 Singapore dollars, she settled for 100. The job was hers.

Before she left for Siam, she sent her daughter, Avis, to boarding school in England. She did so secure in the knowledge that her daughter would be getting the English education that she herself claimed to have. Since Louis was still young, he stayed with his mother. Siam was the first place that Anna lived that was not a British colony. She was venturing into new and unfamiliar territory. Anna didn't meet her new employer until she had been in

Siam for several weeks, and she almost blew it when she cheekily replied to his question about her age by replying that she was 150. Fortunately the king had a sense of humor.

Although she later portrayed him in her books as a combination of Genghis Khan and Krusty the Clown, her new employer, King Mongkut, was a frail and ascetic former Buddhist priest who had ascended the throne upon the death of his half brother. His years as a priest traveling around the country gave him a unique opportunity to see the lives of his subjects up close. Like Anna, he was fluent in several languages, and he was a strong believer in the power of education. King Mongkut wanted his children to be prepared to deal with the West, to have the tools to keep Siam independent. Siam would be the only nation in Asia not to be colonized by the West.

So was there any hanky-panky going on between the king and his new English governess? Sorry to burst musical theater lovers' bubbles, but no. The king was not only pushing sixty, but he had plenty of nubile women in his harem to satisfy his needs. Anna was over thirty, tall, independent, and opinionated. She was also English, of the very people that Mongkut was trying to keep at bay. On Anna's part, her husband was the only man that she had ever loved, and she'd lost him. There would be no other man in her life but her son. The famous waltz scene and the longing glances in the musical and film are just romantic fiction.

Anna had been given a unique opportunity, to educate Mongkut's wives and children, including his heir, Chulalongkorn. She soon found that she was expected not only to teach but also to help Mongkut with his correspondence in English and French and to serve as a sounding board, providing her perspective on Western attitudes and customs. Anna, however, made it clear from the beginning that she was not one of Mongkut's servants. In what could have been a foolhardy move, she insisted on accommodations away from the claustrophobic atmosphere of the palace so that she could have a measure of privacy.

Mongkut had two failings in Anna's eyes. One, he seemed to condone slavery and he required his subjects to grovel on the ground at his approach. The second was the royal harem. Although she wasn't shocked at the idea of the harem itself, she was disturbed at the life the women were forced to lead. It was a life she found intolerable: confined, under constant surveillance, utterly dependent upon the king's whim. Women in the harem included wives, concubines, slaves, the king's sisters and aunts, and dependents of the previous monarch. Anna had free access to the women's quarters. She played with their children, told them stories of life outside the harem, and answered their questions about her life. Soon they saw her as their champion, whispering their grievances in her ear, hoping she would take up their cause with the king.

Anna knew nothing about Siamese history. Because of her ignorance, she had no idea how far Siam had come under Mongkut's reign. The king had hired Western mercenaries to train Siam's troops. He had signed trade agreements with several countries, including England and the United States. Under his reign, Bangkok became an international city as more and more Western businessmen flocked to the country, bringing with them Western technology and innovation, which Mongkut embraced.

Anna's time in Siam might have been more enjoyable if she had kept to her role as governess and secretary. Instead she took him to task about the harem and about the issue of slavery, treating him as if he weren't aware of the need for reform. Anna, who was an admirer of Harriet Beecher Stowe, later claimed that her reading *Uncle Tom's Cabin* to Chulalongkorn led him to reform the

Siamese system of slavery when he became king after Mongkut's death. It certainly wouldn't be surprising if she had used the book in the schoolroom, not as a novel, but as a historical resource, to explain to her students the evils of slavery and their consequences. However, slavery in Siam was different than in the West; often it was voluntary and slaves could buy their freedom.

The king didn't appreciate her sticking her nose where it didn't belong. King Mongkut was an absolute monarch who wasn't used to having his actions questioned, least of all by a woman. In the end her meddling may actually have postponed certain reforms, because the king had no intention of letting Anna think that she had influenced him. To show her who was boss, he refused to give her the agreed-upon raise after she had been there three years and piled on more work.

So why didn't he kick his mouthy governess to the curb? Despite her crusading, the king was pleased with her work and the attention she gave his wives and children. She had taken care of his favorite child, and Anna's favorite pupil, Fa-Ying, when she was dying of cholera. As a sign of his gratitude he had elevated her status to Chao Khun Kru (Lord Most Excellent Teacher), given her an estate, and made her a noble. She inspired his children to learn English, she had an ear for languages, and her help was invaluable with his correspondence.

Anna left Siam in the summer of 1867 on the same ship that had brought her to Bangkok years before. She had had enough. Although her position carried great respect and even a degree of political influence, she was overworked and underpaid and had come to be regarded by the king as a "difficult woman and more difficult than generality." She wasn't well—she'd been ill with cholera twice, and she'd been attacked by unknown assailants twice and threatened more than once. She also missed her daughter, Avis. Five years was a long time to be apart from a child, and Anna dearly loved her children.

The plan was for her and her son, Louis, to travel to England to pick up Avis and then visit her husband's relatives in Ireland, where she would put Louis in boarding school. She would then return to Siam. The plan changed when on an impulse she decided to take Avis on a trip to the United States. It had been a dream of hers ever since she met her first American friend in Singapore. It was a trip that lasted ten years. The question of whether or not to return to Siam was moot with King Mongkut's death in 1868, his son ascending the throne as King Chulalongkorn.

After an attempt at running a school on Staten Island floundered, Anna decided to reinvent herself again, this time as an author. Through a friend she'd met in Singapore she had made the acquaintance of James Field, editor of the *Atlantic Monthly*. Putting pen to paper, Anna began contributing articles about her life in Siam, including "The Favorite of the Harem," which the *New York Times* called in its review "an Eastern love story, having apparently a strong basis of truth." She wrote two volumes of memoirs, which earned her immediate fame, and an entrée to literary circles in New York and Boston where she was able to meet Harriet Beecher Stowe, the woman whose work had inspired her for so long.

Both memoirs, *The English Governess at the Siamese Court* and *The Romance of the Harem*, were heavily fictionalized, exaggerating and fabricating parts of the story to attract a general reader and increase sales. Her accounts ascribed acts of cruelty to King Mongkut, which slandered his reputation in the West, and which unfortunately reinforced the image of the Siamese as backward. While she praised his virtues and reforms, she also wrote that he was "envious, revengeful, as fickle and petulant as he was subtle and cruel," that he bullied his wives, terrorized his servants, and trusted no one. Some reviewers and readers thought her writing showed ingratitude toward the man who had paid her salary and who had been nothing but kind to her and her son. The Thai government allegedly tried to buy up the whole first printing to destroy it. To the Siamese, the portrayal was a sacrilege. Mongkut was considered divine by his people.

In 1897, while traveling in London, she had a reunion with her old pupil King Chulalongkorn. It was an affectionate meeting, the king expressing his thanks in person, but he also took her to task for what she wrote about his father. Her granddaughter Avis Fyshe wrote that the king "expressed sorrow that she had pictured his father as a 'wicked old man' in her books. He said, 'You made all the world laugh at him, Mem. Why did you do it?' 'Because I had to write the truth,' was her answer."

Anna passed away in 1913 at the age of eighty-three, after spending her final three years bedridden after a stroke. The story of Anna Leonowens and the King of Siam might have been forgotten if it hadn't been for an American missionary named Margaret Landon, who discovered Anna's books while living in Thailand. Armed with two hundred pages of a biography by Avis Fyshe, along with letters and other documents, Landon filtered Anna's story through her own perceptions of Thailand. Margaret Landon's book was published in 1944 and became an immediate success, selling over a million copies and being translated into twenty languages. It was later adapted into a movie, *Anna and the King*, as well as the hit Broadway musical *The King and I*.

Anna's story is remarkable in that she was able to successfully reinvent herself and live an independent life in an era when women had very little personal freedom. It took extraordinary courage for her to leave a life that she was familiar with to live and work in a strange country with only her child for company. She had a front-row seat in Siam in the decades when the ruler was trying to bring his kingdom into the modern, Western world while maintaining its independence and traditions. She was not afraid to stand up for her rights and for the rights of those she felt were oppressed. Her writings captured the imagination of the West and created interest in Siam. But as one of the first westerners to write about the country, Anna is now remembered for having created an enduring although largely inaccurate portrait of Siam in the nineteenth century.

# Gertrude Bell
## 1868–1926

*We people of the west can always conquer, but we can never hold Asia—that seemed to me to be the legend written across the landscape.*

—GERTRUDE BELL

They called her "the Desert Queen," but that title scarcely begins to encompass the life of Gertrude Bell or her accomplishments. Leaving her comfortable world behind, she explored, mapped, and excavated the Middle East. At one time, she was considered the most powerful woman in the British Empire. Along with T. E. Lawrence, she not only had a role in the Arab revolt against the Turks during World War I but also helped to shape the modern state of

Iraq. Today she is best remembered as one of the foremost chroniclers of British imperialism in the Middle East.

A tall, imposing redhead with piercing green eyes, Gertrude Bell
was born in 1868 into a life of privilege and ease. From birth it was
clear that she possessed the same intellect, energy, drive, and determination that characterized all the Bells. Smart as a whip, she convinced her parents of the wisdom of further education, enrolling at
Lady Margaret Hall, one of only two women's colleges at Oxford.

Gertrude thrived at Oxford although she chafed at the restrictions on women, including that they be chaperoned when they left
campus. She also had to deal with the misogyny of the male students and professors. One professor required the female students
to sit with their backs to him during class. She was supremely self-
confident from the start and wasn't afraid to debate her professors.
With her boundless energy, Gertrude graduated with a first-class

degree in modern his-
tory in two years, the
first woman to do so.
Her achievement landed
her in the *Times* of London. It would not be the
last time that Gertrude's
accomplishments made
her newsworthy.

Despite her ad-
vanced education, Ger-
trude was still expected
to make her debut in
society, marry well, and
raise children. At the
age of twenty-one, she

was already three years older than the rest of the debutantes. She spent several months under the guidance of her aunt and uncle in Bucharest, polishing her rough edges, turning her from bluestocking into ingénue. A presentation at court and a formal party announced that she was in the market for a husband. In London she made the expected rounds of parties and balls, where she smiled and laughed, but again she chafed against the rules that required a chaperone to attend an exhibition or even to go shopping.

But as much fun as Gertrude was having, it was a difficult time for her. Frankly, most of the young men she met bored her to tears. They were nice enough but none of them were her intellectual equal or as well traveled, nor could they hold a candle to her adored father. After three years, Gertrude was still on the shelf and facing possible spinsterhood. While she enjoyed the company of men, she refused to change her personality to find a husband, to be docile, silent, and always agreeable.

Just when she had given up looking, she fell in love with both a man and a region. The man was Henry Cadogan, grandson of the Earl of Cadogan, first secretary at the British embassy in Teheran. Ten years older than her twenty-four, he was handsome, well educated, charming, and a brilliant sportsman. They spent their days sightseeing, having picnics, and reading Persian poetry to each other. She fell under his spell and the sensuality of the East that he described. He proposed, but her parents made inquiries and discovered that he had gambling debts. A decision was made for the couple to wait until Henry had sufficient income to be able to support Gertrude. When he died a year later from pneumonia, she was heartbroken.

But her love affair with Persia and the Middle East was just beginning. She continued her studies of the Persian language and published her first two books, one a travelogue called *Persian*

*Pictures*, the other a translation of the poetry of the Sufi poet Hafiz. Restless, she left the drawing rooms of Mayfair behind, to conquer unconquerable mountains, removing her skirt to climb in her underclothes. Always a proper lady, she soon put it back on when she'd reached the top. Traveling around the world, she developed a passion for archeology and languages. By her midthirties, Gertrude was fluent in French, German, and Persian and had a working knowledge of Turkish and Italian.

Falling under the spell of the desert, Getrude studied Arabic and was soon riding sidesaddle, wearing a special divided skirt, alone with a guide, a cook, and two muleteers. Traveling in high style, she brought all the comforts of home with her: crates filled with Wedgwood china, crystal stemware, table linens, tea service, volumes of Shakespeare, a fur coat for cold desert nights, and a canvas tub for long, hot baths. To fool officials who might search her luggage, she kept her pistols tucked in her underwear. A clotheshorse, Gertrude saw no reason not to wear an evening dress just because she was in the desert. Plus, she knew the sheiks would judge her by her possessions and gifts and act accordingly. Gertrude was unafraid to venture into areas that few women, let alone men, had penetrated, including the domain of the Druze, a closed Muslim sect, where she befriended their leader Yahya Bey.

Gertrude had the gift of gab; she could talk to anyone about anything. She talked politics and gossiped with the sheiks, sipping strong Turkish coffee and taking turns with the narghileh, a bubble pipe filled with tobacco, marijuana, or opium. Like her hosts, she ate with her hands, and she never flinched at what was served. With an eye for detail and gossip, she kept meticulous notes in her diary of meetings and conversations, comparing what she'd learned in one place with what she learned in another to see the big picture. Gertrude had been looking for a purpose in her life and she found it in the Middle East. She felt at home in the desert in a way that she never had in the drawing rooms of London. The Arabs excited and stimulated her imagination. There she felt she could make a real contribution. She shared her insider knowledge of the local tribes with the British consulates and embassies, and her opinions and recommendations were taken into account by those in power.

Gertrude crisscrossed the desert through the areas that make up most of present-day Syria, Turkey, and Mesopotamia, covering more than ten thousand miles on the map, traveling either by horseback or camel. She targeted her travels on archeological sites in unmapped territories, hoping to make some undiscovered find. Traveling in 1913 from Damascus to the desert of northern Arabia, the Nejd, where no westerner had traveled for twenty years, she was taken prisoner by the emir's uncle in Hayyil and held for nine days before she talked her way out with sheer bravado. Publishing her findings in several books, including *The Desert and the Sown*, her observations opened up the Arab deserts to the Western world.

During World War I, the Admiralty Intelligence Service in Cairo sought assistance from those with knowledge of prewar Arabia. Gertrude's ability to speak the language and her knowledge of the desert tribes made her uniquely qualified. She became the first woman officer in the history of British intelligence, although her designation as major was only a courtesy title. However, she was made a general staff officer, second grade. In Cairo, she became reacquainted with T. E. Lawrence, whom she had first met on an archeological dig in 1913. Her job was to organize and process data about the Arab tribes: her own, Lawrence's, and Major David

Shakespear's. The goal was see if the Arabs could be encouraged to join the British against the Turks, who were allied with the Germans in the war.

In 1916, Gertrude was sent to Basra to advise Sir Percy Cox, the chief political officer with the expeditionary force. She wrote reports on the Bedouin tribes and the Sinai peninsula, some of which were collected and produced as an instruction manual for British officers when they arrived in Basra. Her reports were noted as the clearest and most readable official documents that the Arab Bureau ever produced. In March 1917, after the British took Baghdad, Gertrude was given the title "oriental secretary." Her role was as a facilitator with the various tribes to convince them to support the British administration in the region, to listen to their concerns, and to assure them their rights would be maintained. The tribes trusted her, and called her Khatun, or "Desert Queen," or Umm al Muminin, "Mother of the Faithful," after the Prophet's wife Ayishah.

In 1917, Gertrude was named a Commander of the British Empire but she was not impressed. "I don't really care a button. It's rather absurd, and as far as I can see from the lists there doesn't appear to be much merit in this damn order." Gertrude wasn't dazzled by awards. She found it abhorrent that anyone would think that love of title or honors was her motivation.

After the collapse of the Ottoman Empire, Gertrude was asked to conduct an analysis of the situation in Mesopotamia and the options for future leadership of the region that is now Iraq. Gertrude's report came down on the side of Arab self-determination but her superior, A. T. Wilson, was an old-fashioned colonialist who still believed in the might of the British Empire. In 1921, Gertrude, Lawrence, and Percy Cox were among a select group at a conference in Cairo brought together to find a way to reduce the

British presence in the Middle East after the war. Throughout the conference, she worked tirelessly to promote the idea of creating the nation that we now know as Iraq, to be headed by Faisal, the son of Hassan bin Ali, Sharif of Mecca, one of the instigators in the Arab revolt against the Turks.

Until her death, Gertrude served on the Iraq British High Commission Advisory Group. She became a confidante of Faisal, helping him to achieve his election as king by introducing him to the tribes in the region and earning herself another nickname, "the Uncrowned Queen of Iraq." She founded the British School of Archeology in Iraq, as well as the Archeological Museum in Baghdad. But Gertrude soon found that working with the new king was not always easy. He could be secretive, manipulative, and too easily influenced. Her experience with him led her to declare, "You may rely on one thing, I'll never engage in creating kings again; it's too great a strain." But she remained in Iraq, working through illness and rarely taking vacations, worried that the region was still too unstable for her to leave for long.

Grieving not only the death of her brother Hugo but also another failed love affair, and feeling as if she was becoming irrelevant, Gertrude became depressed. On July 12, 1926, two days before her fifty-eighth birthday, she was found dead by her maid, a bottle of sleeping pills on her night table. It is unclear if it was a suicide attempt or an accidental overdose. There is speculation that on her last trip to England, she may have been diagnosed with a terminal illness, perhaps lung cancer. It would have been within Gertrude's character to end her life to spare her parents any suffering. She is buried in the British cemetery in Baghdad in the country that she loved and gave so much of her life for.

# Amelia Earhart
## 1897–1937

*When I undertake a task over all protest and in spite of all adversity, I
sometimes thrill with the realization that I am doing what I want to do.*

—AMELIA EARHART

Amelia Earhart was eleven when she saw a plane for the first time
at the Iowa State Fair in Des Moines. It was in 1908, only five
years after the Wright brothers made their historic flight at Kitty
Hawk in North Carolina. Airplanes were still unusual and people
were still amazed at the idea of a flying machine. Amelia, however,
was not impressed. "It was a thing of rusty wire and wood and not
at all interesting," she recalled years later. It would be years before
Amelia's passion for flying would be awakened. Nor did she know
that one day she would surpass the Wright brothers in the annals
of aviation.

From childhood, Amelia showed the fearlessness and initiative
that would one day make her America's best-known female pilot.
Amelia once built a roller coaster on the roof of her house after
seeing one at the World's Fair, but her mother made her take it
down. Although her mother would have preferred her to be a bit
more ladylike, she still sewed two gym suits with bloomers for
herself and her younger sister, Muriel. Her father also encouraged
her, taking her and her sister fishing and to play baseball.

While Amelia was working as a voluntary aid detachment
nurse in Toronto during World War I, a former patient, an officer
in the Royal Flying Corps, invited her to watch him fly out at the
local military airfield. Now watching the planes circling and tak-

ing off, as graceful as birds, something took hold inside of her. She soon had a fever for flying; it captured her imagination like nothing else. She spent her rare days off at the local airfield. "I hung around in my spare time and absorbed all I could." Once, while she and a friend were at the airfield, a pilot dove straight at them just for fun. Her friend ran for safety but Amelia stood her ground. "I did not understand it at the time, but I believe that little red airplane said something to me as it swished by."

Despite her new interest in flying, Amelia didn't take her first flight until she moved to Los Angeles in 1921 to live with her parents, who had reconciled there after a separation. It was her father who took her to an aerial meet at Daugherty Field out in Long Beach, paying ten dollars for Amelia to be taken up for her first flight. She had finally found her destiny. "As soon as we left the ground I knew I myself had to fly." When her father balked at the cost, Amelia offered to earn her own money to pay for her lessons. Feeling that a woman instructor would make her feel less self-conscious, Amelia took lessons from pioneer woman pilot Neta Snook. Neta charged her a dollar a minute for lessons. To pay for them, Amelia drove a gravel truck and worked for the phone company.

Before she'd even made her first solo flight, she bought her first plane, a Kinner Airstir named *Canary*, for two thousand dollars. Her first crash landing, in a cabbage patch, didn't dampen her enthusiasm for flying, although it did diminish her fondness for cabbage. Amelia began participating in a few "air rodeo" shows at local airfields. The money she earned help to pay for her expenses. In 1922, Amelia set the women's altitude record by reaching fourteen thousand feet. Although the record was broken only weeks later, it gave Amelia more confidence in her abilities. Soon she was being featured in the newspapers, including a small article in the *New York Times*, which shocked and appalled her relatives back in Kansas. They were of the opinion that a woman only appeared in the paper when she was born, when she got married, and when she died. Unfortunately for them, Amelia in a few short years would never be out of the news.

In 1928, one year after Charles Lindbergh's landmark flight across the Atlantic, Amelia received a phone call that changed her life. A group including socialite Amy Phipps Guest and publisher and promoter George P. Putnam were looking for a girl with the right image to be the first woman to fly across the Atlantic. The explorer Richard Byrd knew of Earhart through aviation circles and recommended her.

Amelia seemed to fit the bill. She had a reputation for being one of the most daring and skilled pilots around, always up for a challenge. It didn't hurt that she bore a striking resemblance to Charles Lindbergh. Despite the fact that she would be only a passenger and would not be paid for the trip, Amelia jumped at the chance to make history. "How could I refuse such a shining adventure?" she said. After a short interview, Amelia was told she was the girl. No one else was even interviewed.

On June 17, 1928, wearing a fur-lined flight suit, she left Trepassey Harbor, Newfoundland, along with pilot Wilmer Stultz and copilot Louis Gordon, on the *Friendship*. They landed twenty hours and forty minutes later at Burry Port, Wales. Since Amelia had no experience flying a plane with instruments, her job was limited to keeping the flight log. "Stultz did all the flying—had to. I was just baggage, like a sack of potatoes. Maybe someday I'll try it alone." But when they finally arrived at Southampton, in England, Stultz and Gordon were completely ignored in favor of Amelia.

Before the flight she was earning sixty dollars a month; now Amelia found herself famous overnight. She was "Lady Lindy" and "First Lady of the Air." After the tragedy of the First World War, America was looking for heroes. Amelia captured attention by being an all-American girl from the heartland. Tall and slim, with a boyish figure; short, tousled curls; and a ready smile, she seemed like everyone's daughter or sister. She struck a chord with the public. Young women were inspired by her and the older generation was reassured by her solid Midwestern persona; she was modest and abstained from alcohol and tobacco. On the surface, initially at least, she seemed shy and nervous about the attention, but underneath lay a core of steel and ambition.

As soon as the ticker tape parades were done, Amelia wrote her first book and embarked on a brutal lecture tour. Since Putnam was now managing Amelia, they were thrown in constant contact with each other and were immediately attracted. They shared the same sense of humor, were adventurous, and were devoted to keeping Amelia's name before the public. There was only one snafu to the burgeoning partnership: Putnam was married, with two children. Soon people began to notice the closeness between the two of them. Putnam's wife got wise to the situation and filed for a divorce.

Newly single Putnam pressed Amelia to marry him, but she wasn't convinced that marriage was for her. Her parents' marriage was no advertisement for the institution and she worried that it would curtail her freedom. "I'm still unsold about marriage. I don't want anything all of the time. . . . I think I may never be able to see marriage except as a cage." Putnam, however, was not a man to take no for an answer. On February 7, 1931, they were married; the only witnesses were one of his uncles and the judge's son. On their wedding day, Amelia handed George a letter, setting out the terms of their marriage. Fidelity was not asked for or required, she wrote, and she asked that they not interfere with each

other's work and keep their private life private. She also asked him
to let her go in a year if she wasn't happy. After the ceremony, there
was no honeymoon, and Amelia was back to work the next day.

Amelia's fame owed a great deal to Putnam. There were other
women flying, like Ruth Nichols and Elinor Smith, but Putnam
made sure that it was Amelia in the headlines. He'd already made
Lindbergh a household name; now he would do the same for her.
He took full advantage of the modern press, especially newsreels.
Amelia's face was everywhere, endorsing everything from chewing
gum to cars. Soon she was making more than thirty appearances a
month across the country. Her lectures, books, and magazine articles paid for her planes and she used them as a platform to promote causes she believed in, such as opportunities for women to
achieve equality in the still young aviation field.

Ironically for someone who achieved so much in the field of
aviation, Amelia was not a natural pilot. Although she was highly
intelligent, enthusiastic, and a fast learner, Amelia often made stupid mistakes, according to her old instructor, Neta Snook. She
once took off for a long flight without checking the fuel tank, and
she would often daydream while flying during a lesson. She never
learned Morse code or radio telegraphy. And she would crash, not
once, but again and again, on landings, on takeoffs. Putnam tried
to keep the news of her crashes out of the media as much as possible. Traveling all the time meant that Amelia's actual flying time
was limited, although she tried to fly to as many of her appearances as possible.

In 1932, Amelia decided on another transatlantic flight, only
this time she wouldn't be a passenger, she would be in the driver's
seat. Despite her fame, Amelia wanted to prove, not only to the
world, but also to herself, that she was the best woman pilot. Although she had set records and had several firsts under her belt,

Amelia hungered for more. Seven women had already perished in the attempt and no man since Lindbergh had flown across the Atlantic alone successfully. Amelia left Newfoundland in her Lockheed Vega five years to the day after Lindbergh left New York for Paris.

But being the first can be hazardous to one's health. The plane staggered through the fog covered in ice; the altimeter broke; gas dripped down her neck; the plane went into a sudden spin and almost plunged into the ocean; and she didn't land in Paris as planned but in Ireland. But she made it. Only Amelia's quick thinking and fast reflexes kept her in the air. After a flight lasting fourteen hours and fifty-six minutes, she landed in a pasture in Culmore in Northern Ireland. Mindful of publicity, Putnam had her restage her arrival for the cameras. For her attempts, Amelia earned the Distinguished Flying Cross from Congress, and the Gold Medal from the National Geographic Society.

Amelia wasn't done yet. In 1935, she became the first person to fly solo from Honolulu, Hawaii, to Oakland, California, winning a ten-thousand-dollar reward for her trouble. She continued her record breaking by becoming the first woman to fly from Los Angeles to Mexico City solo and then on from Mexico City to New York. From 1930 to 1935, Amelia set seven women's speed and distance aviation records in a variety of aircraft.

Amelia and Putnam realized that the public's appetite for record breaking had begun to die down and there were fewer left to break. Still Amelia had one more record that she wanted to make: "A new prize . . . one flight which I most wanted to attempt—a circumnavigation of the globe as near its waistline as could be." There were some who thought that Amelia was tempting fate with this trip but she ignored the criticism.

Since Amelia was on the faculty of Purdue University as a technical adviser to the Department of Aeronautics, the school partly financed the Lockheed L-10E Electra that she would fly in her around-the-world attempt. Putnam publicized her trip as a "flying laboratory" to justify the university's expenditure. Amelia had initially planned on it being a solo venture but she soon realized she needed help. She hired Fred Noonan as her second navigator; he had vast experience in both marine and flight navigation, but he had the reputation of being a heavy drinker.

Amelia made her first attempt on St. Patrick's Day in 1937; when she went to take off, she lost control of the plane and crashed, severely damaging the aircraft. For the first time in her life, she felt fear. While the plane was being repaired, Amelia decided to change her flight plan to travel west to east, leaving from Miami instead. The change in plans was due to changes in global wind and weather patterns. With only Fred Noonan on board, she took off on June 1. But she left behind crucial equipment, including her parachute, life raft, and wireless antenna.

After numerous stops in South America, Africa, India, and Southeast Asia, Amelia and Fred landed in Lae, New Guinea, on June 29, 1937. Amelia had flown for thirty days and twenty-two thousand miles by that point. Physically and mentally she was exhausted. The Electra didn't take off again until July 2, due to adverse weather conditions. Their intended destination was tiny Howland Island, where Amelia expected to refuel. Radio contact between Amelia and the U.S. Coast Guard was intermittent. While they could hear her, she couldn't hear them. The Electra never made it, disappearing somewhere in the Pacific Ocean.

Then began the most intensive search ever for a lost plane. Ten ships and sixty-five planes searched for two weeks but neither the plane nor the bodies were ever found. Theories still abound about what happened that fateful day. Was Amelia Earhart a spy for the government on a secret mission, using the around-the-world flight as cover? Was she rescued by the Japanese and interred in a prison camp during World War II? These are just a few of the imaginative theories surrounding her disappearance.

Amelia Earhart was the first modern American heroine, adored because she was daring and successful in a man's world. The most famous female aviator of the twentieth century, she achieved many firsts and opened up the field for women as pilots and engineers. Ironically, her disappearance kept her in the public consciousness more than if she had completed the flight. Hundreds of articles and books have been written about her in the more than seventy years since her plane disappeared, keeping her accomplishments alive for an entire generation of female aviators. Amelia lived her life as if she were invincible, but in the end she proved to be as mortal as anyone.

# Selected Bibliography

## 1. WARRIOR QUEENS

Chambers, Anne. *Granuaile: The Life and Times of Grace O'Malley c. 1530–1603.* Dublin: Wolfhound Press, 1979, 1998.

Davis-Kimball, Jeannine. *Warrior Women: An Archaeologist's Search for History's Hidden Heroines.* With Mona Behan. New York: Warner Books, 2002.

Holland, Barbara. *They Went Whistling: Women Wayfarers, Warriors, Runaways, and Renegades.* New York: Anchor Books, 2001.

Norton, Elizabeth. *She Wolves: The Notorious Queens of Medieval England.* London: History Press, 2008.

Sjoholm, Barbara. *The Pirate Queen: In Search of Grace O'Malley and Other Legendary Women of the Sea.* Emeryville, CA: Seal Press, 2004.

Swabey, Ffiona. *Eleanor of Aquitaine, Courtly Love, and the Troubadours.* Westport, CT: Greenwood Press, 2004.

Tyldesley, Joyce. *Cleopatra: Last Queen of Egypt.* New York: Basic Books, 2009.

Waldherr, Kris. *Doomed Queens: Royal Women Who Met Bad Ends, from Cleopatra to Princess Di.* New York: Broadway Books, 2008.

Weir, Alison. *Eleanor of Aquitaine.* New York: Ballantine Books, 2001.

## 2. WAYWARD WIVES

Bodanis, David. *Passionate Minds: Émilie du Châtelet, Voltaire, and the Great Love Affair of the Enlightenment.* New York: Crown, 2006.

Denlinger, Elizabeth Campbell. *Before Victoria: Extraordinary Women of the British Romantic Era.* New York: New York Public Library/Columbia University Press, 2005.

Douglass, Paul. *Lady Caroline Lamb: A Biography.* New York: Palgrave Macmillan, 2004.

Hodge, Jane Aiken. *Passion and Principle: The Loves and Lives of Regency Women.* London: John Murray, 1996.

Lovell, Mary S. *A Scandalous Life: The Biography of Jane Digby.* London: Fourth Estate, 1995.

Milford, Nancy. *Zelda: A Biography.* New York: Harper & Row, 1970.

Mitford, Nancy. *Voltaire in Love.* London: Hamish Hamilton, 1957.

Nicolson, Nigel. *Portrait of a Marriage: Vita Sackville-West and Harold Nicolson.* New York: Atheneum, 1973.

Schmidt, Margaret Fox. *Passion's Child: The Extraordinary Life of Jane Digby.* New York: Harper & Row, 1976.

Souhami, Diana. *Mrs. Keppel and Her Daughter.* New York: St. Martin's Press, 1996.

Wagner-Martin, Linda. *Zelda Sayre Fitzgerald: An American Woman's Life.* New York: Palgrave Macmillan, 2004.

Wallace, Irving. *The Nympho and Other Maniacs: The Lives, the Loves and the Sexual Adventures of Some Scandalous and Liberated Ladies.* New York: Pocket Books, 1971.


## 3. SCINTILLATING SEDUCTRESSES

Andrews, Allen. *The Royal Whore: Barbara Villiers, Countess of Castlemaine.* Philadelphia: Chilton, 1970.

Bentley, Toni. *Sisters of Salome.* New Haven, CT: Yale University Press, 2002.

Cawthorne, Nigel. *The Sex Lives of the Kings and Queens of England: An Irreverent Expose of the Monarchs from Henry VIII to the Present Day.* New York: Smithmark, 1994.

Denny, Joanna. *Anne Boleyn: A New Life of England's Tragic Queen*. New York: Da Capo Press, 2006.

Fraser, Antonia. *The Six Wives of Henry VIII*. New York: Random House, 1992.

Herman, Eleanor. *Sex with Kings: 500 Years of Adultery, Power, Rivalry, and Revenge*. New York: HarperCollins, 2004.

———. *Sex with the Queen: 900 Years of Vile Kings, Virile Lovers, and Passionate Politics*. New York: HarperCollins, 2006.

Hodge, Jane Aiken. *Passion and Principle: The Loves and Lives of Regency Women*. London: John Murray, 1996.

Morton, James. *Lola Montez: Her Life and Conquests*. London: Portrait Books, 2007.

Seymour, Bruce. *Lola Montez: A Life*. New Haven, CT: Yale University Press, 1996.

Shipman, Pat. *Femme Fatale: Loves, Lies, and the Unknown Life of Mata Hari*. New York: HarperCollins, 2007.

Starkey, David. *Six Wives: The Queens of Henry VIII*. New York: HarperCollins, 2003.

Williams, Kate. *England's Mistress: The Infamous Life of Emma Hamilton*. London: Arrow Books, 2006.

## 4. CRUSADING LADIES

Blackman, Ann. *Wild Rose: The True Story of a Civil War Spy*. New York: Random House, 2005.

Farquhar, Michael. *A Treasury of Foolishly Forgotten Americans: Pirates, Skinflints, Patriots, and Other Colorful Characters Stuck in the Footnotes of History*. New York: Penguin, 2008.

Gordon, Lyndall. *Vindication: A Life of Mary Wollstonecraft*. New York: HarperCollins, 2005.

Grace, Fran. *Carry A. Nation: Retelling the Life*. Bloomington: Indiana University Press, 2001.

LaPlante, Eve. *American Jezebel: The Uncommon Life of Anne Hutchinson, the Woman Who Defied the Puritans*. New York: HarperCollins, 2004.

Morgan, Edmund S. *The Puritan Dilemma: The Story of John Winthrop*. New York: Longman, 1999.

Ross, Ishbel. *Charmers and Cranks: Twelve Famous American Women Who Defied the Conventions.* New York: Harper & Row, 1965.

Tomalin, Claire. *The Life and Death of Mary Wollstonecraft.* New York: Penguin, 1992.

Vowell, Sarah. *The Wordy Shipmates.* New York: Riverhead Books, 2008.


## 5. WILD WOMEN OF THE WEST

Canfield, Gae Whitney. *Sarah Winnemucca of the Northern Paiutes.* Norman: University of Oklahoma Press, 1983.

Hudson, Lynn. *The Making of "Mammy Pleasant": A Black Entrepreneur in Nineteenth-Century San Francisco.* Urbana: University of Illinois Press, 2003.

Iversen, Kristen. *Molly Brown: Unraveling the Myth.* Boulder, CO: Johnson Books, 1999.

McLaird, James D. *Calamity Jane: The Woman and the Legend.* Norman: University of Oklahoma Press, 2005.

Riley, Glenda, and Richard W. Etulain, eds. *By Grit and Grace: Eleven Women Who Shaped the American West.* Golden, CO: Fulcrum, 1997.

———. *Wild Women of the Old West.* Golden, CO: Fulcrum, 2003.

Shirley, Gayle C. *More Than Petticoats: Remarkable Colorado Women.* Guilford, CT: TwoDot, 2002.

Temple, Judy Nolte. *Baby Doe Tabor: The Madwoman in the Cabin.* Norman: University of Oklahoma Press, 2007.

Turner, Erin H. *More Than Petticoats: Remarkable California Women.* Helena, MT: TwoDot, 1999.

———, ed. *Wise Women: From Pocahontas to Sarah Winnemucca, Remarkable Stories of Native American Trailblazers.* Guilford, CT: TwoDot, 2009.

Zanjani, Sally. *Sarah Winnemucca.* Lincoln: University of Nebraska Press, 2001.


## 6. AMOROUS ARTISTS

Ayral-Clause, Odile. *Camille Claudel: A Life.* New York: Abrams, 2002.

Bogle, Donald. *Brown Sugar: Over One Hundred Years of America's Black Female Superstars.* New York: Continuum, 1980, 2007.

Grunfeld, Frederic V. *Rodin: A Biography.* New York: Da Capo Press, 1998.

Herrera, Hayden. *Frida: A Biography of Frida Kahlo.* New York: Harper & Row, 1983.

Kurth, Peter. *Isadora: A Sensational Life.* New York: Little, Brown, 2001.

O'Meally, Robert G. *Lady Day: The Many Faces of Billie Holiday.* New York: Arcade, 1991.

Paris, Reine-Marie. *Camille: The Life of Camille Claudel, Rodin's Muse and Mistress.* Translated by Liliane Emery Tuck. New York: Little, Brown, 1989.

Rose, Phyllis. *Jazz Cleopatra: Josephine Baker in Her Time.* New York: Doubleday, 1989.

Rummel, Jack. *Frida Kahlo: A Spiritual Biography.* New York: Crossroads, 2000.

## 7. AMAZING ADVENTURESSES

Cordingly, David. "Anne Bonny (1698–1782)," in *Oxford Dictionary of National Biography.* New York: Oxford University Press, 2004.

Farquhar, Michael. *A Treasury of Foolishly Forgotten Americans: Pirates, Skinflints, Patriots, and Other Colorful Characters Stuck in the Footnotes of History.* New York: Penguin, 2008.

Gibb, Lorna. *Lady Hester: Queen of the East.* London: Faber and Faber, 2005.

Howell, Georgina. *Gertrude Bell: Queen of the Desert, Shaper of Nations.* New York: Farrar, Straus and Giroux, 2008.

Jones, Victoria Garrett. *Amelia Earhart: A Life in Flight.* New York: Sterling, 2009.

Keay, Julia. *With Passport and Parasol: The Adventures of Seven Victorian Ladies.* London: BBC Books, 1989.

Lovell, Mary S. *The Sound of Wings: The Life of Amelia Earhart.* New York: St. Martin's Press, 1989.

Morgan, Susan. *Bombay Anna: The Real Story and Remarkable Adventures of the King and I Governess.* Berkeley: University of California Press, 2008.

Yolen, Jane. *Sea Queens: Women Pirates Around the World.* Watertown, MA: Charlesbridge, 2008.

# On Page and Screen

The following is a brief list of the films and fiction featuring the scandalous women in this book to whet your appetite:

## CLEOPATRA

### Film

*Antony and Cleopatra* (1983), with Timothy Dalton and Lynn Redgrave
*Caesar and Cleopatra* (1945), with Claude Rains and Vivien Leigh
*Cleopatra* (1934), with Claudette Colbert, Henry Wilcoxon, and Warren William
*Cleopatra* (1963), with Elizabeth Taylor, Richard Burton, and Roddy McDowell
*Cleopatra* (1999), with Billy Zane, Timothy Dalton, and Rupert Graves
*Rome*, two seasons (2005–2007), with James Purefoy, Ciarán Hinds, and Polly Walker

### Fiction

*Antony and Cleopatra*, by Colleen McCullough
*Asterix and Cleopatra*, by Rene Goscinny, illustrated by Albert Uderzo
*Hands of Isis*, by Jo Graham (This book is more about Cleopatra's handmaiden Charmian but it's a wonderful look at the Cleopatra story through others' eyes.)

*Kleopatra*, by Karen Essex
*The Memoirs of Cleopatra*, by Margaret George
*The October Horse*, by Colleen McCullough
*Pharaoh* (*Kleopatra* volume II), by Karen Essex

## BOUDICA

### Film

*Warrior Queen* (2003), with Alex Kingston

### Fiction

The Boudica quadrilogy, by Manda Scott: *Dreaming the Eagle, Dreaming the Serpent-Spear, Dreaming the Hound, Dreaming the Bull*
*Boudica, Queen of the Iceni*, by Joseph E. Roesch
*Marion Zimmer Bradley's Ravens of Avalon*, by Diana L. Paxson
*Warrior Queen: The Story of Boudica, Celtic Queen*, by Alan Gold

## ELEANOR OF AQUITAINE

### Film

*The Lion in Winter* (1968), with Peter O'Toole, Katharine Hepburn, and Anthony Hopkins
*The Lion in Winter* (2003), with Patrick Stewart, Glenn Close, and Jonathan Rhys Meyers

### Fiction

*The Book of Eleanor*, by Pamela Kaufman
*Captive Queen*, by Alison Weir
*The Courts of Love*, by Jean Plaidy
*Duchess of Aquitaine*, by Margaret Ball
*Eleanor the Queen*, by Nora Lofts
The Henry II/Eleanor of Aquitaine trilogy, by Sharon Kay Penman: *When Christ and His Saints Slept, Time and Chance, Devil's Brood*
The Justin de Quincy mysteries, by Sharon Kay Penman (Eleanor of Aquitaine

is a featured character): *The Queen's Man, Cruel as the Grave, Dragon's Lair, Prince of Darkness*
*The Queen's Pawn*, by Christy English
*The Secret Eleanor*, by Cecelia Holland


## JOAN OF ARC

### Film

*Joan of Arc* (1948), with Ingrid Bergman and José Ferrer
*Joan of Arc* (1999), with Leelee Sobieski and Chad Willett
*The Messenger: The Story of Joan of Arc* (1999), with Milla Jovovich, John Malkovich, and Faye Dunaway

### Fiction

The Joan of Arc Tapestries series, by Ann Chamberlin (this series is historical fantasy, not straight historical fiction): *The Merlin of St. Gilles' Well, The Merlin of the Oak Wood, Gloria: The Merlin and the Saint*
*Warrior Girl: A Novel of Joan of Arc*, by Pauline Chandler


## GRACE O'MALLEY

### Fiction

*Grania: She-King of the Irish Seas*, by Morgan Llywelyn
*The Pirate Queen: The Story of Grace O'Malley, Irish Pirate*, by Alan Gold
*The Wild Irish*, by Robin Maxwell


## LADY CAROLINE LAMB

### Film

*Byron* (2003), with Jonny Lee Miller
*Lady Caroline Lamb* (1972), with Sarah Miles, Jon Finch, and Richard Chamberlain

**Fiction**

*Passion*, by Jude Morgan

## VIOLET TREFUSIS

**Film**

*Portrait of a Marriage* (1990), with Cathryn Harrison, David Haig, and Janet McTeer

## ZELDA FITZGERALD

**Film**

*Last Call* (2002), with Jeremy Irons and Sissy Spacek
*Last of the Belles* (1974), with Richard Chamberlain and Blythe Danner

**Fiction**

*Save Me the Waltz*, by Zelda Fitzgerald

## ANNE BOLEYN

**Film**

*Anne of the Thousand Days* (1969), with Richard Burton and Geneviève Bujold
*Henry VIII* (2003), with Ray Winstone, Charles Dance, and Helena Bonham Carter
*The Other Boleyn Girl* (2003), with Jared Harris, Jodhi May, and Natascha McElhone
*The Other Boleyn Girl* (2008), with Natalie Portman, Scarlett Johansson, and Eric Bana
*The Private Life of Henry VIII* (1933), with Charles Laughton and Merle Oberon
*The Six Wives of Henry VIII* (1970), with Keith Michell and Dorothy Tutin
*The Tudors*, seasons 1 and 2 (2007 and 2008), with Jonathan Rhys Meyers, Jeremy Northam, and Natalie Dormer

### Fiction

*Brief Gaudy Hour*, by Margaret Campbell Barnes
*The Concubine*, by Nora Lofts
*A Lady Raised High*, by Laurien Gardner
*Mademoiselle Boleyn*, by Robin Maxwell
*Murder Most Royal*, by Jean Plaidy
*The Other Boleyn Girl*, by Philippa Gregory
*The Queen of Subtleties*, by Suzannah Dunn
*The Secret Diary of Anne Boleyn*, by Robin Maxwell

## BARBARA PALMER

### Film

*The Lady and the Highwayman* (1989), with Hugh Grant and Emma Samms
*The Last King* (2003), with Rufus Sewell, Helen McCrory, and Rupert Graves

### Fiction

*The Loves of Charles II*, by Jean Plaidy
*Royal Harlot*, by Susan Holloway Scott

## EMMA HAMILTON

### Film

*I Remember Nelson* (1982), with Kenneth Colley, Geraldine James, and Tim Pigott-Smith
*That Hamilton Woman* (1941), with Vivien Leigh, Laurence Olivier, and Alan Mowbray

### Fiction

*Losing Nelson*, by Barry Unsworth
*Milady Hamilton*, by Robert Kail
The Nelson and Emma trilogy, by David Donachie: *On a Making Tide*, *Tested by Fate*, *Breaking the Line*

*Too Great a Lady: The Notorious, Glorious Life of Emma, Lady Hamilton,*
by Amanda Elyot
*The Volcano Lover,* by Susan Sontag

## LOLA MONTEZ

### Film

*Lola Montès* (1955), with Martine Carol, Peter Ustinov, and Anton Walbrook

### Fiction

*An Invitation to Dance,* by Marion Urch

## MATA HARI

### Film

*Mata Hari* (1931), with Greta Garbo, Ramon Novarro, and Lionel Barrymore
*Mata Hari* (1985), with Sylvia Kristel and Christopher Cazenove

### Fiction

*The Red Dancer: The Life and Times of Mata Hari,* by Richard Skinner
*Signed, Mata Hari,* by Yannick Murphy

## ROSE O'NEAL GREENHOW

### Film

*The Rose and the Jackal* (1990), with Madolyn Smith Osborne and Christopher Reeve

## MARY ELLEN PLEASANT

### Fiction

*Free Enterprise,* by Michelle Cliff
*Sister Noon,* by Karen Joy Fowler

## CALAMITY JANE

### Film

*Buffalo Girls* (1995), with Anjelica Huston and Melanie Griffith
*Calamity Jane* (1953), with Doris Day, Howard Keel, and Allyn Ann McLerie
*Deadwood*, three seasons (2004–2006), with Ian McShane, Timothy Olyphant, and Robin Weigert
*The Paleface* (1948), with Bob Hope and Jane Russell
*The Plainsman* (1936), with Gary Cooper, Jean Arthur, and James Ellison
*Wild Bill* (1995), with Jeff Bridges and Ellen Barkin

### Fiction

*Buffalo Gals*, by Larry McMurtry
*Deadwood*, by Pete Dexter
*Little Big Man*, by Thomas Berger

## ELIZABETH "BABY DOE" TABOR

### Fiction

*All for Love: Baby Doe and Silver Dollar*, by John Vernon

## MARGARET TOBIN BROWN

### Film

*A Night to Remember* (1958), with Kenneth More and Tucker McGuire
*Titanic* (1996), with Catherine Zeta-Jones and Marilu Henner
*Titanic* (1997), with Leonardo DiCaprio, Kate Winslet, and Kathy Bates
*The Unsinkable Molly Brown* (1964), with Debbie Reynolds, Harve Presnell, and Ed Begley

## CAMILLE CLAUDEL

### Film

*Camille Claudel* (1988), with Isabelle Adjani, Gérard Depardieu, and Katrine Boorman

## ISADORA DUNCAN

### Film

*The Loves of Isadora* (1968), with Vanessa Redgrave, James Fox, and Jason Robards

## JOSEPHINE BAKER

### Film

*The Josephine Baker Story* (1991), with Lynn Whitfield, Rubén Blades, and David Dukes

## BILLIE HOLIDAY

### Film

*Lady Sings the Blues* (1972), with Diana Ross, Billy Dee Williams, and Richard Pryor

## FRIDA KAHLO

### Film

*Frida* (2002), with Salma Hayek, Alfred Molina, and Geoffrey Rush

## ANNE BONNY AND MARY READ

**Fiction**

*The Only Life That Mattered: The Short and Merry Lives of Anne Bonny, Mary Read, and Calico Jack Rackham*, by James L. Nelson
*Pirate Spirit: The Adventures of Anne Bonney*, by Jeffery S. Williams

## LADY HESTER STANHOPE

**Film**

*Queen of the East* (1995), with Jennifer Saunders

## ANNA LEONOWENS

**Film**

*Anna and the King* (1999), with Jodi Foster and Chow Yun-Fat
*Anna and the King of Siam* (1946), with Irene Dunne and Rex Harrison
*The King and I* (1956), with Deborah Kerr and Yul Brynner

**Fiction**

*Anna and the King of Siam*, by Margaret Landon
*The Story of Anna and the King*, by Cecelia Holland

## AMELIA EARHART

**Film**

*Amelia* (2009), with Hilary Swank, Richard Gere, and Ewan McGregor
*Amelia Earhart: The Final Flight* (1994), with Diane Keaton and Bruce Dern
*Night at the Museum: Battle of the Smithsonian* (2009), with Ben Stiller, Owen Wilson, and Amy Adams

## Fiction

*Breathe the Sky: A Novel Inspired by the Life of Amelia Earhart*, by Chandra Prasad
*Flying Blind*, by Max Allan Collins
*I Was Amelia Earhart*, by Jane Mendelsohn

# CREDITS

Lady Caroline Lamb, page 45: "Portrait of Lady Caroline Lamb" (oil on canvas) by Sir Thomas Lawrence, c. 1827: © Bristol City Museum and Art Gallery, UK/The Bridgeman Art Library.

Jane Digby, page 54: "Jane Digby" by Joseph Carl Stieler: Berrington Hall, Herefordshire, UK/National Trust Photographic Library/John Hammond/ The Bridgeman Art Library.

Violet Trefusis, page 61: "Violet Trefusis" (b/w photo) by Pamela Chandler: by kind permission of the National Portrait Gallery (London, England).

Barbara Palmer, page 89: "Barbara Villiers, Duchess of Cleveland as St. Catherine of Alexandria" (oil on canvas) by Sir Peter Lely, c. 1665–70: Private Collection/The Bridgeman Art Library.

Lola Montez, page 102: "Lola Montez" (photograph, daguerreotype plate), c. 1851: Museum of Fine Arts, Boston. (Gift of Edward Southworth Hawes in memory of his father Josiah Johnson Hawes, 43.1396 © 2010 Museum of Fine Arts, Boston. All rights reserved.)

Mary Wollstonecraft, page 130: "Portrait of Mary Wollstonecraft Godwin, Author of a Vindication of the Rights of Woman" (engraving) by W. T. Annis, pub. 1802 (b/w photo) by John Opie: Private Collection/The Bridgeman Art Library.